The Whole Church

The Whole Church

Congregational Leadership Guided by Systems Theory

Ken Reeves

An Alban Institute Book
ROWMAN & LITTLEFIELD
Lanham · Boulder · New York · London

Published by Rowman & Littlefield
An imprint of The Rowman & Littlefield Publishing Group, Inc.
4501 Forbes Boulevard, Suite 200, Lanham, Maryland 20706
www.rowman.com

6 Tinworth Street, London SE11 5AL, United Kingdom

British Library Cataloguing in Publication Information Available

Library of Congress Cataloging-in-Publication Data
Names: Reeves, Kenneth, 1955- author.
Title: The whole church : congregational leadership guided by systems theory / Kenneth
   Reeves.
Description: Lanham : Rowman & Littlefield, 2019. | Includes bibliographical references
   and index.
Identifiers: LCCN 2019005088 (print) | LCCN 2019018817 (ebook) |
   ISBN 9781538127322 (ebook) | ISBN 9781538127339 (cloth : alk. paper) |
   ISBN 9781538127346 (pbk. : alk. paper)
Subjects: LCSH: Pastoral theology. | Christian leadership. | Church management. |
   System theory.
Classification: LCC BV4011.3 (ebook) | LCC BV4011.3 .R44 2019 (print) | DDC
   253.01/1—dc23
LC record available at https://lccn.loc.gov/2019005088

♾™ The paper used in this publication meets the minimum requirements of American
National Standard for Information Sciences—Permanence of Paper for Printed Library
Materials, ANSI/NISO Z39.48–1992.

Dedicated to Jean and May

Contents

Acknowledgments

Writing *The Whole Church* has been a labor of love. It has been great to put systems theory into a form that I hope is helpful to ministers.

The labor is made sweet by you who are reading this. Thanks!

I also appreciate all who have read sections of the manuscript and given me their feedback and valuable input: Dan Hotchkiss, Maggie Lewis, Jeff Jones, Jay Heinrichs, Stephen Ott, Steven Drake, Jean Chandler, Gary Miles, and Don Southworth. I extend special thanks to Sue Sterling who read the entire manuscript and offered great suggestions.

Thanks to the professional editors whose input strengthened the manuscript: Beth Ann Gaede and Marly Cornell.

Thanks to Densis Pena of Serried Rock Studios for translating my pencil scratches into actual diagrams.

Thanks also to Rowman & Littlefield, the Alban Institute, and Rolf Janke for thinking *The Whole Church* was worth publishing. Thanks to the copy editor Sudha Soundrapandiyan who spared me considerable embarrassment by making needed corrections before anyone else could read this book. Thanks to Ramanan Sundararajan for his gracious help and flexibility with the production process. Thanks to Courtney Packard at Rowman for answering my many questions.

I want to thank all the seminary students and ministry colleagues who took my classes and attended my workshops. Thanks for exploring with me the dynamics of congregational leadership and for giving me a sounding board that helped clarify and strengthen the ideas in *The Whole Church*.

I am grateful to all the people in all the congregations with whom I ever interacted. Thank you for your participation in your church communities. (Any names in this text are fictitious).

I thank my father, Alex, who knew good writing, and my mother, Ruth, who supported reading. I thank my beautiful wife Jean and daughter May for letting me disappear into my office for hours and for welcoming me back.

Introduction

People need each other. Happily, we have been learning, over the course of history, to meet each other's needs with increasing success. Systems theory contributes to this development.

Successful human relations began when the members of hunter-gatherer clans shared with each other whatever food they found. Later in history, farmers began to trade with each other their surplus crops in return for commodities they lacked. Larger societies, needing order and public safety, developed laws. Jesus called people to love each other, and Paul, in his epistles, offered guidance in how to love. Confucianism promoted manners and social protocols. Western authors offered etiquette manuals. Philosophers and preachers championed moral behavior. Nations instituted religious tolerance. During the nineteenth century, most countries abolished slavery. Many nations developed democracy. The twentieth century saw the development of marital, parental, and conflict-resolution skills. Warfare has declined. Systems theory has added its understanding of patterns of human relatedness, providing further insight into how to relate well, and, indeed, love one another.

This macro development of relationship skills parallels my own individual development. I have experienced human relationships as the most important aspect of my life, yet sometimes as difficult. I am usually pleasant and agreeable, other times less agreeable than I like to admit.

When relationships were difficult, isolation used to appeal. As a Boy Scout I climbed mountains to forest fire lookout towers, where I would think I could do that—live alone on a mountaintop watching for fires. Of course, at the time I was hiking with other boys, including a kid named Buster who, one day for a laugh, shoved me into a creek as I filled my canteen. Dripping wet and wanting to retaliate, being alone looked simpler than this mess.

Yet other times the interactions were great. I remember camping on a warm, clear night, a few of us lying on a domed hilltop looking up at the stars, and experiencing a union among friends as we contemplated the infinite.

I realized that if I were isolated, I would miss these peak interpersonal experiences. Furthermore, experiencing a union with my brothers and sisters inspired my caring for them. I also found meaning in conversations with people about things that mattered: emotions, beliefs, and the contents of the inner life. I observed my congregation's minister having just those conversations, and I thought: That's what I really want to do.

Therefore, I do not to live on a mountaintop but work as a minister and a psychologist. This vocation has called me to grow personally so as to develop supportive harmony with others and to moderate the inevitable snarls and snags that occur in relationships; to learn, as humanity has learned, among other skills: to share, love, and resolve conflicts.

While practicing ministry, I learned of Murray Bowen's version of systems theory at a lecture by Rabbi Edwin Friedman, author of *Generation to Generation*. This theory added to my understanding of how people are connected and helped me strengthen those connections.

I applied Bowen theory as a minister, which helped my leadership. To understand this useful theory further, I researched it while earning my PhD in psychology. But as I practiced psychology and taught systems theory at seminaries, I found myself less beholden to Bowen theory and more interested in the essence of systems theory.

Essentially, systems theory views any system as a whole, its elements engaging in patterns of interaction to compose that whole. According to systems theory, a problem in a system is caused not by some errant member of that system, but by a problem embedded in the whole system. For instance, an uncaring action somewhere in a congregation reflects a congregation-wide problem with caring.

To ameliorate this systemic problem, the minister employs the relationship patterns described by systems theory. Addressing the situation above, the minister knows that a change in one element of a system influences the entire system. Therefore, the minister demonstrates increased caring, which results in more caring system-wide.

The Whole Church presents this essential systems theory as a guide for pastors in leading their congregations toward health. In my view, systems theory orients pastors toward two health-promoting goals: the congregation's wholeness and its being a safe home for its members. Whole and safe, the congregation can fulfill its purposes: to support its members and fulfill its spiritual mission. Then it is a healthy community in which people's needs for each other, as well as for spiritual support, are met.

1

Systems Theory

While in parish ministry, I served two congregations. My first settlement was pretty easy. My second settlement tested me and my systems theory-based leadership skills.

My first church had been a lay-led fellowship that had grown, thrived, bought a small church building, expanded that building, then watched their membership decline. As their numbers shrank, they considered bringing on a minister to help them reverse that course. Not a simple slam-dunk decision, they debated it for five years. Eventually, they broke down and applied to the denomination for a minister trained in supporting membership growth. The denomination appointed me.

I arrived to find my denomination underrepresented in this midsized city, making the demographics for membership growth easy. I did not have to do much more than show up and speak in complete sentences for the church to grow and the ministry to proceed smoothly.

After five years at that congregation, I was ready to push on to new horizons. I entered the search hoping to be appointed to another congregation that wanted to grow, and received such an appointment.

My second congregation had spun off from a big, thriving church in the downtown of another midsized city. Demographically, my denomination was already well represented in the region. Also, this congregation's members had not debated whether to hire a minister for five years. Indeed, one founding member pushed that decision into effect. Someone later told me that to him the decision had felt "railroaded."

Nevertheless, my first year with this congregation was a honeymoon. I settled in. During this year, I attended a seminar on Bowen systems theory by Rabbi Edwin Friedman. We twenty-five clergy listened to Friedman wax on about systems theory and church leadership. That seminar saved my ministerial life.

As the second year of my settlement began, the congregation elected a new board president, Betty, whom I had observed complain about the church but not contribute proposals. I viewed the nominating committee's elevation of a complainer into leadership as a symptom of anxiety in the congregation. As I anticipated sharing leadership with her, I had a sinking feeling.

At the first board of trustees meeting of that program year, Betty informed us that some people in the congregation were unhappy with me, but she would not say who they were or what they were unhappy about. She further wanted members to be free to complain about me behind my back. My sinking feeling sunk lower. I did not want to bless this secret complaining, so I expressed my vision for open, direct communication, knowing this vision would be dismissed, at least by Betty.

Along with Betty, two others on this seven-member board seemed hostile toward me. I picked up wary looks, chilly comments, and closed-off body language. To my surprise, one of the seemingly hostile board members requested that I report on my ministerial goals for the year at the next meeting. I thought this was a great suggestion and an opportunity to offer self-defining leadership.

At that meeting, I brought my goals. They were pretty standard: a thriving religious education program, quality worship, and membership growth. I expected the board to tinker with them, add something of their own, and otherwise give them a nod and proceed to other business. Instead, the hostile members tore the goals apart, as if I had proposed turning the church into a casino. I listened to this thrashing and kept my cool, but over my head a thought bubble held the question: *What the ... ?*

I left that meeting angry and afraid and took a walk into the night to ponder the situation. I remembered Edwin Friedman describing congregational leadership as akin to riding a bucking bronco. Now I was on that crazy horse. The board members' fury told me something was not well in my congregation, and that for me to hang on for dear life and then guide the church into health, I needed to muster my best leadership based on sound leadership theory. I considered first principles ...

THE VALUE OF LEADERSHIP

I had felt called to become a minister to use my influence to support a congregation's members and its mission. I knew a leader's influence, or power, could support or destroy. Lord Acton warned of leaders' destructiveness: "Power tends to corrupt, and absolute power corrupts absolutely. Great men are almost always bad men."[1] Leaders can be egotistically inflated by the praise they receive from their followers, leverage their office for personal gain, or use their power to enact ill-conceived and impossible schemes, sometimes with tragic outcomes for multitudes of people.[2] Some ministers play fast and loose with their power, leaving damaged congregations in their wakes, which I did not want to do.

Ideally, a leader offers a compelling vision of greatness and guides people there. For example, John Winthrop, in 1630, envisioned that his fellow Pilgrims would:

> Followe the Counsell of Micah, to doe Justly, to love mercy, to walke humbly with our God, for this end, wee must be knitt together in this worke as one man, wee must entertaine each other in brotherly Affeccion ... wee must delight in eache other, make others Condicions our owne, rejoyce together, mourne together, labour, and suffer together, allwayes haveing before our eyes our Commission and Community in the worke, our Community as members of the same body ... for wee must Consider that wee shall be as a Citty upon a Hill, the eies of all people are uppon us.[3]

Given leaders' influence, there used to be the "great man" theory of leadership that viewed a leader as an autonomous superhuman agent making things happen.[4] In Shakespeare's *Henry IV*, Glendower, believing he is such a "great man," boasts, "I can call the spirits from the vasty deep."[5]

But post-WWII scholars concluded that there were more factors causing the world's recent madness than the persons of Hitler, Stalin, et al.[6] These scholars de-emphasized the superhuman leader to focus on followers, groups, and systems that imbue their leaders with power. According to this view, it was not Hitler who compelled Germany into war, but the larger German system that found in Hitler a leader who would support its bellicose agenda.

I believe power lies in both leaders and followers, such that they work together like two riders on a tandem bicycle. Both provide pedal power, take turns steering, and together they go places.

Sometimes leadership involves managing. Managers attend to the running of an operation.[7] They ask: "How well are we doing what we are supposed to be doing?" In a congregation, managers oversee the budget, ensure the facilities are maintained, make sure volunteers fulfill their appointed tasks, etc.

My recalcitrant board did not need a manager but rather the second kind of leadership that is concerned about the group's purpose, identity, and mission, and its faithfulness to those principles. These leaders ask, "What is the point of what we are doing?" My congregation's mission of spiritual support was lost on my anti-supportive board; they needed a leader to help them remember that mission.

Along with supporting the group's mission, a leader supports people's positive emotions.[8] The leader generates trust and optimism, which motivates and inspires people to execute that mission. My anxious and irritable board needed a leader to help them feel better.

Congregations need both management and leadership. Without management, *i*'s are not dotted, *t*'s are not crossed, and jobs fall through the cracks. (Where is my paycheck?) Without leadership, people flail about aimlessly and in despair. My people needed leadership.

IS THERE A THEORY IN THE HOUSE?

To lead effectively and not just shake my fist at the night sky, I needed a theory to guide me. A theory makes sense of things. The *Dictionary of Psychology* defines a theory as "a principle or body of interrelated principles that purports to explain or predict a number of interrelated phenomena."[9] A theory predicts the future. If I let go of a pen, the theory of gravity predicts it will fall to the floor. A good theory is backed by evidence. Every time I let go of that pen, its fall to the floor adds evidence to the theory of gravity. A good theory guides action toward successful outcomes. If I want a pen on the floor, I know what to do.

As leaders, we may have good instincts to guide our actions, but I think we are stronger when we can also articulate a theoretical rationale to explain those actions and predict their effects. Such a theory would be like a compass reliably guiding a minister to one's chosen destination.

I began ministry using the mechanistic theory, by which the world is composed of separate elements. Indeed, this keyboard, this desk, and this phone all appear separate. Each person in a congregation also appears independent of the others. Influence, according to mechanistic theory, is simple: one party changes another party, like a cue ball sending an 8-ball into the corner pocket (see Figure 1.1).

Given that at first glance elements appear separate from each other, and given its simple method of influence, mechanistic theory is commonly held. But mechanistic theory left unexplained the gratifying oneness I could sense when the congregation joined in worship. Furthermore, if mechanistic theory

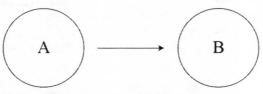

Figure 1.1   Influence according to mechanistic theory.

were accurate and my hostile board members were autonomous malefactors, I would have to influence them with a reform campaign, which seemed destined to fail, or excommunicate them, which would violate my mission to support the members of my congregation.

In search of a better theory to guide my pastoral leadership, I looked into secular leadership literature, but with limited success. Some writers emphasized how to be, suggesting characterological virtues. For example, Bill Bradley, former basketball player and US senator, offered this ideal: "Leaders should be collaborative, modest, and generous."[10] Fine, but what effect would those virtues have on the group being led? I read that good leaders are sensitive to the emotions of the group.[11] Nothing wrong with that, but what concept guides such sensitivity? I found long lists of personality virtues correlating with leadership success: adaptability, adjustment, alertness, ascendance, assertiveness, attractiveness, cooperativeness, dominance, educational level, energy, through the alphabet to: tact, tolerance of stress, tough-mindedness, and verbal fluency.[12] However, no single quality stood out as a consistent way for a leader to be.[13] I could strive to cover the laundry list of leaderly virtues, but tagging all those bases would require enormous mental energy, and, knowing me, would likely fail, and, furthermore, in the process I could lose sight of the people I hoped to serve.

Other theories discussed what leaders should do. Kouzes and Posner suggested leaders "model the way, inspire shared vision, challenge the process, enable others to act, and encourage the heart."[14] These are great suggestions, but what principle or concept provides a rationale for these behaviors?

Friedman introduced me to leadership guided by Bowenian systems theory and offered valuable insights. I began to apply those Bowenian ideas, but still stumbled around with questions. For instance, Friedman added to the list of a leader's virtues, describing good leaders as clever, deft, and possessed of a rare genius for leadership, but he seemed to imply that such genius is innate.[15] Could I learn it? Indeed, when people believe their personal qualities are fixed, they underachieve; but when people believe they can grow, they strive and achieve.[16] I wanted a path to leadership achievement. Friedman further added what leaders should do: be aware of the systemic processes of the group.[17] Fine, but from all my exposure to his work, I still wondered: what is a system, and what is a process?

Additional authors applied systems theory to churches. Peter Steinke described systems, and distinguished healthy from unhealthy congregations, but seemed to imply that congregations became unhealthy as a result of mistakes.[18] Not wanting to make mistakes, I wondered what thinking patterns could lead to errors, and what thinking patterns would result in wise decisions. Ron Richardson described emotional systems and viewed the source of their ills as a "heightened level of anxiety in the system" that throws off the "togetherness/individuality" balance in that system.[19] Sounds good, but what raises anxiety? What lowers anxiety?

I still looked for a guiding principle, other than to be smart and virtuous (because I am not always smart and virtuous) that could reliably guide my leadership. Systems theory offered valuable ideas, but questions lingered regarding what it meant and how it could guide me. Not seeing such clarity elsewhere, I decided to look anew at systems theory and give it that clarity myself.

Here goes …

SYSTEMS THEORY

Introducing the new and improved systems theory! (*Applause.*) While other leadership theories list who a leader should be or what a leader should do, I want to present systems theory as providing a leader a way to think. And instead of a catalog of potential thoughts, systems theory offers the leader one thought: the central principle of systems theory, that the system is a whole. When leading a system, be it a congregation, a nation, or a family, the leader guided by systems theory remembers: the system is a whole. Understanding and appreciating the system's wholeness, that leader acts to maintain, support, and develop its wholeness. When the leader is mindful of and supporting the system's wholeness, the leader's virtues follow. For instance, the leader would fulfill Bill Bradley's suggestions to be "collaborative, modest, and generous," by collaborating in a modest, self-effacing way, generously sharing power such that the whole community benefits from one's leadership.

The system explained by systems theory is "a collective entity consisting of a set of interrelated and interacting elements that have been organized together to perform a function."[20] If a group of people stood in a circle, and someone grasped the trailing thread of a ball of yarn and tossed the ball to another, who took the thread and tossed the ball to another until they formed a network of threads, those people would compose a system. Interrelated and interacting—if one of them moved, everyone would be affected.

A system is more like salad than oatmeal. A salad contains distinct elements: lettuce, broccoli, tomatoes, and maybe those tiny ears of corn. People usually do not run salad ingredients in a blender; if they did, it would no longer be a salad. Analogously, a system of people, such as a congregation, is composed of distinct individuals who each bring their unique flavors to compose the whole.

Systems theory explains systems. It holds that patterns and principles characterize all types of systems.[21] Therefore, the same patterns and principles would characterize an ecosystem, a country's economy, the nations of the world, the solar system, an individual body, a beehive, a family, or a congregation.

Regarding these systemic patterns and principles, each element in a system fulfills a function, interacting with and influencing every other element to create that system. The various organs and cells in your body function in interaction with each other to form you. The various individuals and groups in a congregation function in interaction with each other to form that congregation.

Any one relationship within a system is affected by all the other relationships in the system. The relationship between minister and board president is influenced by the relationship between the music director and the choir and between the religious education director and the kids. Harmony in one relationship increases harmony system-wide. "We are caught in an inescapable network of mutuality ...," observed Martin Luther King Jr. "Whatever affects one directly, affects all indirectly."[22]

Changes in any one element, or in any one relationship, produce changes through the rest of the system. The butterfly flapping its wings in China affects weather around the world. In a congregation, the enthusiasm generated from a successful rummage sale ripples through the system.

In a system, there can be both direct and immediate effects, indirect and delayed effects, and expected and unexpected effects. You teach Christian history; directly people learn about the Nicene Creed. Indirectly people appreciate their religious identity, which makes them more welcoming to visitors, causing the membership to grow.

Given that the system is composed of many elements all interacting with and affecting each other, influence in a system is nonlinear. Each element affects and is affected by each other. Element A affects and is affected by B. Element B affects and is affected by A. Element C affects and is affected by A and B. Additional elements create additional influences. See Figure 1.2.

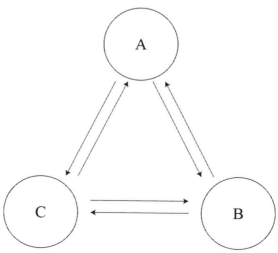

Figure 1.2   Influence according to systems theory.

A system settles into homeostatic stability. The planets in the solar system maintain consistent orbits around the sun. The members of a congregation settle into behavioral norms and patterns, giving them a homeostasis. Planets in their orbits, a congregation in its patterns—a system's homeostasis resists change.

Systems theory attends to what the elements in a system are doing as they affect each other, or to the process of the system's interactions. For example, in an ecosystem, rain falls and sun shines; those processes cause plants to grow.

Humans also interact via various processes, although, unlike the rest of nature, our interactions often involve speaking. What we say to each other would be the contents of our interaction. What our words are *doing* as we say what we are saying would be the process of our interaction. If, for example, Charlie announced he would be leaving a committee, the contents of this utterance would be the indication that Charlie would be leaving the committee. The process would involve what Charlie was doing by making this announcement. Was this a passive-aggressive move to upset the rest of the committee? Was it a benediction at the conclusion of his years of sterling service? Was it an escape from some difficult work the committee was doing? Was it a move to jettison some tasks as he adjusts his lifestyle balance?

There are some destructive processes, such as shunning, blaming, escalating tensions, pressuring, and invalidating. Other processes are constructive, such as compromising, collaborating, brainstorming, listening, and validating.

Systems theory holds that patterns describe, define, and characterize all systems. Its central principle: the system is a whole. Therefore ...

- Elements interact with and affect each other.
- Any one relationship affects and is affected by all other relationships.
- Changes in one element influence all.
- Effects can be direct and indirect, immediate and delayed.
- Influence is nonlinear.
- The system establishes a homeostatic stability.
- Process matters.

MINISTRY SUPPORTS PUBLIC HEALTH

Informed by the systems theory view that the system is a whole, I interpreted my board's hostility as representing something unhealthy within my whole congregation. I then saw as my job to raise the tide of health in the congregation, enabling boats now unhappily mired in mud to float freely. Indeed, a healthy congregation provides a context in which its members feel good, function well, and experience support for their spiritual journeys. It supports healthy relationships and families. It supports people as they grieve losses and celebrate triumphs. It is pleasant place to work.

Attending to the health of the whole system uses ministerial time and energy efficiently. Rather than helping each individual and thereby, in theory, creating a healthy congregation, the minister does the reverse: supports the congregation's health, making it a community in which everyone thrives. The healthy congregation then becomes a pastoral vehicle, supporting the health of all its members. Supporting systemic health is analogous to supporting public health, which occurs via indirect yet effective interventions. Just as cleaning smoggy air would likely bring greater benefit than hundreds of physicians treating asthma, so would creating a healthy community improve people's lives more than hundreds of pastoral care appointments.

STILL SMARTING FROM THAT BOARD MEETING

As I reflected on my difficult board meeting, the systems theory theme that all elements in a system influence each other caused me to realize that, as I sought to influence the congregation, the congregation (through its hostile board of trustees) was influencing me, causing me to feel scared and angry.

In terms of process, I thought their hostility toward my goals could be an unconscious move to scare and silence me, ultimately pushing me out of the congregation, or to goad me into a battle they would win—outcomes detrimental to both the congregation and me. To support better outcomes, I decided to move in the opposite direction: to keep speaking, to assume I am secure in my pastorate, and to refrain from battling them. At the November meeting, on behalf of speaking securely and noncombatively, I offered the board another self-definition: my theory of worship. They trashed that. In December, I offered another self-definition: my visions for the church, which they shredded. Each time, I felt bad and needed to apply late-night ambulatory ice packs to my psychic bruises. Still, as I experienced pressure to be silent, I kept defining myself. Pressured to leave, I assumed I would be their minister for as long as I wanted. Goaded into battle, I did not attack them or defend myself.

What buoyed me was that I saw myself offering something healthy for the church: clear, affirming leadership on behalf of which I was willing to take some hits. I was also glad their blows were coming at me, a trained professional, and not causing a member of the congregation to suffer. In January, February, and March, I brought additional self-definitions to the board meetings. Each time, they took what I offered, tore it to shreds, threw the shreds on the floor, and ripped up the floor.

As the year proceeded, I met with the board president every month to talk over matters at the church—a healthy practice, I believe. I entered these meetings feeling tense, but would still offer Betty my proposals for the church. She dismissed them, while advocating for people to complain about me.

Outside the board meetings, additional dramas were unfolding. The board president and the previous president scheduled a "we need to talk" meeting with me. Remember that sinking feeling? I was in an express elevator, going down.

At this meeting, they told me that I should not involve myself in church business and not meet with committees—just preach and offer pastoral care. I took notes and read back what they had said to make sure I was hearing them accurately. I said little else, except that I would think about what they had told me.

Wanting to support the congregation's committees, I continued to make myself available to any that invited me to their meetings. I acted as if that meeting with the presidents had never occurred. I expected a follow-up "we need to talk" session in which the two would apply greater pressure on me, but they remained quiet.

Around the same time, the board formed a committee, composed of four parishioners who were not on the board, to deal with the problem of me. By some miracle, this new committee let me meet with them. I sensed that they would be open to insight, so I offered one. I drew a triangle on a piece of paper. At the three points of the triangle, I placed myself, the people who wanted to complain about me, and the rest of the congregation to whom the complainers would complain. I asked the committee whether they wanted this indirect style of communicating. They said no.

The committee and I set up opportunities for people to give me direct feedback. Not everyone who was unhappy with me used this forum, but some did; and for them, the direct feedback cleared the air.

To support additional direct communication and self-definition, I proposed to meet one-on-one with each board member to ask them for their visions for the church. Six of the seven met with me. I took notes and reflected back their visions to make sure I heard them accurately. The board president declined to meet with me but agreed to articulate her visions in a newsletter column. Fine. Self-definition would still be happening. I called it a victory.

At the next board meeting, I read back their visions for the church, including the president's. She took offense, as if her visions had been private. I reminded her I was reading them from the newsletter. She *humphed* and was quiet. I could do no right. We proceeded to discuss the various visions with civility but with no big breakthroughs or choruses of *Kumbaya*. Still, people were defining themselves and being heard. I was not the only one practicing self-definition.

And so the church muddled along. At the May board meeting, the president advocated again for people to complain behind my back. I did not criticize her, complain about her, or beg for mercy. I said I still envisioned a church in which people spoke directly to each other. With this, she burst into tears, slammed her hand on a table, and said, "You are making this so hard for us!"

I felt a little shock but realized I was making it hard for her. I was not acquiescent, nor silent, nor goaded into a battle with her. I felt pleased I had not been lured into these leadership missteps, but also felt sad for her and did not know how to support her. She composed herself. The board moved on to other business.

Soon thereafter the nominating committee did not select Betty for her expected second term as board president. I had not complained to anyone about Betty. I had not spoken to anyone on the nominating committee. I had offered no hint about possible nominees for the president's job, nor about replacements for the two hostile board members who were retiring. The next fall began with a new board president and two new (and cooperative) board members, all a pleasure to work with. The congregation became easy and relaxed. Betty and the other difficult former board members appeared less and less often at church.

This is my testimonial. Systems theory helped me weather a stormy year and guide the congregation a few steps toward becoming a safe, trusting community.

SYSTEMS THEORY GUIDES INTERVENTIONS

The systems theory-based minister thinks of one's congregation as a whole, and supports that wholeness. During my difficult year, I supported the congregation's wholeness by interpreting the board's hostility not in personal terms—their fault or mine—but as a symptom expressing illness in the whole system, that symptom charging head-on into me.

Not seeing the problem as their fault, I did not attack perceived enemies, which would have escalated the conflict. I did not seek allies to support me against my detractors, which would have split the church. I did not complain or beg the big meanies to be nice to me, which would have been pathetic. I did not try to reform my detractors, which would have been futile.

Not seeing the problem as my fault, I did not slink away, hide, go quiet, or quit, which would have split me from the church and rewarded the practice of pressuring ministers until they crumble.

Regrettably, though, I failed to support wholeness—everyone staying together—by neglecting to care pastorally for my challengers, who then left the church. As my board members were angry with me, I could have listened to them and validated their predicament, albeit still not giving in to their pressure. They might then have felt supported and remained in the congregation.

Regarding the hostile board members and the lay leaders who forbade me from involvement in committees, I could have seen them as representing the whole congregation's anger about having a minister imposed on them and taking some of their power. I could have acknowledged the bind they were in between wanting professional leadership to help their church thrive, versus wanting to be the sole leaders of their church. I could have validated their opinion that authority in the church should go to those with the longest tenure, which did not include me. Also, instead of going behind their backs to meet with committees, I could have taken the more vulnerable and respectful route of reporting back to them that I was still meeting with committees against their wishes, then faced their pushback.

In addition to supporting its wholeness, the systems-based minister supports the congregation's members's experience of safety. When safe, people in a community can relate to each other with clarity and transparency, everyone defining himself or herself and understanding each other. Unfortunately, people in my congregation had felt unsafe. They naturally responded with self-protection, manifested when they elevated into board presidency a self-protectively complaining member.

I supported safety in my congregation by being vulnerable, rather than self-protective, by defining myself—my goals, visions, and priorities. I also offered proposing, envisioning leadership, rather than the relatively self-protective complaining or critiquing leadership. My vulnerable self-definition contradicted the anxious assumption that everyone had to be afraid and self-protective.

The system's homeostasis fought back by anxiously resisting my security-based transparency, pushing me to merge with the system in self-protection. Nevertheless, by holding firm in my vulnerability month after month, I demonstrated trust in my security. Witnessing my vulnerability, people could realize, consciously or unconsciously: "If Reeves does not have to protect himself here, we may be safer than we assume."

When I had asked the board members for their visions, I was inviting others to define themselves. I thought that if they feared transparency but managed to be transparent anyway (and lived to tell the tale), they would emerge with less fear, lowering the system's anxiety.

Furthermore, my congregation was familiar with being "railroaded." They may have perceived my listing of goals as another locomotive bearing down on them, to which they responded by lashing me to their tracks and stoking coal in their locomotive. I did not want to railroad them and silence their voices, nor did I want them to railroad me into silence. Instead I chose to be self-defining, while listening to them. Then they could experience safe, non-railroading interaction.

Reflecting the congregation's easing of anxiety, the nominating committee elevated to leadership calmer, more cooperative board members.

And yet I could have supported safety further by validating Betty and her wish for indirect communication. For some people and cultures, indirection is normal and effective.[23] My preference for working out differences directly is fine, but not the only way.

Furthermore, I could have validated how risky it is to complain directly to someone, especially to a male authority figure. Cultural and familial history, even trauma history given men's abuse of women, could have made such complaining appear forbidden, if not dangerous. I could have supported safety by paradoxically endorsing Betty's wariness of me by telling her that she was performing an important and self-sacrificial service: to protect people from me. I could have invited her to maintain her role, while acknowledging I would maintain my job of advocating for open communication. I regret not taking these leadership actions.

CONCLUSION

Systems theory offers a minister a way to think, by providing one thought: the system is a whole. This perspective guides the minister in intervening to invite the whole congregation into safety. Whole and secure, the congregation supports its members' spiritual lives and lives its mission.

QUESTIONS FOR REFLECTION

Regarding the congregation described in this chapter, what other leadership initiatives might have supported its wholeness and safety?
How would supporting a congregation's wholeness make your ministry easier?
How would it complicate your ministry?

NOTES

1. John Emerich Edward Dalberg-Acton, "Letter to Bishop Mandell Creighton," April 5, 1887, in *Historical Essays and Studies*, ed. J. N. Figgis and R. V. Laurence (London: Macmillan, 1907).

2. Warren Bennis, "The Challenges of Leadership in the Modern World," *American Psychologist* 62, no. 1 (January 2007): 2–5.

3. John Winthrop, "A Modell of Christian Charity," a sermon written in 1630 on board *The Arbella* on the Atlantic Ocean (Boston: Collections of the Massachusetts Historical Society, 1838).

4. Bennis, "The Challenges of Leadership."

5. William Shakespeare, "Henry IV," in *The Oxford Shakespeare: The Complete Works*, 2nd edition, ed. John Jowett, William Montgomery, Gary Taylor, and Stanley Wells (Oxford, UK: Oxford University Press, 2005).

6. Bennis, "The Challenges of Leadership."

7. Gilbert Rendle, *Leading Change in Congregations: Spiritual and Organizational Tools for Leaders* (Herndon, VA: Alban Institute, 1998).

8. Daniel Goleman, Annie McKee, and Richard Boyatzis, *Primal Leadership: Realizing the Power of Emotional Intelligence* (Boston: Harvard Business School Press, 2002).

9. *Dictionary of Psychology*, 2nd edition, ed. Gary Vandenbos, s.v "theory" (Washington, DC: American Psychological Association, 2015).

10. Bill Bradley, "Bill Bradley Quotes." ThinkExist.com, http://thinkexist.com/quotes/billbradley, accessed January 21, 2015.

11. Goleman, McKee, and Boyatzis, *Primal Leadership*.

12. R. M. Stogdill, *Handbook of Leadership: A Survey of Theory and Research* (New York: Free Press, 1974).

13. R. D. Mann, "A Review of the Relationship between Personality and Performance in Small Groups," *Psychological Bulletin* 56, no. 4 (1959): 241–70.

14. James Kouzes and Barry Posner, *The Leadership Challenge: How to Make Extraordinary Things Happen in Organizations* (San Francisco: Jossey-Bass, 2012).

15. Edwin Friedman, *Generation to Generation: Family Process in Church and Synagogue* (New York: Guilford Press, 1985).

16. Lisa S. Blackwell, Kali H. Trzesniewski, and Carol S. Dweck, "Implicit Theories of Intelligence Predict Achievement across an Adolescent Transition: A Longitudinal Study and an Intervention," *Child Development* 78, no. 1 (January–February 2007): 246–63.

17. Friedman, *Generation to Generation*.

18. Peter Steinke, *Healthy Congregations: A Systems Approach* (Herndon, VA: The Alban Institute, 2006).

19. Ronald Richardson, *Creating a Healthier Church: Family Systems Theory, Leadership, and Congregational Life* (Minneapolis: Fortress Press, 1996).

20. *Dictionary of Psychology*, 2nd edition, ed. Gary Vandenbos, s.v. "system" (Washington, DC: American Psychological Association, 2015).

21. Ludwig von Bertalanffy, *General Systems Theory: Foundations, Development, Applications* (New York: George Braziller, 1968).

22. Martin Luther King Jr., *Letter from the Birmingham Jail* (San Francisco: Harper, 1994).

23. Kristen Behfar and Christina Black, "In Defense of Indirect Confrontation: Managing Cross-Cultural Conflict," *Leadership and Organizational Behavior*, University of Virginia, Darden School of Business (April 3, 2017). https://ideas.darden.virginia.edu/2017/04/in-defense-of-indirect-confrontation-managing-cross-culture-conflict.

2

Diagnosis

When everything is going a little crazy, people naturally try to make sense of such events, their interpretations to guide their responses, a process known as diagnosing.

The word "diagnosis" comes from the Greek, "dia," meaning: through, across, or between, as in "diagonal"; and "gnosis," meaning: knowledge.[1] A diagnosis would be knowledge gained by going through or from within.

To make a good diagnosis, one needs a diagnostic theory, or lens, through which to view and interpret a problem accurately, that interpretation guiding interventions that actually help. When diagnosing a human system such as a congregation, there are two theoretical options: the personality-problem diagnosis and the systems diagnosis.

The personality-problem diagnosis views one element of the system as bearing a rotten personality and therefore causing troubles. This diagnosis follows the mechanistic assumption that systems are composed of parts that do not interact nor affect each other; therefore, when a problem occurs, it is due to an isolated broken part, which can be fixed, removed, or replaced. If your car does not start, the diagnosis: a dead battery. Replace it: *vroom, vroom*. Indeed, the mechanistic diagnosis applies well to simple systems, such as a car.

Option two, the systems diagnosis, interprets a problem as a symptom revealing illness in the whole. Analogous to a perfect storm, caused by the interactions of humidity, temperature, wind speed, and other factors, in a congregation, elements of history, stress, congregational identity, its minister's and members' flaws and foibles, the larger world, etc., all collaborate to create the sometimes-stormy symptoms that buffet that system. You pull out one thread of a tangle to pronounce it as *the problem* and find the rest of the system is attached, including you.

15

THE MINISTER AS DIAGNOSTIC INSTRUMENT

Because you, as minister, live in the system, you are affecting it and affected by it. Affected by it, you experience what it is like to belong to your system, which gives you diagnostic information. Systems theory gives you a lens through which to view the system by making you the lens. You understand the system by observing how you feel and behave as part of the system. You are like a meat thermometer in the roast. At times, it is hot in there, and you sweat. At other times, frozen, you shiver. Hopefully there will be the just right Goldilocks times as well.

If, in your church, you feel afraid, that tells you some threat is lurking about in the system and that others are likely afraid as well. People communicate their fear, not by saying, "Gee, Rev., I feel kind of afraid here," but by being scary. It requires discernment to notice your experience and through that to understand your system, but that's your job as congregational diagnostician.

In my church, Betty, feeling scared, angry, and powerless, complained. Hearing her complaints, the congregation, consciously or unconsciously, sensed her fear, anger, and powerlessness. They then appraised her as a good representative of its fear of authority and its anger about losing power to a minister who was railroaded onto them, so they elevated her into leadership.

I, as a diagnostic instrument, interacted with the congregation in part through my contact with Betty. In that interaction, especially as she advocated for a secret complaining, I was afraid of her. (As she wanted to complain in secret, she was probably afraid of me.) Furthermore, as she resisted my proposals, I felt powerless and angry, just as she felt. My fear, powerlessness, and anger gave me diagnostic information about the anxiety, powerlessness, and anger being experienced system wide. Thanks, Betty, for helping me understand my congregation.

A GOOD DIAGNOSIS BEGINS THE CURE

A good diagnosis not only explains events accurately, but also begins a cure by seeing symptomatic behavior in the context of an understandable, valid human story. Validating a symptom is like saying, "What you are doing, at first glance, looks crazy, but still I will understand it." When the causal factors are understood, it makes sense that people are running around with their hair on fire. Indeed, Betty did not land here from Bizarro Planet to do bizarro things. She was doing what a normal, sane person would do as a part of her congregation.

Seeing people's behavior as valid calms the diagnostician, as one watches people and their flaming hair. One's calm presence calms the system.

Interventions made while calm, rather than while panicked, furious, or confused, would be constructive and healing.

For example, two sides in a congregational conflict berate each other. The personality-problem diagnosis views both sides as dysfunctional. The cure: a pox on both their houses. (In Shakespeare's *Romeo and Juliet*, the dying Mercutio curses both the Montagues and the Capulets, crying: "A plague o' both your houses!"[2] often quoted as "A pox on both your houses.")

The alternative, systemic view sees the conflicting congregation as partisan and as tending to see differences as requiring a winner and a loser. As you sleuth around about this conflict, you learn more details and fine-tune the focus. Maybe you learn the system has bottled up resentment, which is now emerging. Maybe the system lacks grievance procedures, leading to the bottling up of resentment. Maybe the system used to be "bossed" and hierarchically controlled, and now, with the absence of a boss, people's resentments are free to surface. Maybe the congregation was created in opposition to some other group and, still looking for opponents, finds them among themselves. Maybe the system was once traumatized by ethical transgressions and now views all problems as ethical transgressions. Maybe the system successfully blamed and eliminated a member in its past and continues to look for people to blame and eliminate. These validating interpretations calm the diagnostician and support interventions that do more to heal than delivering poxes.

SYSTEMIC ANXIETY, REACTIVITY, AND THE CONTINUUM OF HUMAN MENTAL FUNCTIONING

One way to validate a systemic problem would be by framing it within the concepts of systemic anxiety and reactivity. Reactivity is nature's way of helping us respond to threats.[3] Crossing a street, a car racing at you, reflex is triggered. Your emotion is anxious, behavior reactive, you leap out of its way. Without reactivity, you become a hood ornament.

The trigger does not have to be this dramatic. Preparing for a meeting, wondering about your job security, doubting your worth, numerous situations can trigger reactivity. Its intensity can range from mild unease to terror and panic, its duration lasting from a fleeting flash to a constant. Indeed, regarding duration, defensive reactivity assists survival in an emergency but becomes a liability when habituated, because that habitual reactivity becomes a defensive stance used even when one is safe, and defensiveness impedes authentic interpersonal contact.[4]

Let's say there is a continuum of human mental functioning; at one end, thought; at the other end, reflex. See Figure 2.1. At any given moment of the day, one stands somewhere on this thought–reflex continuum.

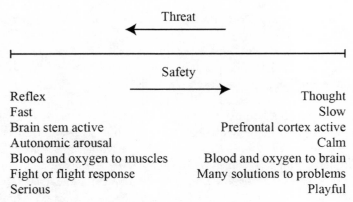

Figure 2.1 Thought–reflex continuum.

On the reflex side, people react fast to a perceived threat. If an automobile is careening toward you, reflexive speed saves your life. Moderately paced thinking can wait. One gains speed but loses flexibility. Acting on reflex, people have only two options: fight or flight. To hide or freeze are versions of flight.

To generate the fight-or-flight response, the body's sympathetic system releases stress hormones: adrenaline, noradrenaline, and cortisol, which increase heart rate and blood pressure and direct blood and oxygen to the large muscles, which are good for fighting and running.[5] Less blood and oxygen remain for maintenance organs, such as the stomach, which places it on hold, leaving nausea or a sensation of butterflies.

The brain is another maintenance organ, not needed in flight or fight, so it too receives less blood and oxygen. People can then feel dizzy or confused. In addition, when brains are flooded with cortisol, people have trouble thinking; their minds can "go blank." They also do not learn abstract or complex information, because the hippocampus, the brain structure that transfers short-term memories into long-term memories, goes offline during emergencies.[6] Although after a scare, people do learn to fear threats.

Additional physiological responses aid in this emergency. The pupils dilate to let in more light. Rapid metabolism leaves one feeling hot and flushed. Muscles tense in preparation for fight or flight, causing aches or trembling. If one cannot actually fight or run, such as during a meeting, foot tapping hints at one's wish.

In reflex mode, the brain stem is active. According to one theory, our brains contain three evolutionary stages: reptilian, mammalian, and human.[7] The brain stem is reptilian, and reptiles are serious. You don't see turtles or iguanas wagging their tails and skipping through the meadows. When people are at the reflex end of the continuum, they are serious, and attempts at humor fall with a thud before this dour, reptilian audience.

After the emergency, one remains keyed up. Adrenaline and noradrenaline take a while to metabolize out of the system. In the primitive wild, one danger could be followed by another, so it made sense to stay alert and scan for threats.

When safe, people's parasympathetic system, a metabolic governor, brings calm. People then swing to the thought side of the continuum.

On the thought side, as noted, people move at a moderate pace. The prefrontal cortex, our most evolved brain structure, is active. Its thinking is creative and flexible, leading to the development of many solutions to a problem. The hippocampus engages, and abstract learning occurs. No longer reptilian, people can be mammalian, and mammals play; see puppies and kittens.

If a lion walked in on you right now, you would likely perceive this as a threat, which would trigger reflexive fight or flight. On the other hand, meditating on the salvific beauty of the divine would support safety and the prefrontal cortex's thoughtfulness, flexibility, and creativity.

Entire systems, such as families, nations, or congregations, can be located on this mental functioning continuum, somewhere between reflex and thought.[8] If you could give your congregation a test of its members' level of reactive arousal and then distribute the results along the continuum of mental functioning, you would likely see a bell curve, as shown in Figure 2.2, with some people higher in arousal, some lower, most in the middle.

The bell curve of a highly anxious congregation (system A in Figure 2.3) would swing to the reflex side of the continuum. In this system, you might sense anxiety like the whiff of a gas leak. You then feel anxious, breathe shallowly, and take care to avoid sparking a flare-up. Your behavior, rather than based on your values or principles, is about guarding against threat.

In such an anxious system, the smallest spark could trigger a crisis. When in a crisis, people feel angry, confused, disturbed, distressed. You believe you have to fix it now, but your words blurt, your actions race, and effective thinking seems to stop. Instead of cooling the crisis, you seek safety via the

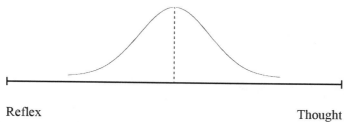

Reflex   Thought

Figure 2.2   System on the thought–reflex continuum.

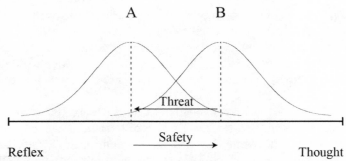

Figure 2.3   Anxious system = A; Calm system = B.

quickest, most familiar route. Creative solutions do not come to mind, just escape routes. Therefore, amid high anxiety, you might feel anxious, lose your breath, walk on eggshells, forgo your values, protect yourself, stop thinking, and jump as fast as you can to safety.

A system may remain anxious, living in Threatworld for months or years. Ideally though, effective leadership supports the anxious system in easing to the thought side of the continuum, where system B stands in Figure 2.3.

SYMPTOMS OF SYSTEMIC ANXIETY

An anxious system, be it reacting to an emergency or chronically anxious, experiences a catalog of symptoms, all stemming from what people feel and do when threatened and reactive.

Chaos

In a calm system, people can think about their community—that thought generating its structure. In an anxious system, thought is absent, and so is structure, leaving instead chaos.

In a chaotic system, one element of structure, truth, is fluid or ambiguous. Facts are disputed. What is up is down, left is right. Trying to hold on to something true is like grasping smoke. In a church, the minister preaches contradictory sermons that say nothing. Without grounding in something agreed to as true, life makes no sense.

The chaotic system lacks rules. A rule defined one day is broken, or its opposite stated the next. People bend or subvert rules to their benefit. They interpret the rules to suit themselves, ignore rules that do not suit them, make up rules as they go along, or distract others from the rules. They don't need no stinkin' rules. Without rules, in a chaotic family, parents violate their marital bonds, no one follows daily procedures, and people commit violence.[9] In a chaotic church, the minister conducts affairs with parishioners, the treasurer embezzles money, and broad swaths of church life are conducted capriciously, if at all.

A system in chaos blocks success. In this no-win system, brainstormed suggestions are reflexively negated, or invalidated, even by the people who had just proposed them. Moderate ideas are rejected as extreme.[10] If you offer, "Let's think this over and consider it tomorrow," and you hear: "*No!* That's a terrible idea. How could anyone imagine doing that?" you have a little chaos on your hands. With no route for success, the members of a system in chaos experience confusion, futility, and fear. Potentially effective leaders see the system as unhealthy and avoid it.

Escalation

When faced with a problem, people can solve it or escalate. Solving it requires moderation, but perceiving threat, people react with arousal and escalate any problem into the stratosphere. They verbally attack each other, threaten lawsuits, and storm out of meetings.

Extremes of Love and Freedom

Relationships occur along a continuum, with love, union, belonging, and warmth on one end and freedom, autonomy, uniqueness, and energy on the other, as shown in Figure 2.4. In the middle, people find a sweet spot and experience both love and freedom, being close and being oneself. An anxious congregation, though, swings to extremes.

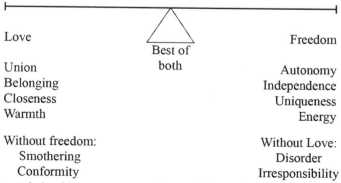

Figure 2.4   Relationships occur on a continuum between love and freedom.

Extreme love sacrifices freedom. This anxious system gathers into a herd and seeks rescue in rules and conformity. The novel, *1984*, depicts such a society that, following a war, allowed no independent thought.[11] The anxious church could similarly push for togetherness, huddle in uniformity, and fear disharmony. The church might not be *1984*, but people would watch what they say for fear of upsetting others or getting into trouble. A more theologically conservative congregation might swing to this extreme and fear unconventional thought.

Extreme freedom sacrifices love. This anxious system throws up its hands, rolls its eyes to the back of its collective heads, and surrenders all order. The novel, *The Lord of the Flies*, describes such a system of shipwrecked boys competing for survival with a ruthless, free-for-all disregard for each other.[12] The anxious church could "let it all hang out" and allow freedom, no matter how hurtful. Caustic words, stingy pledging, and boundary violations would reflect a free but not loving system. A more theologically liberal church might swing to this extreme and allow irresponsible behavior.

Swings to Opposites

Ideally, change is based on thought, and the contents of thought would include the congregation's identity and mission. The anxious congregation, on the other hand, makes changes without thought and instead swings between opposites. The bouncy, in-your-face Rev. Tigger is replaced by the dour Rev. Eeyore. The call for a revolution, a flood, a cleaning of house, suggests the congregation is seeking the opposite of where it is now, without thoughtful attention to its identity or mission.

The Intense Cure

A thoughtful cure begins with the least-intrusive intervention. Without such thought, there is the intense cure. The treasurer sneezes—someone calls an ambulance. A board member violates a clause in the board covenant—the board delivers reprimands, sanctions, and holds a hearing before a star chamber of stern-faced judges. There are firings, excommunications, and inquisitions.

Speed

Unless the building is on fire, most church problems can be addressed at a moderate pace. But a threatened, reactive congregation will want to move fast. You might see blasted emails and immediate solutions that diverge from the congregation's identity, mission, or vision. You might face pressure: "Do it now. Do it yesterday! Don't just stand there, do something!"

The Boss Takes Over

Ideally, people work together to solve problems. But in response to chaos, out of the dust and rubble one strong man (or woman) can take charge.[13] Mussolini becomes dictator and makes the trains run on time. Chaos is indeed improved by the strict control of a tyrant, but then people have a tyrant on their hands.

A chaotic system, needing structure and leadership, is vulnerable to exploitation by a tyrant. When people are flailing around and cannot think, they look to anyone for guidance. In this anxious system, someone loud, aggressive, and exploitive can declare themselves The Solution and be given power. One way the tyrant seizes power is by warning of the chaos that would occur without that tyrant's control. Indeed, the tyrant can gin up threat for political gain. With chaos knocking at the door, the tyrant's control is needed, or so the tyrant claims.

Furthermore, when people fear a threat, they seek the most paranoid or alarmed to protect themselves. What if there is a real attack? The most paranoid would be vigilant, the most alarmed, quickest to retaliate. Unfortunately, though, the same paranoia and alarm that elevated the tyrant keeps that figure in power by intimidating would-be challengers. See the *Wizard of Oz* head, flaming and intimidating.

Such tyrants make rules, based not on principles but on the tyrant's self-interest. They impose controls not only on people's behavior but also on their thoughts and emotions.

Fighting

Dwelling on the thought side of the thought–reflex continuum, people generate many responses to a problem. When reflexive, there are two: fight or flight.

When the solution is fight, the loud and aggressive foment and escalate conflict. Their escalation throws any opponents back on their heels and leaves them flummoxed or cowering. So make it a battle! No, make it a war!

Scapegoating

A healthy system is whole. An anxious system might seek relief by removing parts of itself—let's kick out Buster—otherwise known as scapegoating. Scapegoating is a process of loading the system's problems, or sins, onto one person, persons, or goat, and then complaining about, blaming, attacking, and banishing that scapegoat.

Problems accompany scapegoating. If people solve a problem by removing one problem person, when the next problem arises, they would scapegoat again. Then everyone would worry about becoming the next scapegoat.

Scapegoating is analogous to removing organs from one's body. You could get away with removing an appendix, but if the solution to each successive illness is to remove another organ, eventually the body weakens and dies. Analogously in a congregation, scapegoating results in less systemic wholeness, more illness.

Furthermore, the easiest person to scapegoat is the system's most vulnerable member—the miner's canary in the system. Attacking that individual creates a toxic environment for the scapegoat, but in an interconnected system, if the scapegoat/canary can't breathe, everyone's atmosphere is tainted. Paul acknowledged this interconnected system: "If one member suffers, all suffer together" (I Corinthians 12:26, English Standard Version [ESV]).

Invalidation

Ideally, a congregation is a support community for its members. Less ideally, in an anxiously fighting congregation, its members invalidate each other. As they invalidate, people apply erratic, extreme responses to each other.[14] They are overly involved in each other's lives, about which they dispense criticism. They disregard each other's painful emotions, or attribute those emotions to socially unacceptable traits: "You're just being over-reactive." They claim authority regarding others' emotions: "You are feeling angry, but won't admit it."

Heroes and Villains

The systems diagnosis views everyone as part of the problem and as, potentially, the cure. An anxious congregation using the mechanistic diagnosis divides those roles, blaming a villain for their pain and commissioning a hero to alleviate that pain.

Ministers can be hooked into the hero role, which may seem appealing at first. But in the drama of heroes and villains, to remain the hero becomes a high-wire act. Indeed, if you fail at being the hero, your next role: villain.

Sometimes the hero appears virtuous but powerless, tormented by the evil villain. If this hero cannot vanquish the villain, at least the hero gains moral standing by being more virtuous than the villain. This beleaguered hero gains another victory by garnering pity and accumulating allies against the villain: "You fight that big, bad villain on behalf of little, innocent me."

The Partisan System

While a calm system is whole, an anxious system, in fight mode, polarizes into partisan camps. Each side then lobs bombs at the other, decrying the other's terrible behavior, while describing their own behavior as justified in response to the other's evil. They would entice any remaining neutral party with "Don't you agree that we're right, and they are wrong?"

Pressure, or The Reform Campaign

Within a safe system, if I have a problem, I can change myself to improve my life. In a threat-filled system, I protect myself by hunkering down into my personal status quo. But I remain in pain, so something has to change. To relieve my pain while protecting myself, I reflexively move to change someone else, such as Buster. Let's look at what is wrong with him and change him. Facing a reform campaign, Buster is not accepted as he is, leaving him unsafe, adding to system-wide anxiety.

Flight

Within a safe system, people are comfortable being seen and heard. On the other hand, an anxious system can feel like a whack-a-mole game in which people are liable to be attacked, criticized, reformed, or scapegoated, so people keep their heads down. Engaging in flight, people usually do not bolt from committee meetings but hide in plain sight.

People hide by using self-protective silence or complaint, rather than the transparency that accompanies making proposals or asserting their wishes. When my congregation elevated Betty into leadership, someone who complained without proposing, that represented its collective impulse to hide.

Members of a congregation can hide also by avoiding their differences with each other. People mouth the approved platitudes or speak only with their allies.

Relatedly, people avoid directly addressing those with whom they have concerns, instead pulling in third parties to whom they address their concerns. The impulse to complain about me to third parties reflected my congregation's anxiety and reflexive flight. As a system's anxiety intensifies, the third parties multiply: former ministers, judicatories, attorneys, and the press.

Fearing attack, people protect themselves by erecting defenses: explanations, withdrawals, resentful accommodation, or phony niceness.

A whole congregation can hide by avoiding its problems. Indeed, problems, and the conflicts they generate, are scary. Who knows what will happen? Then problems go underground, fester, and erupt later in more dramatic form.

Finally, a congregation can hide by being vague about its identity. No one articulates why the congregation exists and what it is here to do. Without the meaning identity provides, morale, motivation, energy, and esteem all decline.

Fight and Flight

In a safe system, people express who they are and cooperate with each other. In an anxious system, people hide and fight at the same time. For instance, I passive-aggressively refuse to talk to Buster, which protects me, while my avoidance drives him nuts. I huddle with my cabal to deplore the nefariousness of Buster's cabal, fighting my enemy, while protected by my allies. I fight proposals and hide by offering none of my own.

Rigidity

Thinking done by one's prefrontal cortex is flexible and creative, developing many solutions to a problem and welcoming serendipitous possibilities. On the other hand, brain-stem thinking is rigid and myopic. People consider two solutions: fight or flight. They resist new ideas and stifle brainstorming.

Dependence

In a safe system, people's brains function well; when threatened and reactive, not so well. When people can't think, they want you to think for them, and ask you what to do. If they are new at a task, or need some one-time advice in a crisis, being told what to do and how to do it helps them learn the task or function in the crisis. But when people chronically cannot think or learn, that reflects their dependence.

You can sense their dependence when people seem perennially helpless and lost. You feel pressure to do more, solve more of their problems, meet more of their needs, and rescue them. Or the congregation makes requests and demands that you are afraid not to meet. You then find yourself, in Friedman's terms, "overfunctioning" as they "underfunction."[15] As you solve their problems and tell them what to do, that feeds and rewards their underfunctioning dependence.

This overfunctioning minister would be codependent. The codependent depends on the dependent for one's role and purpose. Guided by the motto "You matter; I don't," the codependent neglects one's own needs to take care of the dependent.[16] The dependent has infinite demands, so for the codependent, it is difficult to rest and conclude, "Job well done." Eventually the codependent burns out at which point one's motto becomes, "Nothing matters."

Codependence is difficult to avoid in ministry because congregations rightfully expect services: pastoral care, stimulating worship, newsletters, etc. But the anxious community in which people cannot think demands overabundant services, setting up this dependency-codependency relationship.

Another version of codependence occurs when people forgo their principles in reaction to each other. You can hear this codependence in statements such as "He said X, so I had to say Y." Or "She did A, so I had to do B." Or, humorously, "The devil made me do it."

Worry, Fear, Pessimism

Within a safe system, people are optimistic. In an unsafe system, people experience worry, fear, and pessimism. As you would guess, people can look and sound worried, exaggerate the congregation's problems, and dread the dire consequences of failure. They might also behave in ways that cause you to worry, such as with threats of pay cuts if pledging falls short. They might be scary, such as by proposing anonymous complaining about you. They might pessimistically doubt progress could ever occur.

To understand pessimism, researchers studied how an animal would be affected by a problem out of its control. They administered a mild shock to a lab animal and gave it no way to stop the shock.[17] They administered the same shock to another animal but gave it a bar it could press that would stop the shock. A third animal received no shock. The animals were moved to new cages, where they each could jump out, and were given that same mild shock. The first received the shock and did nothing. The second looked around—no bar—but looked further, saw a way out, and jumped. The third received the shock and jumped out. The researchers concluded that the first unfortunate animal had learned helplessness and pessimism. Your congregation could also have experienced shocks over which they had no control, leaving them helpless, displayed by worry, fear, and pessimism.

No Insight

In a safe system, people's prefrontal cortexes and hippocampi are active, and they can learn. When threatened, brain stems engaged, people cannot grasp complex thinking or insight.[18]

Ministers often try to heal by teaching, pulling for insight, hoping people will "get it." In Threatworld, they don't. Your brilliant observation, the best idea ever, hits people's emotional flames, ignites (*pfft!*), and then floats away as ineffectual ashes. Say goodbye to insight as a curative strategy.

Furthermore, insight involves looking inward. If the minister's insights are outward and all about the congregation, that minister is not safe enough to consider one's own participation in the congregation's ills.

Seriousness

In a safe system, people play, laugh, and are humored. Under threat, the brain stem, or reptile brain, is active, and people become reptilianly serious.[19] When everyone is earnest, and when playfulness, joking, or laughing is just out of the question, it is a tense, anxious system. For example, during my unit of CPE (Clinical Pastoral Education), death and tragedy consumed my hospital chaplaincy, and my supervisor joshed around and coaxed me to lighten up. I thought he was nuts. Living in a dire world, my reptile brain active, I was serious.

We Know the Rules—Implicit Obligation

Ideally in a congregation, people negotiate for what they want. Less ideally, they are bound by implicit obligation. As the rule of an autocrat improves chaos, a system bound by implicit obligation improves autocracy. The system does not need a tyrant bossing everyone around, because everyone knows what they "have" to do.[20]

In a family, obligation imposes implicit rules upon its members. The husband's rule might be "A good husband spends all his free time with his family." If this husband wants to go golfing with a friend, he would have a conflict between being the good husband vs. having fun with a buddy. If he announces, "I am going golfing with Joe," his wife might voice the obligation: "Buster, a loving husband would want to be home with his family." If he defies the rule for husbands, he feels guilty. If he stays home, he loses his freedom.

In a congregation, people would similarly know what they are obligated to do. If a minister says, "I have to meet with the Women's Alliance," there might not be a tyrant issuing this order, nor a law requiring it, nor even a request by the Women's Alliance, but still they "know" they must meet with the Women's Alliance.

A congregation and its minister might collude to impose implicit obligations on the minister. Together they know that a good minister is never ill, is always agreeable, wears modest clothes, has polite children, and drives a Subaru. If the minister wheels into the church parking lot ensconced in a cherry-red Corvette, eyebrows would rise to the heavens.

On one hand, internalized rules simplify decision-making. Also, in a church, it makes sense that individuals sacrifice some individual wishes for the good of the whole. On the other hand, implicit obligation prevents people from being free to do what they might want to do. No golfing. No Corvette. Thwarted desires fester resentment. Furthermore, closeness occurs when clearly defined people contact other clearly defined people, all negotiating for what they want, which does not happen when people forgo their wishes to fulfill implicit obligations.

YOU ARE A DIAGNOSTIC INSTRUMENT

As a minister and part of the congregation, you are subject to being infected by its illness, which gives you diagnostic information.

If you fear taking stands, or if any stand you take is demolished, you might be in a chaotic system.

If you are angry and want to pull out the big guns and blast your opponents, you could be in a system that escalates.

If you want to impose uniformity, you could be in a system that is unified at the expense of freedom.

If you want to rebel and defy other people, you might be in a system that is free at the expense of unity.

If you advocate for dramatic solutions that diverge from the congregation's traditions, you could be in a system that swings to opposites or that demands intense interventions to its problems.

If you feel pulled to solve problems fast, you could be in a reactive system demanding speed.

If you want to take control and set everything to right, you might be in a chaotic system that is pulling for a boss.

If you find yourself angry with people in your congregation and imagining scenarios in which they lose and suffer, you might be in a congregation that fights.

If you find yourself condemning one element of your congregation and wishing it were gone, you might be in a system that scapegoats.

If you find yourself judging and labeling your perceived opponents, you could be in a system that invalidates.

If you see yourself as your congregation's messiah and as the only one who can solve its problems, and if you target Buster as your foe, you might be in a congregation pulling for a hero to battle its villains.

If you find yourself wanting to be right and on the good side of every controversy, opposing the bad people on the other side, you could be in a partisan system.

If you want to change or fix other people, your congregation could respond to problems with reform campaigns.

If you are avoiding vulnerability, hiding your principles, defensively explaining everything you do or talking about others behind their backs, you could be experiencing a system in flight.

If you complain about your congregation while resisting its lay leaders' proposals, you might be in a system that practices fight and flight at the same time.

If you keep promoting one and only one solution to a problem, you might be in an inflexible, rigid system.

If you feel pulled to rescue the congregation and solve all its problems, or fear failing to meet people's demands, if you are working too hard and burning out, you might be serving a dependent system.

If you feel compelled to react to what others are doing at the expense of your principles, you could be dealing, again, with a dependent congregation.

If you feel afraid, worried, or pessimistic about your congregation, you could be reflecting its fear, worry, and pessimism.

If your insightful reflections to the congregation fall on deaf ears, if the people don't "get it," or if you notice your insights are all about them and not about yourself, you might be in a system that is not thinking reflectively and not amenable to insight.

If you cannot be anything but earnest and serious in your church, you could be in a system in which everyone is guided by their reptile brains and moving turtle-like through church life.

If you impose "shoulds" and obligation onto others, or if you feel compelled to do what you "should" do, justifying your overwork with the phrase "I have to …" you might be in a system ruled by implicit obligation.

A DIAGNOSTIC SITUATION: THE ANXIOUS TREASURER

For example, an anxious system might have a treasurer who expresses his worry: "I don't know if we can afford this. Maybe we shouldn't be spending … ."

You say, "But we have grown 40 percent in the past year. Our income has doubled in two years."

"But we could stop growing, and we have to replace the roof, and our staff costs are rising with our growth."

You think everyone is basking in this congregation's growth and vitality, if only this treasurer could be fixed or dismissed.

But the treasurer's worry reflects the congregation's worry. People remember posting the church's utility bills on the bulletin board and pleading for members to pay them. Worried this could happen again, they appointed a worrier for treasurer, hoping he will worry on their behalf and keep their finances sound.

Or the worry has little to do with money. Maybe there is anxiety about you, the new minister—you're so different from the Rev. Buster. If someone donates a million dollars to the congregation and the treasurer still worries, you realize that underneath money lies a deeper anxiety.

Viewed with the personality-problem diagnosis, this treasurer is sick. A million bucks, and he's still worried! Viewed through the systems lens, the treasurer expresses the congregation's anxiety about its history of financial insecurity, or about you.

WHAT IS THE THREAT?

The calm and calming diagnostician views the anxious system in the context of an understandable story in which there is a good reason people are anxious: they are threatened by a valid threat. There may be an actual crisis upon the congregation. The building burns down, or a van filled with its youth crashes on the highway. There could also be a crisis in the larger society. Terrorists attack the World Trade Center, or a man with a gun shoots up a school. Under such terrible circumstances, people naturally feel threatened and become anxious and reactive.

It's a Stage

As a second valid source of threat and disturbance, the congregation could be going through a stressful stage. A toddler in full tantrum blistering paint off the walls is going through a stage. Knowing it is a stage, the parents can then relax … a little. You could be like Moses leading people through what seems like forty years through the wilderness. If so, it is a stage that, like the terrible twos, will pass.

Peck described communities as going through four such stages of development.[21] The first stage is a honeymoon, which over time grows stale and phony. At stage two, differences erupt, and people push each other to change. But those being pushed do not want to change, and push back. This is a painful stage marked by tension and wrangling. Then at stage three, people stop pushing, listen, and practice vulnerable disclosure. This openness leads to stage four, which Peck calls true community. In the midst of stage two, though, life is painful, people are behaving badly, and everything can appear wrong. Still, it is just a necessary stage preceding stages three, openness, and four, community.

Also, the congregation could be in a transition, involving three stages.[22] First there is an ending, saying goodbye to old ways and assumptions—a painful stage of loss. Next comes emptiness. It is difficult to accept emptiness, to wait and consider what might be next. Then comes a new beginning, and people's spirits lift.

A congregation can also go through a loss and bereavement. Bereavement is a painful, wrenching deviation from the usual experience of everyday life. Despite how painful it is, bereavement is a normal response to a loss that takes a course along which healing occurs.

A congregation going through Peck's stage two, or a transition, or a bereavement, experiences stress that could trigger systemic anxiety. Nevertheless, if you frame their behavior as reflecting their process through a stage, you see the people as normal, their dramatic behavior understandable. Seeing people as normal lowers your tension and anxiety around them, enabling you to offer them patient, supportive guidance through the stages.

The Survival of the Fittest

When anxiety is chronic or coming from no obvious source, there is a third cause of reflexive behavior: the implicit threat posed by the survival-of-the-fittest organization of the world.

As Darwinian theory suggests, animals and plants compete for resources and for the ability to pass along their genes.[23] Two male elk clashing antlers in the mountains are working out which is more fit and thereby qualified to win the waiting harem of females. The stronger elk wins and gets to father the next generation of similarly fit elk.

In this hierarchical organization, the optimal location is on top, the alpha position, where survival is pretty secure, at least for the moment. Other individuals, such as the defeated elk, slip down in the hierarchy. Their survival is less secure, and so they live with anxiety. Those who are up have it better for now, but can't really relax. That winning elk will get old and next year might be overthrown by the buck he just defeated.

This survival-of-the-fittest hierarchy also occurs among humans. Kings and autocrats rule serfs and slaves. Capitalism decrees that the fittest are the wealthiest. Adults dominate children. Humanity dominates nature. In a patriarchy, men dominate women. Some theologies have the saved and the condemned, suggesting that correct belief is a form of fitness. Caucasians reap more benefits from society than African Americans. Heterosexuals have held more rights than homosexuals. Even in a family, sometimes the most love, support, and material wealth go to the oldest male. In this hierarchical organization, personal flaws reveal one as less fit for survival, so people hide them. In the end, there are winners and losers, the winners seeming to deserve to win, the losers to blame for losing.

If we distilled the many-runged hierarchical ladder down to two rungs, there would be a dominant party and a subordinate. Each would have their own script.

The dominant party has power.[24] He or she, often he, speaks easily and freely, confident in the importance of his views. He controls, using pressure, intimidation, even violence. The dominant party judges or labels, using name-calling or blaming. The dominant party can dismiss with joking, teasing, heckling, and excluding. When there is kind intent, the dominant party would be paternalistic. A leader with kind intent could also become corrupted by one's power, become self-aggrandizing, and dismiss the needs of one's followers. When there is hostile intent, the dominant party would inflict harm ruthlessly. This party wins, but remains wary of being overthrown.

The subordinate party has their script. He or she, often, she, accommodates and pleases to keep the dominant happy. Because the dominant has power over the subordinate's life, she pays attention to the dominant. A servant can claim to be good at her job because she knows the master so well, she knows what the master wants before the master knows.

The subordinate is stressed because she has little control over her destiny. The janitor, subject to the control of others, is more stressed than the CEO, who controls his destiny. The subordinate can complain, but that leaves the power to fix the problem in the hands of the dominant. One can plead, still leaving power with the dominant. One can express anger, but that anger can be dismissed as sound and fury signifying nothing. One can sabotage or do a slow-walk, without directly challenging the boss. One can find a shred of control as one helps and pleases. One can seduce. One can find sympathetic allies among other powerless people.

With no power to change her status, the subordinate endures helplessness, hopelessness, and depression. When she breaks the dominant's rules, the subordinate experiences guilt. Being low in the survival-of-the-fittest hierarchy, due to being supposedly more flawed and less fit than the dominant, one experiences shame. As the dominant is violent, in a complementary fashion the subordinate becomes self-destructive, such as by abusing substances. Indeed, the shame implied by being down in the survival-of-the-fittest hierarchy is so painful that people sometimes seek relief through suicide.

In this hierarchy, the dominant party is also stressed by having to work hard, keep competing, and stay vigilant to remain on top.

For everyone, love and cooperation do not occur up or down the rungs of a hierarchy. Competing against them for survival, people do not care about their opponents.

Even when people have food, shelter, and clothing, the survival-of-the-fittest hierarchy implies that for both dominants and subordinates, survival is not secure. Their survival threatened, people live on the reflex side of the thought–reflex continuum.

Living with chronic reflexive arousal, people experience high blood pressure and a rapid pulse, resulting in chronic illness. This condition would be analogous to a motor idling at high revs; it runs hot and breaks down sooner than a motor put-putting along.

The lower people descend on the hierarchy, the more insecure their survival, the more they live on the reflex side of the continuum, experience chronic anxiety, and suffer illness. Research conducted at a corporation revealed that low-ranked clerks were three times more likely to die of any cause than higher ranked coworkers.[25] Furthermore, with each step down the company ladder, workers' risks for heart disease, stroke, diabetes, obesity, addictions, infectious disease, and some cancers increased.

Living in the survival-of-the-fittest world, people learn and internalize difficult assumptions:

> There are winners and losers.
> One has to fight hard to win.
> Only the few have power and a voice.
> The loser has no power, no voice.
> The loser is flawed and so deserves to lose.
> One is alone.
> One is not safe.
> Not being safe, one has to protect oneself.
> One's needs will not be met.

The survival of the fittest causes additional problems: war, injustice, and environmental destruction. I think that the root of all human problems is our historical and ongoing emphasis of the survival of the fittest.

Nevertheless, hierarchies do have value. The stronger elk fathering the next generation benefits his species' vitality. Competition prods athletic and business achievement. A leader offers efficient decision-making. Ideally, the best ideas rise to the surface.

Because hierarchies have value, bee colonies have queens and wolf packs their alpha individuals. Human organizations also structure into hierarchies. People elect leaders and find security in a division of labor.

Nevertheless, when emphasized, this survival-of-the-fittest organization of the world exacts tragic consequences.

A congregation living with hierarchical assumptions is being consistent with the larger system—the world around them. The congregation can assume and even emphasize this hierarchical structure by fostering debates, arguments, and elections that determine winners and losers. Dominant parties, such as the minister, can apply pressure and judgment. As it lives out the survival-of-the-fittest logic, the congregation will perceive threat and experience chronic systemic anxiety.

Even if the congregation de-emphasizes the survival-of-the-fittest organization, the world around it retains survival-of-the-fittest hierarchies, giving the congregation a threatening context, which can infect it with systemic anxiety.

WHY DO WE EMPHASIZE HIERARCHY?

We could apply the personality-problem diagnosis to humanity and accuse ourselves of having a personality problem that causes us to emphasize survival-of-the-fittest hierarchies. Instead, I suggest that we validate ourselves by seeing our emphasis of the survival of the fittest as understandable.

A story can be told about the human species assuming power and becoming corrupted by it. The earliest humans fit with the other species into nature's balance. They gathered foods and hunted small animals—a successful hunt might bring home a rabbit.[26] Or they might find an already-dead animal (*yum!*).[27] Other animals preyed on them, which kept their population in check. They probably saw big animals, mastodons, and salivated but knew that poking a mastodon with a stick would have been suicidal. Still their big brains pondered how to fight off predators and how to slaughter an animal big enough to provide steaks for the whole clan.

At some point, people's big brains figured out how to advance in hunting skills so as to fight off predators and kill big animals and live to tell the tale. They could then hunt down almost any animal, and did, wiping out mastodons, giant beavers, flightless birds, and other such prey.[28] When they had killed off local prey, unlike other predators, humans could switch their diet to plants.[29] Their hunting skills and omnivorousness allowed humans to survive by exempting themselves from nature's we're-all-in-this-together balance.

Humans made another move to dominate nature when they developed agriculture and controlled plants to meet their needs.[30] When they developed the container and could store surplus food, they became more immune to natural crop fluctuations.[31]

Separation from nature continued with the construction of city walls, in part to wall out nature.[32] People smelted metals, built machines, and harnessed fossil fuels, to become increasingly healthy, wealthy, comfortable, and increasingly separate from nature's balance. Surviving via superiority and separation from nature was enshrined in Genesis in which the creator gave humanity "dominion" over the earth (Genesis 1:28, ESV).

The dominance that worked with plants and animals people applied to each other. They emphasized winner vs. loser hierarchies, with rich over poor, kings over serfs, males over females, the saved over the damned. Humanity in many circumstances continues to use this survival-of-the-fittest, winner vs. loser organization because it helped us survive. A survival mechanism is valuable and hard to de-emphasize, even though it extracts tragic costs.

CONCLUSION

Systems theory presents a diagnostic principle: a symptom represents illness in the whole system generated by a valid cause. That validating diagnosis begins the cure.

QUESTIONS FOR REFLECTION

In your experience, what examples of systemic anxiety have you witnessed, and what symptoms have you observed in such systems?

When have you felt an emotion as a member of a group or system? What was your emotion? What did that emotion indicate about the health of the group?

NOTES

1. *Oxford English Dictionary*, 3rd edition., s.v. "diagnosis."

2. William Shakespeare, "Romeo and Juliet" in *The Oxford Shakespeare: The Complete Works,* 2nd edition, ed. John Jowett, William Montgomery, Gary Taylor, and Stanley Wells (Oxford: Oxford University Press, 2005).

3. Louis Cozolino, *The Neuroscience of Psychotherapy* (New York: Norton, 2010).

4. Pat Ogden, "Emotion, Mindfulness, and Movement" in *The Healing Power of Emotion*, ed. Diana Fosha, Daniel Siegel, and Marion Solomon (New York: Norton, 2009).

5. Ibid., 204–31.

6. Daniel Siegel, *The Developing Mind* (New York: Guilford Press, 1999).

7. Paul MacLean, *The Triune Brain in Evolution* (New York: Springer, 1990).

8. Edwin Friedman, "Bowen, Theory and Therapy." In *Handbook of Family Therapy, vol. II*, ed. A. Gurman and D. Kniskern (New York: Brunner/Mazel, 1991), 134–70.

9. Maggie Scarf, *Intimate Worlds* (New York: Ballantine Press, 1997).

10. Jay Heinrichs, *Thank You for Arguing* (New York: Three Rivers Press, 2013).

11. George Orwell, *1984* (New York: Alfred Knopf, 1992).

12. William Golding, *Lord of the Flies* (New York: Berkeley Publishing Group, 1954).

13. Scarf, *Intimate Worlds*.

14. Marsha Linehan, *Cognitive Behavioral Treatment of Borderline Personality Disorder* (New York: Guilford Press, 1993).

15. Friedman, "Bowen Theory and Therapy."

16. Fred Lehr, *Clergy Burnout* (Minneapolis. Fortress Press, 1991).

17. Martin Seligman, *Learned Optimism* (New York: Vintage Books, 2006).

18. Cozolino, *The Neuroscience of Psychotherapy*.

19. MacLean, *The Triune Brain.*

20. Scarf, *Intimate Worlds.*

21. Scott Peck, *The Different Drum* (New York: Touchstone, 1998).

22. William Bridges, *Transitions* (New York: Da Capo Press, 2004).

23. Charles Darwin, *The Origin of the Species* (London: J. Murray, 1859).

24. Carol Pierce and Bill Page. *A Male/Female Continuum: Paths to Colleague-ship* (Laconia, NH: New Dynamics Publications, 1986).

25. R. G. Wilkinson, *Unhealthy Societies: The Afflictions of Inequality* (London: Routledge, 1996).

26. Jared Diamond, *Guns, Germs, and Steel* (New York: Norton, 1997).

27. Ian Tattersall, *Masters of the Planet* (New York: Palgrave Macmillan, 2012).

28. Diamond, *Guns, Germs, and Steel.*

29. Tattersall, *Masters of the Planet.*

30. Ian Morris, *Foragers, Farmers, and Fossil Fuel* (Princeton: Princeton University Press, 2015).

31. Frederick Turner, *Beyond Geography* (Rutgers, NJ: Rutgers University Press, 1992).

32. Ibid.

3

The Healthy Church

We pastors are congregational therapists called to support the healthy functioning of our congregations. Therefore, it behooves us to envision that health toward which we are working.

At first glance, we know what a healthy congregation looks like. It would have an optimistic tone, happy congregants, meaningful worship, and vital programs and services for its members and for the community. It would support people's spiritual lives. There would be not merely an absence of symptoms, but the presence of well-being.

THE CONGREGATION IS WHOLE AND SAFE

A healthy congregation would also be whole. The minister offering therapy or healing to a congregation supports that wholeness. Indeed, the word "heal" comes from the Old English word "haelen" meaning "to cure, save, and make whole."[1]

In a whole congregation, people would assume: "We're in this together and we cooperate and collaborate." This we're-in-this-together assumption contrasts with the assumption that congregational life is a survival-of-the fittest competition, which pits people against each other and raises anxiety. The cooperation and collaboration engendered by being in the same boat together supports everyone's sense of safety within that boat.

Not just congregations, but the world is organized in these two ways: the survival-of-the-fittest and we're-in-this-together. See figure 3.1. We're-in-this-together occurs in nature as particles collect to form atoms, atoms into molecules, cells into bodies. Animals group into packs, schools, and flocks.

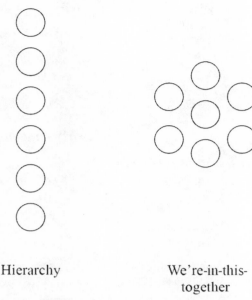

Hierarchy   We're-in-this-
                             together

Figure 3.1 Two ways the world is organized.

The aggregate of all the earth's interdependently related species forms a we're-in-this-together world.

In human circles, we're-in-this-together occurs in communities in which people accept and support each other despite their flaws and foibles. Such societies are guided by laws and policies that apply to everyone equally and that treat everyone fairly. People address differences with listening and negotiate win-win outcomes, resulting in peace. Spiritually, we're-in-this-together communities teach that God loves us all equally and infinitely.

Although hierarchies divide people and raise anxiety, they have an upside: skilled leaders offer good ideas, implementing them efficiently. Therefore, a healthy system balances hierarchy with we're-in-this-together. Indeed, a system guided only by the survival-of-the-fittest has a self-aggrandizing leader who makes expeditious decisions, but whose decisions hurt the followers. On the other hand, a system guided only by we're-in-this-together might host conversations like: "It's Sunday. What do you want to do?"

"I don't know. What do you want to do?"
"I don't know. What do you want to do?"

Without leader suggesting, "Let's have a worship service," this community could drift without a rudder, everyone shrugging their shoulders and looking blankly at each other. A parish minister balances both worlds by being the leader in the alpha position who works on behalf of everyone, thus supporting the we're-in-this-together wholeness of the congregation.

In the end, within that well-led and still whole congregation, people can trust their belonging and experience a safe and supportive spiritual fellowship.

Communication Goes Well

In a healthy congregation, people communicate well. Healthy communication involves the exploration of ideas from various points of view. As people explore, all are equal on a quest for truth. As matters are explored deeply and collaboratively, insights transcend individual understandings, people experience closeness with each other, and everyone wins.

There is admittedly a note of la-la land in the paragraph above because communication in a community is difficult. Complicating communication are the underlying and unspoken questions running through any group: Who's in? Who's out? Who's up? Who's down?[2] While communicating, people are maneuvering for positions in which they are up and in, seeking esteem, power, and closeness with others. Down and out is where they sing the blues.

People can bring a gauzy naivete about communication. They can assume that communication involves simply conveying objective information to which others are responding objectively. Sorry, but much is occurring subjectively and emotionally as people maneuver around inclusion and power.

People can also naively assume they know what another person means when they say X and that others know what they mean when they say Y. When feelings are intense, conflicts are occurring, or the stakes are high, think again. To ask: "What did you hear me say just now?" can reveal that the other heard little of, or the opposite of, what was just said.

After failures at communication, people can feel pessimistic. Assuming communication will fail, they stake inflexible positions, defend themselves, or withdraw.

To address these challenges, people acknowledge that communication in groups bears attention. They might attend to communication by verbalizing what they just heard. "I hear you saying X. Is that correct?" Furthermore, when they have said something they think might be hard to hear, or misinterpreted, or when its response comes from out of left field, they ask: "What did you hear me say?"

Groups support healthy communication by setting standards. For instance, they create a covenant, which includes such items as "We make I-statements" and "We listen openly." The leader can articulate standards as well, such as "We are a support community, therefore let us support each other by respecting each other's ideas."

To monitor its communication, sometimes a group enlists a process observer who notes and reports at intervals: Are we coming closer together or further apart? Are we moving toward an agreement or stuck?

A group supports healthy communication when its people greet new ideas with curiosity. They see what can be built out of the new idea, analogous to helping at a barn raising.[3] "Let me help you construct this idea. I'll raise this supporting beam. And how do we provide space for cows?" To help construct someone else's idea, one defers for the moment one's own idea. That deferment does not mean abandoning one's idea or agreeing with something one questions. It does mean giving the other a turn to explore their idea. One's own turn can come later. Indeed, if both parties are vying to express their ideas at the same time, no one is heard. Instead, when people collaborate on building an idea, with two or more brains at work, the result might be better than if one person developed it alone. Furthermore, the barn-building conversation leaves participants feeling good about their creativity and close to each other.

When people in a healthy community communicate emotions, those feelings are understood as important information about how well people's needs are being met. Therefore, people do not seek to silence each other's emotional expressions but affirm them. If someone is angry, the rest of the community understands that that anger expresses unmet needs. They validate the anger and then negotiate how to meet that person's needs, alongside everyone else's, resulting in general contentment.

Feedback Is Constructive

A healthy congregation gives healthy feedback. Giving positive, behavioral feedback affirms effort and improvement, which rewards people and increases the odds that such behavior will recur.[4] For example: "You worked hard on this year's canvass, and we raised our pledge income by 10 percent. Congratulations!"

When you have to offer negative feedback, it works best when it is specific to one occasion and reveals the effects of an observed behavior. "When you said X, I felt Y" provides useful information.

Congregations often give their clergy feedback in such forms as the "Every Member Survey," a bump-in-the-night phenomenon that sends chills down ministers' spines. These ratings assume that a minister provides services, which congregational consumers evaluate. Such surveys often use a Likert scale to measure a minister's success at pleasing everyone. An item might read: "Rate the minister's sermons on a scale from 1 to 5, 1 being 'dislike;' 5 being 'like very much.'" The minister might learn how many 1's, 2's, etc., they received and/or a cumulative rating such as 2.5. If one received a 2.5, that could nag at the minister with the sense that their sermons are not hitting the ball out of the park, while giving the minister no information on how to improve one's preaching. (All is not lost, though. That minister could interpret their own anxiety as reflecting the congregation's anxiety and address that anxiety.)

A more informative form of feedback asks parishioners: What from our minister would you want more of? Less of? And the same? These questions invite guidance for the minister's behavior. Receiving the feedback "I'd like more sermons about the moral and political questions of the day and related spiritual implications" could guide the minister's preaching. If the minister receives a suggestion that violates one's goals and principles, one can decline it. If Betty had asked for more blessings on anonymous complaining, I could have viewed this as interesting and then continued to support open communication.

A second form of a constructive feedback assesses the minister's progress toward stated goals. At the beginning of the program year, the minister and board can agree on the minister's goals for the year. At the end of the year, everyone can gauge how well those goals were met.

Third, everyone is evaluated. Why let the minister have all the fun? Everyone considers: How are we doing on our jobs? They look back: What did we accomplish? They look forward: How could we improve?

People Experience Love and Freedom

Healthy congregations balance love and freedom. I think communities live on a continuum with love at one end, freedom at the other. On the love side, people share responsibility for their community and give each other support. They are unified by a mission. They are contained by an organizational structure. Policies exist and are followed. The congregation is guided by behavioral standards. This love gives people belonging and warmth.

On the freedom side, people can be their autonomous and unique selves. They can speak freely and disagree with each other. They can take stands and influence their system. This freedom gives people energy.

Individuals in a group want to be uniquely themselves and to securely belong. A congregation can offer that best-of-both-worlds experience.

There Is Structure

Healthy congregations are well-organized, guided by clear, effective policies, procedures, and roles (see Chapter 5, "Church Structure").

Thought Occurs, Problems Are Solved

Within a safe community, people dwell on the thought side of the thought–reflex continuum. There people use moderation to solve problems, rather than escalate into wars. People's prefrontal cortexes are engaged, which supports creative thinking, generating many solutions to a given problem.

The Congregation Develops

A healthy congregation develops. Sometimes this development means growing in membership from family size, to pastoral, to program, to corporate.
The congregation expands its building and adjusts its organizational structure
to accommodate new members.

Sometimes development involves a community's progression, described in
Chapter 2, "Diagnosis," from a honeymoon (that grows stale), to a stage at
which people pressure each other to change, to a stage of mutual openness,
to an authentic community.

The Congregation's Identity Is Apparent

A healthy congregation lives into the fullness of its identity. Its unity unites;
its activism activates; its spirituality deepens. Indeed, one indication that a
congregation is secure and living on the thought side of the continuum is that
it knows and reveals its identity. This congregation would clearly be itself, not
trying to be all things to all people, nor reflexively hiding.

Oswald and Lees define congregational identity as the persistent set of
beliefs, values, patterns, symbols, stories, and style that makes a congregation
distinctive.[5] A congregation's identity is analogous to an individual's identity: an amalgam of one's history, beliefs, desires, likes, values, principles,
achievements, and more. Identity is harder to identify than the more visible
church programs, but like gravity is quietly present and powerful.

Its identity gives a congregation benefits. Identity coheres a community
just as a cell membrane coheres protoplasm into a cell. The identity says
"yes" to that which the community affirms and "no" to that which is antitheti-
cal to the community.

Its identity provides a grounding or a stabilizing ballast. With that ballast,
the congregation can weather storms with confidence.[6]

Its identity boosts a congregation's esteem. "Go Mudville!" generates more
enthusiasm than "Go... *um*... somebody...whomever we are."

A clear identity supports congregational growth. Oswald and Lees
affirm, "What seems to be more important than anything else is that growing congregations have a positive personality, which shows through in the
church's (a) energy, (b) belief in inclusion, and (c) sense of having a unique
identity."[7]

Identity informs a congregation's programs. Church life occurs in a cycle,
depicted in Figure 3.2, beginning with identity—who we are—leading to
mission—what we are here to do—and vision—where we are going. With
identity, mission, and vision clear, a church sets goals, specified in objectives. There could be a five-year goal—double the membership size—with

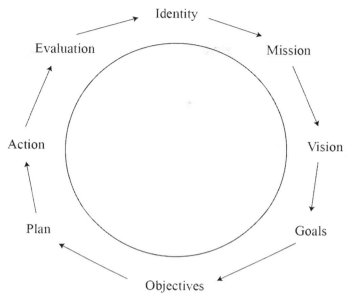

Figure 3.2   Identity cycle.

objectives: grow by 20 percent each of the five years. With objectives clear, committees or boards plan how to meet their goals and objectives, deciding who does what, when, and with what resources. With a plan, action follows: a program, a worship service, something happens. Then people evaluate: Did the action move us toward our goal? Was it consistent with our identity, mission, and vision? Does this alter our identity? Then they are back to considering their identity. The identity, mission, and vision of the congregation provide meaning and answer the "So what?" question. Someone asks: "We are meeting for worship and are hosting service programs, but so what?"

> "Well, we do so because we are a community of faith in God. We worship together to remind us of our faith, and we express our faith by caring for others."
> "Oh! I see. That makes total sense. Thank you."

On the other hand, when people do not see the meaning of their communal enterprise, they lose interest. The thrill is gone, and they complain of burnout.

If the point is missing, it is time to articulate the identity, mission, and vision of the church. Indeed, every Sunday you occupy a pulpit from which to name why we all bother to convene for worship, run programs, and care for each other. It may seem self-evident, and hardly worth articulating, nevertheless that articulation reminds the people of their collective purpose.

Furthermore, holding up a mirror to the congregation so they can see themselves more clearly helps them develop further into who they are.

It may seem difficult to name one unifying identity. A congregation would have its polarities: old members and new, or traditional and innovative, but some common denominator brings people together Sunday after Sunday. What would that be?

You may also want to invite the congregation to recognize and name their identity themselves. When they articulate it, they can more fully embrace that identity.

To support you in articulating and eliciting your congregation's identity, here are its facets.

ELEMENTS OF CONGREGATIONAL IDENTITY

Functions

A church has many functions.

It is a small nonprofit, with a staff, a budget, a building, policies, and procedures.

It is a social club, where people make friends and enjoy each other.

It is a chosen family into which people willingly join and give each other a home and belonging.

It is a home for values, such as values for love, altruism, or the divine.

It is an informal therapy group, where people heal and grow.

It is a school, offering lifelong learning.

It is a group of do-gooders, contributing to others.

It is a political action committee, influencing the larger body politic.

It is an artists' colony, where people create beauty, such as a choir making music.

It is a showcase, where people can achieve greatness and display their best qualities.

It is a camp, where people have fun, play, and make noise.

Many secular and sacred communities fulfill these functions. But I define the unique function of the church as this: the church is a support community for people on various journeys toward ultimate goals, such as love, or peace, or liberation.

While hopefully every congregation fulfills all these functions, Congregation A might emphasize the fellowship function, Congregation B might emphasize social action, and Congregation C might focus on its institutional strength.

Mission

Akin to its function, a central aspect of a congregation's identity is its mission. To clarify its mission, you might ask your congregants what your church does for them. They might appreciate its spiritual support, its accepting community, and its contribution to the world. They would then be articulating its mission as they experience it. Pooling everyone's experience of what their church does for them would reveal its mission themes. To clarify mission further the *Handbook for Congregational Studies* offers four missions.[8]

Guided by the sanctuary mission, the church provides an opportunity to withdraw from the trials of daily life and receive spiritual support within a community of fellow believers. Its worship taps into the sacred, inspiring its members.

The civic congregation supports existing social and economic structures. To address hunger, the civic congregation could host a soup kitchen. It takes up social issues by providing a forum within which those issues can be discussed, enabling members to act, but on their own.

The activist congregation, on the other hand, engages in corporate action to transform social and economic structures with the goal of a just and loving society. Rather than offer a soup kitchen, it lobbies for justice.

The inviting/evangelical congregation seeks to bring people into the faith. It offers others the community's saving message of hope, love, freedom, or meaning.

In identity workshops, I have invited participants to vote for which of these missions they saw their congregation fulfilling. If the group observes their congregation emphasizing the sanctuary and civic missions, that could be reflected back to them: "You are a congregation that seeks to give its members spiritual sustenance, and to contribute to the community." They would respond: "That's us."

Story

A third aspect of a community's identity is its central story or stories. To clarify a congregation's story, *The Handbook*, cites the theory that in all the literature of the world, there are only (spoiler alert) four stories.[9]

The cosmic story emphasizes the oneness, union, and harmony underlying apparent differences. Taoism tells this story with its emphasis on the Tao as a unifying presence and its counsel to go with its flow and receive its energy. Statements like "It will all work out" or "Let go and let God" express this cosmic union. The Hollywood love story reflects this union theme. At the beginning of the movie, the couple appears incompatible, but in the final scene they embrace.

In the tragic story, forces conspire to cause the individual's diminishment. Tragedy is resolved not by winning but by accepting loss. Mortality is a tragic story, and there is nothing we can do to stop it. An elderly person memorializing loved ones and encountering one's own physical limits could be living this tragic story.

The journey story tells of the hero's or heroine's venture out from the familiar and safe, into the unknown but promising. One enters the wilderness and there struggles through complications and vicissitudes on a quest for something great: love, power, a boon for the world. The Gospel recounts Jesus's journey through death and saving rebirth. The Hebrews' journeying to the Holy Land, immigrants coming to America, or young adults embarking on their journey of life emphasize this story.

In the empirical story, what you see is what you get. This story expresses the search for truths that can be observed through the senses and measured. In this story, there are no heroes or heroines, no mystery. The world has natural explanations for everything. "Let's be honest and realistic" is an empirical plea. The scientist measuring data, or Sherlock Holmes gathering clues, would be empirical.

Members of a congregation might conclude that they resonate with the union and journey stories, indicating that they are sharing a journey toward union and harmony.

Purpose and Authority

Another aspect of identity involves a congregation's purpose and source of authority.[10] There are four options.

For a house of worship, worship is central and done well. During worship, people explore transcendence and mystery. In the worship service people can experience intimacy, but if people gather for worship only, it is easy to remain anonymous. There is not much conversation after church; friendship is optional. Power is held by clergy, staff, and administrative committees. A Roman Catholic church is likely a house of worship, as the priest and staff make decisions; the people receive the Mass then go home.

The family congregation emphasizes support for its close-knit circle of members. It calls itself a family. Its Sunday worship provides a ritual confirmation of the church as family. During worship, time is taken for family matters within the congregation. Coffee hour is seen as a part of worship. Families have homes, and so the family congregation values its building. The family congregation tends to suppress conflict because when conflict does occur, it becomes personal and intense.

In a family congregation, power is vested in those with the longest tenure. Someone who pronounces: "My great-grandfather laid the cornerstone of this church ..." is claiming pedigree and therefore tenure, as if to say: "therefore I have the power to make decisions around here." The pastor, holding less tenure than longtime members, may offer pastoral support but is excluded from power.

The community congregation strives to be a harmonious, close community. It develops interpersonal closeness through small fellowship groups. It cares for members' needs. To maintain harmony, the community congregation practices a democratic process that spreads authority and participation through its membership. When there is a conflict, members strive to achieve consensus by incorporating all views to arrive at a decision that meets everyone's needs. The pastor facilitates and guides a healthy decision-making process, leaving the outcome of those decisions to the membership.

The leader church is activist, speaking out on social issues. Its pastor applies influence both in the community and within the congregation. In a leader church, authority is gained not from an official role (house of worship), tenure (family church), or shared agreement (community church), but from doctrine, scriptures, and tradition. The pastor is the steward of these sources of authority and so speaks in a commanding, directive way, citing texts and tradition to promote the morally correct outcome.

Reviewing these purposes and sources of authority, people might conclude: "We are a family congregation, and when is our next potluck?"

History

Its history provides another aspect of a congregation's identity. In identity workshops, participants chart on a roll of butcher paper a timeline of the church's history, including events in the larger world that affected the congregation.

Looking at their timeline, people can observe relevant themes through the sweep of their history. They might conclude: "We have been through a lot. The building burned down in 1810. We rebuilt. The Civil War caused a rift that took decades to heal. Rev. Smith philandered during his brief tenure in the 1920s, but Rev. Jones brought us three decades of stability. We grew in the sixties, declined in the seventies, and re-grew in the eighties. There must be something here that keeps us going." Indeed, they would be observing their resilience.

Doctrine

A congregation's identity includes which doctrines it considers most important. At an identity workshop, I would ask which elements of their denomination's creed or doctrine their congregation emphasizes. If the church follows the Nicene Creed, it might emphasize the son-ship of Jesus; another church, the fatherhood of God.

Symbols and Rituals

A congregation's identity includes its symbols and rituals. A symbol or ritual is like an arrow pointing to something profoundly meaningful, or a vehicle bringing people to salvation.

To clarify their congregation's symbols, people could ask:

What are the symbols and rituals seen here at this congregation?
How do we symbolize love?
How do we symbolize power?
What are our symbols of transcendence?
How do we ritualize rites of passage: death, coming of age, marriage, child
    dedication, joining?
How do we celebrate holidays?
Who is responsible for symbols and rituals?

Maybe for one church its altar, candles, cross, and open Bible symbolize divine support for its people. In another church, its crowded bulletin board symbolizes its activity in the world. A church's pews could be symbol of tradition. Another church could see its folding chairs as a symbol of its innovation and flexibility.

A congregation could assess its worship in terms of its simplicity vs. intricacy. A very simple worship involves resting in the presence of God—Quakers sitting quietly in an unadorned room and speaking when the spirit moves them. A more intricate worship involves abundant images and symbols, such as a high Mass with Bach on the organ, celebrants wearing vestments, and sunlight shining through stained-glass windows.

Rules

A congregation has rules regarding how people are supposed to behave. Some rules are explicit, spelled out in covenants, policies, and bylaws. Others are implicit and "known" by everyone, or almost everyone, as revealed when someone breaks such a rule and people are then "shocked, shocked!"

People could create an "Insider's Manual" for their church that would include rules or norms around:

Communal behavior
Money
Level of personal sharing
Alcohol
Political expression
Inclusion of outsiders and members of minorities

Commitment to the congregation
Conflicts
Other important rules

Demographics

Demographics influence a congregation's identity. Demographics statistically describe the congregation's members according to age, gender, ethnicity, education, marital status, social class, sexual identity, religious background, etc. A church composed of many gray-haired folks has a different identity than one with families and kids running around. A church of African American people differs from one with Korean or Latino people.

Size

A congregation's identity changes with its membership size.[11]

The family-sized church has up to 100 members active and attending worship. Its members experience intimacy, as they all know each other well, and informality, as there is not much to organize. Its "parents," the patriarchs and matriarchs, lead. Power is often de facto and held by those who, through their long and worthy service, have earned the trust of the community. The pastor, often being new, has less authority.

The pastoral-sized church has 50 to 150 members. Its size and complexity call for more organized leadership. The membership organizes itself into a few subgroups. The pastor would be the central leader in close contact with everyone.

The program-sized church has 150 to 350 members. The clergy is no longer able to be in contact with everyone, but they develop programs and delegate pastoral and leadership duties to the laity.

The corporate-sized church has over 350 members. The senior pastor is a symbol of unity and stability amid complex congregational life. That pastor is seen as presiding over something majestic and impressive. People relate to each other within small, intimate subgroups. The church is involved in various aspects of people's lives, providing daycare, recreation, or retirement services.

Finances

A congregation's relationship to money constitutes another aspect of its identity. A congregation with a large endowment supporting its operating expenses differs from one that depends on pledges.

Questions related to finances could include the following:

What are the sources of our congregation's money?
On what do we spend it?
How do we talk about it?
What is the process of deciding how we raise and spend money?

Character and Style

A congregation's character and style approach hard-to-measure qualities regarding how its members work and play together. To explore a congregation's style, its members could ask:

What sort of program really clicks here?
When do we feel most together?
How does this congregation deal with a challenge or a crisis?

Some themes will likely emerge, such as "We are a congregation that likes to have fun, but also likes a challenge. We take on the challenge and handle it well. When we accomplish the challenge, we celebrate and have a good time."

A second way to explore character and style considers the degree to which the congregation is laid back or bustling, cautious or bold, energetic or reserved, tentative or confident, consensual or hierarchical, cool or warm, casual or formal, and pessimistic or optimistic. Feel free to add other stylistic qualities.

In the end, a healthy church is clear and transparent about its identity. One congregation might conclude: "We are a community congregation on a journey toward wholeness and oneness with God. We have a range of ages and ethnicities, although economically we tend to be middle class and well-educated. We teach the fatherly nature of God with moderate formality, preferring classical music to contemporary. Our long history and our large endowment give us security."

Another congregation might conclude: "We are an inspired and enthusiastic African American leader church, here to serve our members and the community through programs and advocacy. Our worship is energetic and intended to energize us into action. Our membership has both the well-educated and white-collar and the less-educated and blue-collar. We are a new congregation working on establishing ourselves and evangelically inviting others to join us."

Segue to Vision

In my experience, as a congregation explores and names its identity, the conversation naturally flows around the identity cycle to vision. Seeing who they are, people speak of where they would like to go. Put differently, being grounded and secure in their identity, people can trust and risk envisioning their shared horizon. Therefore, they might propose: "We are nicely civic, but we could journey into greater activism. Let's really address some issues."

When members express visions for their church, that would empower them and enhance their ownership of the congregation. Then you might find yourself in a virtuous cycle: clarity about identity grounding the congregation in its source of meaning, giving people security, leading to their willingness to risk envisioning, giving them ownership of that vision, leading to enthusiasm and meaningful action. The word "enthusiasm" originates from the Greek: "enthous" meaning: to be filled with God.[12] If your ministry guides people into clarity about their identity, which generates enthusiasm for their vision, not bad for a day's work.

THE CONGREGATION SUPPORTS ITS MEMBERS

A healthy congregation provides a context in which its members find support with which they function well, feel good, and go forth on their spiritual journeys. The congregation itself is the elixir for its members. It's high tide, and all boats are tacking in the breeze.

Back to the thought–reflex continuum, in a healthy system, people feel safe enough to think slowly and reflect on matters, and such reflection supports maturation. Furthermore, their stress is low, and so people's blood pressure and heart rate are low, resulting in fewer stress-induced chronic illnesses and longer life spans.[13]

Church involvement supports self-discipline, which correlates with health and success.[14] Self-discipline is called upon when lazing around on Sunday mornings is tempting. The belief that God is watching, or that a community is aware of how you're doing, creates accountability, which further helps self-discipline.

The religious practices of meditation and prayer strengthen the part of the brain that handles self-regulation. Individuals benefit when their self-regulation helps them think before they act, and the world benefits from well-regulated individuals. (Poorly regulated people leave destruction in their wakes.) These practices, and religious involvement in general, support people's psychological and physical well-being,[15] life satisfaction,[16] and their ability to cope with stress.[17]

Being religious is further associated with healthy family functioning, lower levels of spousal conflict, and more consistent parenting.[18] Religiousness is also linked to forgiveness,[19] kindness,[20] compassion,[21] and altruism.[22]

Furthermore, a healthy congregation is an informal therapy group. Indeed, many of the emotional benefits people find in a church parallel the benefits of group therapy, as follows.

Hope

Hoping a therapy group will be helpful has the placebo effect of making it helpful.[23] Furthermore, group members boost each other's hope by revealing their own progress.

To a congregation, people also bring hope for support, salvation, and meaning. Hearing what new members are seeking, you can respond, "Yes, I think you'll find that here." To add support for that hope, you can encourage testimonials celebrating all the love, growth, acceptance, etc., people have found. When its members believe in the congregation's efficacy, that congregation is efficacious.

Universality

Someone suffering can feel alone, as if they were the only one who ever _____ (fill in the blank). The shame of being alone intensifies one's suffering. But in a therapy group, people find others who have struggled with the same issues. What a relief!

People might come to a church feeling alone and lonely. No one else has my questions, doubts, or particular beliefs. Ideally, though, they find a church in which they commune with like-minded souls. To invite such communing, the minister, knowing the universality of people's experiences, supports people's openness with each other. The minister does so by offering one's own vulnerability in the pulpit, which shows people they too have the safety they need to be open and vulnerable. Small reflection groups, retreats, and the sharing of joys and concerns during worship all provide forums for vulnerability leading to the realization: "I am not the only one."

Information

In group therapy, people receive helpful information, such as the benefits of exercise or the name of a good psychiatrist.

A church can also impart information, such as about what to expect during bereavement, what happens in transitions, or how to support children's spiritual development.

Information differs from advice—a mild form of pressure. Information describes how the world works, letting someone use that information to choose one's own behavior. Advice might be fine and well intended, and if someone asks for advice, I'll give it (this book is full of advice), but simply giving information about how the world works and letting people decide what to do with it is helpful.

Altruism

In a therapy group, members give each other active listening, support, and the box of tissues. When people give to others, their esteem and experience of meaning increase.

Congregations are natural places for altruism. Simply placing a dollar in the collection plate is altruistic. People can, of course, serve on committees, teach Sunday School, bring a casserole to bereaved parishioner, or be altruistically involved in the larger community.

Social Learning

In a therapy group, people develop social skills, such as how to take turns or how to speak honestly. Likewise, in a church, people can learn elementary skills, such as how to sit quietly during worship; or intermediate, such as assertiveness; or advanced, such as how to lead a capital campaign. In a church, people can try new behaviors, knowing if they stumble, they won't get fired. The church can also host classes on social skills, such as parenting.

Ministers can make the church a safe place to try new skills by understanding that not everyone comes to church with advanced social skills. We can then forgive when someone stumbles or applaud when someone succeeds.

Ministers have a special entrée with lay leaders, whom they can teach leadership skills, such as how to run a meeting. The minister can ask a lay leader what one might like to learn during their leadership tenure. If, for instance, a committee chair would like to strengthen her conflict resolution skills, you both could agree on ways you could support such development.

Modeling

Someone with a snake phobia improves when watching someone else handle a snake. In a therapy group, people watch and imitate the healthy and constructive behavior they observe.

In a church, people also watch each other and learn. A shy person benefits from seeing another shy person speak during worship. A committee member watches the chair lead meetings, preparing oneself for that role.

Group Cohesion

The more attracted its members feel toward their group, the more beneficial the group turns out to be. The same applies to a church. A congregation that is proud of its identity feels good to belong to. When it feels good to come to church on Sundays, that's therapeutic.

Catharsis

In group therapy, people express their feelings and find relief. In a church, there can also be opportunities for such catharsis. During memorial services, hopefully, mourners feel safe enough to weep and find healing from their tears. Worship elements such as joys and concerns, impassioned prayers from the pulpit, or evocative sermons all support people's emotional expression. As people express their feelings, such emotions shift from tears to relief, from anger to humor. As they allow themselves to feel their feelings, those emotions, not being disowned, become integrated, and the people become whole. Furthermore, people who express strong, honest feelings with each other experience vibrant relating and bond with each other.

Emotional freedom can swing too far; venting and ranting can hurt people. Then it is time for covenants and standards, such as "We say what we feel, with respect for each other."

The Disconfirmation of Dreaded Outcomes

In a therapy group, people take risks to express something that in their history would have been invalidated. Someone expresses sadness, expecting to be mocked, but now is comforted. What one had dreaded does not happen, leaving a little less dread.

Similarly, in a congregation, someone might fear being misunderstood but risk saying what one thinks or feels. When one's listener understands, the dreaded outcome does not occur and is disconfirmed. The individual goes on to interact with others more freely and deeply.

You can support such risk-taking with standards that reassure people that they are safe enough to be vulnerable. You can reinforce any openness you observe. If someone comes to you fuming with anger, you can applaud their courage. Not only would that disarm them, but also it would disconfirm their fear of challenging an authority.

CONCLUSION

When a congregation whole and safe, it is healthy. It dwells on the thought side of the thought-reflex continuum, where it functions well and benefits its members. It is secure enough to integrate and express its identity.

QUESTIONS FOR REFLECTION

Taking stock of a congregation with which you are familiar, how and when is it transparent about its identity? How could it be more transparent?

Given that congregation, how might you describe its identity using the terms of this chapter?

This chapter discusses the benefits of a healthy congregation for its members. What are the benefits of a healthy congregation for its minister?

NOTES

1. *Oxford English Dictionary*, 3rd edition, s.v. "heal."

2. Donelson Forsyth, *Group Dynamics*, 6th edition (Belmont, CA: Wadsworth Cenage Learning, 2014).

3. Michael Kahn, *The Tao of Conversations* (Oakland, CA: New Harbinger Publications, 1995).

4. B. F. Skinner, *The Behavior of Organisms* (New York: Appleton-Century, 1938).

5. Roy Oswald and Speed Leas, *The Inviting Church* (Herndon, VA: The Alban Institute, 1987).

6. Ibid.

7. Ibid.

8. Jackson Carroll and Carl Dudley, *Handbook for Congregational Studies* (Nashville: Abingdon Press, 1986).

9. Ibid.

10. Penny Becker, *Congregations in Conflict* (Cambridge, UK: Cambridge University Press, 1999).

11. Arlin Rothauge, *Sizing up a Congregation for New Member Ministry* (New York: The Episcopal Church Center, 1983).

12. *Oxford English Dictionary*, 3rd ed., s.v. "enthusiasm."

13. Roy Baumeister and John Tierney, *Willpower* (New York: Penguin Books, 2012)

14. Ibid.

15. Neal Krause, "Religion, Aging, and Health: Current Status and Future Prospects." *Journals of Gerontology: Series B* 52B, no. 6 (1997): 291–3.

16. C. Ellison, D. Gay, and T. Glass, "Does Religious Commitment Contribute to Individual Life Satisfaction?" *Social Forces* p. 68 (1989): 100–23.

17. P. Handal, W. Black-Lopez, and S. Moergen, "Preliminary Investigation of the Relationship between Religion and Psychological Distress in Black Women." *Psychological Reports* 65 (1989): 971–5.

18. G. Brody, Z. Stoneman, D. Flor, and C. McCracy, "Religion's Role in Organizing Family Relationships: Family Process in Rural, Two-Parent African American Families." *Journal of Marriage and the Family* 56 (1994): 878–8.

19. M. S. Rye, et al., "Religious Perspectives on Forgiveness" in *Forgiveness: Theory, Research, and Practice*, ed. M. E. McCullough, K. I. Pargament, and C. E. Thoresen (New York: Guilford Press, 2000), 17–40.

20. C. Ellison, "Are Religious People Nice People? Evidence from the National Survey on Black Americans." *Social Forces* 71 (1992): 411–30.

21. R. Wuthnow, *Acts of Compassion: Caring for Others and Helping Ourselves* (Princeton, NJ: Princeton University Press, 1991).

22. V. Hodgkinson, M. Weitzman, and A Kirsch, "From Commitment to Action: How Religious Involvement Affects Giving and Volunteering." In *Faith and Philanthropy in America: Exploring the Role of Religion in America's Voluntary Sector*, ed. Robert Wuthnow, Virginia Hodgkinson (San Francisco: Jossey-Bass, 1990).

23. Irwin Yalom and Molyn Lesczc, *The Theory and Practice of Group Psychotherapy* (New York: Basic Books, 2005).

4

Working on Yourself

To calm and heal an anxious system, you, as minister and therapist for your congregation, have as a central task to remain secure. As the system perceives threats, you trust your safety. To your congregation's immoderation, you respond moderately.

Because the congregational system is a whole, each element affects each other; therefore you affect the rest of the system. When you live on the thought side of the thought-reflex continuum, and when your congregation's anxiety fails to lure you to the reflex side, the congregation will join you on the thought side. As you resist pressure to be as reactive as the rest of your system, you create a less reactive and thereby healthier environment for everyone. As you cook a nourishing meal in the overheated kitchen of the congregation, the system will be fed, cool off, and graduate into health. When you are secure, your leadership strategies and techniques are effective.

MINISTRY IS STRESSFUL

Leading an anxious congregation into health can embroil a minister in tension and drama, akin to riding a bucking bronco. Leadership then may seem impossible but does not have to be. At best, a secure minister interprets the congregation's tensions as opportunities and happily proceeds with a healing ministry. At worst, the congregation's illnesses interact with the minister's insecurities to trip up that ministry, exacerbate the congregation's problems, and drive the minister insane.

In ministry, happiness and insanity are woven fine.[1] The good news: research finds that the occupation with the happiest people is the ministry, with 67.2 percent of ministers very happy. The highest job satisfaction of any profession is the ministry, with 87.3 percent of ministers reporting feeling very satisfied with their jobs.[2]

On the other hand, pastors experience depression at a higher rate than the general population,[3] 45 percent of pastors report depression or burnout causing them to take a leave of absence from ministry,[4] 80 percent report that pastoral ministry affects their marriages and families negatively, and 90 percent of pastors work 55 to 75 hours per week.[5]

Another study found that compared to the general population, pastors had higher rates of diabetes, arthritis, asthma, hypertension, and obesity.[6]

A minister, after a few 60–70-hour work weeks, might feel so whipped as to end another day collapsed in a heap and not feel able to move a muscle.

Like parenthood, ministry is a wonderful calling, and it's exhausting. Ministers want to care for people, form communities, speak of the holy, and support salvation, and so we invest our hearts and souls into it, often to an unhealthy extreme.

Congregational pressure causes some of this stress. For example, one minister reports: "The advisory committee of my congregation told me to keep my sermons to ten minutes, tell funny stories, and leave people feeling great about themselves."[7] If this minister accommodates to such pressure and forgoes his integrity to preach cute sermonettes, that would be stressful.

Self-sacrifice to meet pastoral needs adds stress. One researcher finds that clergy "tend to be driven by a sense of a duty to God to answer every call for help from anybody, and they are virtually called upon all the time, 24/7."[8] To say "no" would seem selfish.

This sense of duty could be exacerbated by ministers' belief that the church depends on them. Maybe, but behind the belief that the church needs the minister, could be the minister's need to be indispensable.

Pastors might measure their success by church growth, yet face shrinking memberships due to factors beyond their control. As they try to reverse what they cannot control, they judge themselves as failures and experience stress.

Bearing internal conflicts adds stress. Clergy often experience a conflict between their personal needs vs. the church and its needs. Ministers can experience a conflict between their calling to work for God, think lofty thoughts, and reach for the infinite vs. the mundane tasks of church management. A third internal conflict occurs between the persona ministers present to the world—happy, energetic, and emotionally present—vs. a sometimes-different internal reality. It is stressful to prop up a persona that conflicts with internal reality.

Clergy also experience the stress that accompanies a subordinate position in a social hierarchy. Clergy used to hold a dominant position, where they could decry sin and condemn sinners. Puritan preachers had the power to sermonize for two hours or more,[9] with lay enforcers poking drowsy parishioners with sticks.

But there has been a revolution resulting in lay people becoming dominant. Fueling this revolution is the freedom lay people have to church-shop or leave organized religion. Within Protestantism, 34 percent of American adults currently have a religious identity different from the one in which they were raised. Furthermore, almost 20 percent of American adults who were raised in a religion are now unaffiliated.[10] People can demand comforting, amusing fare, or they'll go elsewhere. Compelled to please their mobile, dominant consumers, clerical life becomes stressful.

ADDICTION

One usually does not think of ministry as addictive, but it can be. Ministry does deal with ultimate matters, so it should be a path to salvation. Seeking salvation, one starts down the ministerial road, and it is satisfying. People listen to one's sermons; one gets to think lofty thoughts; and sometimes one experiences peak, heavenly moments.

Then one has to do mundane work; the congregation has tension; some people are sourpusses; and where is the heaven? One can try to grab a little heaven by working harder to please others. As one works harder to earn heaven, that begins an addiction.

Addiction can be defined as the investment of one's desire for salvation into something finite, which one can control, such as hard work, as if that would bring salvation.[11] Such investment wastes that desiring energy and disappoints because the finite vehicle does not result in salvation. As clergy seek salvation through working ever harder, they find themselves further from the salvation they had hoped for and, adding insult to injury, exhausted.

Working to earn salvation fulfills the "doing" contract people can have with the world. By that contract, salvation is earned, "So, do, do, and do." This contract parallels the Pre-Reformation Roman Catholic recipe for salvation: "Work really hard and hope for heaven." Ministers and congregations can together assume the doing contract, resulting in the minister burning out or, in addiction parlance, bottoming out.

If they do burn out, ideally, ministers recognize that a ministry based on serving and pleasing is unsustainable. They remember that The Reformation has occurred, giving them salvation by grace and a second contract with the world: "You can be yourself and let what you do emerge from who you are." They realize: "Being myself means guiding people toward God." They then devote energy to that infinite salvific vehicle, God, and guide people on their spiritual journeys to experience divine love. In the end, they strike a sustainable balance between providing services (which still need to be done) and being themselves by guiding people's spiritual journeys. They can even add: "Being myself also means considering my needs." They then balance service with self-care.

In addition to offering spiritual guidance, ministers can guide people in exploring who they are as a community and how the minister and laity could work together to mutual satisfaction. The pastor who was told to preach ten-minute stories could ask: "How might this style of sermons support your salvation?" This minister could add to the conversation his theory of preaching and salvation. Everyone could consider how the minister could preach the sermons he is called to preach, while meeting the congregation's needs.

THE DEVELOPMENT OF SECURITY

The minister journeys, too. You learn, gain awareness, and alter your behavior in a chosen direction to become more fully, and more securely, yourself. Having journeyed and grown, you know and trust your selfhood, your flaws, foibles, and capacity. Trusting yourself, you are willing to make your self available and vulnerable on behalf of your ministry.

There is no simple technique for learning security. Much of it comes from secure parents who support their child's brain development. Babies are born with a fully developed amygdala, but their prefrontal cortex takes twenty years to complete.[12] One of the amygdala's jobs is to detect threats and trigger fight-or-flight reactivity.[13] One of the cortex's jobs is to discern a threat from a non-threat and decide effective responses. The amygdala can overgeneralize its perceptions of threat, causing amygdala-guided children to perceive many threats, triggering many meltdowns. In the midst of such meltdowns, contact with an adult cortex helps the child develop one's own cortex. The child whose cortex develops grows into an adult who can accurately distinguish threats from non-threats and can reassure one's amygdala, resulting in security.

Furthermore, the parents' calm is based on their healthy assumptions—like "we can solve problems" or "we are here to support each other"—which their children internalize.

Even with security internalized from childhood, a congregation's insecurity can still trigger a minister's reactivity. Therefore, one augments childhood security with further personal growth and professional training, analogous to athletic training. The athlete has physical gifts but trains further to make their body a well-tuned athletic instrument. The minister possesses gifts but works further, completing seminary and developing through one's lifetime, to become a well-tuned pastorally therapeutic instrument.

Paradoxically, working on yourself to be yourself involves acceptance of yourself.[14] Self-acceptance supports safety, which draws people to the thought side of the thought–reflex continuum, where they reflect, gain insight, and develop. Conversely, the implication that one is flawed and therefore low on the survival-of-the-fittest hierarchy is threatening. Threats push people to the reflex side of the continuum where insight and growth shut down. Instead of that, you are perfect; now change.

HAPPINESS AND MEANING

One goal of personal development is to live with happiness and meaning. Happiness comes when one's needs are met and one's thoughts are healthy. Meaning comes when one is invested in something greater than oneself, which one values.

It's pretty easy for a minister, investing in valued concerns such as the congregation and God, to find meaning. Happiness is different story. Giving to others, one's own needs are not easily met. One might also view oneself critically or the world with cynicism.

A minister's happiness matters. Buechner described ministry as "the place where your deep gladness and the world's deep hunger meet."[15] The world hungers for spiritual liberation. Your deep gladness reveals your liberation and shows the world a way to that liberation. Furthermore, happiness and security make you immune against infection by the congregation's anxiety. Therefore, it's time to get serious about happiness.

WAYS TO BE HAPPY #1: MEET YOUR NEEDS

When people's needs are met, they feel happy. People need food, clothing, and shelter. After that, people need intangibles, such as love, safety, and freedom.[16]

Meeting one's needs is complicated by other people, who have their needs—the rascals. Unfortunately, the rest of the human population is not poised and waiting to attend to what you need. At times, someone else's needs will even conflict with yours.

Hoping that meeting others' needs will indirectly meet their own, ministers sometimes work hard to meet others' needs. Meeting others' needs would meet one's need for meaning, although other unasserted needs would likely go unmet.

Sometimes people neglect their needs. They might not know what their needs are or doubt they have a right to have their needs met. Doubting someone else would care to meet their needs, they might not ask to have them met. A subordinate in the dominant/subordinate world is trained to assume their needs will go unmet.

Although neglected, the unmet needs remain. If one has not eaten, hunger gnaws. With emotional needs unexpressed and unmet, one might feel depressed, anxious, and resentful. The unmet needs might gain expression in indirect ways: silent martyrdom, complaint, sarcasm, and furious explosions from time to time.

When one's unmet needs are expressed so indirectly, they likely remain unmet. I suppose a heroically helpful person could find the unmet need hiding behind someone's silence, complaint, sarcasm, or hostility, and then meet that need. But what are the odds of that miracle occurring? Pretty low.

Successfully meeting one's needs in relationship with others (who have their needs) involves a negotiation. One begins by stating what one needs: "I need to feel valued." One can add what it would do for them to be valued. "I would then feel happy and energetic." Realizing the importance of this need, the other would want to meet it.

Then how? So the two brainstorm what action could meet that need. One proposes, "If you gave me a high-five whenever I washed the dishes, I would feel more valued."

The other person might agree to the high-fives or might amend the proposal. That party might offer, "How about if I say: 'Good job,' when you do the dishes?" The first agrees. When they both like their plan, it will likely be implemented, making it a successful negotiation.

Enacting the plan, the first person's needs are met, and they are happy. The second person knows they have succeeded, which makes them happy. They can then turn to the second person and their needs.

Assertiveness

To negotiate for needs requires assertiveness, which involves asking for what you want or saying "no" to what you do not want. Assertiveness begins with knowing what you want and believing you have a right to express your wish. You describe the current situation, any associated feelings, and then make a behavioral and observable request. You can add the benefits that will come with the other's cooperation.

An assertive request for a raise might sound like this: "I believe I am paid less than I deserve for my work (current situation), and that is lowering my morale (associated feeling). I would like a salary increase of 5 percent (the request). I think the increase would improve both my morale and my output (the benefit)."

Meeting a Goal

Another way to meet a need involves setting and working toward a goal, a popular activity every New Year's Day. To increase the odds of success it helps to break a goal down into smaller objectives. It is motivating to keep in mind the good news you will experience when you meet your goal. Logging daily steps taken toward your goal mark accumulated progress. Letting others know of your goal, and informing them of your progress, builds in accountability. After an accomplishment, you can enjoy a reward.

Self-discipline, or willpower, helps one meet a goal. Willpower is like a muscle, which grows stronger with exercise, but still has limits.[17] To use willpower well, one applies it to meeting one's goal, rather than waste it on trivial matters. Furthermore, if you run a willpower marathon, great, but then, like the marathoner's muscles, willpower needs rest and nourishment.

It helps to work on one goal at a time. When people attempt a lifestyle revolution, they slide back into old ways. Instead, if one devotes willpower to one goal, until it becomes habit and no longer requires willpower, that goal will likely stick. Then one can apply that willpower to another goal.

Lifestyle and Self-Care

The body is an organism that needs to move, eat healthily, and rest. A nourishing and balanced lifestyle meets these needs and creates a foundation for a healthy, happy life.

Exercise

When we move, our bodies repay us with health. An exercise practice lowers resting heart rate and blood pressure. Lowering one's rate of metabolism is like slowing the idle speed of an engine, which extends its life.

One's low resting heart rate and blood pressure reflect one's low baseline level of arousal. Given that low baseline, it would require a dire emergency to trigger reflexive fight or flight. Indeed, one's ability to remain thoughtful in an anxious system could be measured by one's resting heart rate—the lower the rate, the more thoughtful and less reactive one would be.

Exercise also activates the brain and supports the formation of new neural connections, which support mental alertness, learning, and memory.[18]

Pushing one's limits when exercising strengthens not only the body but also one's sense of personal agency. Possessing agency improves one's mood and increases self-confidence and self-esteem.

Exercise helps one lower stress. Under stress the body releases stress hormones, such as cortisol and adrenaline, which help us fight or run in an emergency, but when they are floating around in our bodies chronically, they contribute to illness and make us more reactive. Moderate exercise metabolizes and breaks down these chemicals, leaving you relaxed afterward.[19]

Exercise develops the neurons that release the neurotransmitter GABA, which quiets and calms the brain. Research comparing active to sedentary mice finds that when both are stressed, dunked in cold water in these experiments, they get fired up and aroused. But the exercised mice, their brains bathed in GABA, calm down sooner than the sedentary mice.[20] A consistent exercise practice could help you calm down too, after you've been dunked in cold water.

Meditation

Meditation can be an additionally calming facet of a person's lifestyle. Meditation is the act of sitting still for a length of time, five to twenty minutes is common, and observing thoughts and emotions without judging or acting on them. One learns to pause and observe, rather than react.

As one meditates, the mind naturally wanders. People have about 20,000 thoughts per day,[21] which do not stop when one meditates. Therefore, to notice thoughts and feelings busily crossing the mind does not mean one is meditating badly. One simply sits and possibly draws attention to the breath. Then, of course, the next thoughts come barging in. Oh well. This neutral acceptance allows one's thoughts and emotions to do what they naturally do: shift and flow through one's mind.

Meditation helps one be aware of one's feelings, which gives a minister diagnostic information. "I am noticing my anxiety. Maybe my anxiety reflects my congregation's anxiety."

Meditation helps one feel good. It increases activity in the left side of the prefrontal cortex, where pleasant feelings are experienced.[22] Furthermore, "It may be that mindfulness leads to an increase in self compassion," says Stuart Eisendrath, MD, of the Depression Center at the University of California, San Francisco.[23]

As with exercise, a meditation practice lowers one's baseline blood pressure and heart rate, resulting in a healthier heart,[24] longer life, and moderated arousal.

Meditation strengthens the connection between the amygdala and the prefrontal cortex.[25] As noted above, the amygdala is good at detecting and reacting to threats. The prefrontal cortex is good at discerning a threat from a non-threat. Walking along a path in the woods, you might see a long thin shape on the ground. The amygdala registers "snake!" and sends signals to your legs, which propel you into the air such that you could dunk a basketball for the first time in your life. Then the connection to the prefrontal cortex engages, the "snake" turns out to be a stick, and you settle and continue your walk. The stronger connection between prefrontal cortex and amygdala supports one's general calm.

As an interpersonal benefit, meditating Tibetan Buddhists show increased activity in the brain's temporoparietal junction and posterior cingulate cortex, which supports empathy.[26]

Rest

The body needs a balance of activity and rest. To rest, ministers can take retreats or simply do nothing. Idleness may seem wrong, but resting is like sharpening the saw, after which you work more easily and efficiently.

You are a model for your congregation. You can model frenetic activity or balance. Your church may push you to do more, but as you model balance, you would be offering them something more important than the completion of every given task.

Sleep

Sleep restores, rejuvenates, and energizes the body and brain. Research finds that for full alertness, good moods, mental acuity, creativity, and energy, our bodies need to spend one third of life asleep.[27]

As one sleeps, one goes through sleep cycles. Through the course of each cycle, sleep deepens. Stage 3, the deepest phase, is the most restorative for the physical body. At this stage, the muscles are completely relaxed, their blood supply increased, tissue growth and repair occur, and the immune system fights toxins.

Next comes Rapid Eye Movement (REM) sleep also known as dreaming. During REM sleep, the brain transfers short-term memories from the motor cortex to the temporal lobe where they become long-term memories. While dreaming, the brain replenishes the neurotransmitters that organize the neural networks that remember, learn, and solve problems, improving mental focus and quickening reaction time. While dreaming, the brain balances its hormones, enzymes, and proteins, and cleanses itself of amyloids, mental junk, the buildup of which is associated with Alzheimer's disease.

People sleep through (hopefully) four or five cycles per night. During each successive cycle, the time spent in stage 3 and REM sleep increases, with greater physical and mental benefits resulting. Therefore, one's last hour of sleep is the most beneficial.

If an alarm clock is interrupting your dreams, and if you need coffee to function, your sleep is probably inadequate. Over time, inadequate sleep is analogous to inadequate nutrition, starving you.

Friends

People need friends. We are made to connect.[28] The support of a listening ear can help your emotions shift. After expressing anger, fear, or sadness, you might find yourself laughing.

Collegial Support

Ministers who belong to a small, supportive collegial group fare better than those who do not.[29] In my difficult year of ministry, I could have benefited from such a group, learned from their reflections, and found support in their concern.

Diaphragmatic Breathing

Our bodies need oxygen. When anxious, people tense and constrict their bodies to prepare for fighting or running. This tension constricts their breathing. Shallow breathing maintains anxiety.

To calm themselves, people breathe.[30] Optimal breathing engages the diaphragm—muscles in the chest that pull air into the entire lungs. When your belly expands with each intake of air, that indicates diaphragmatic breathing. When the entire lung is taking in air, the body receives the oxygen it needs, which calms it. When the body is calm, the mind becomes calm.

Self-Definition

People need to be themselves in relationship to others. It is easy when alone to be oneself, and easy in a relationship to be who others want one to be, but I want to be myself and be close. To be yourself, it helps to know who you are. Ideally, ministerial formation supports your looking inward to clarify who you are. Clear about who you are, you can be yourself with others, not pretending or hiding behind a persona. You can articulate your identity, beliefs, principles, and what you will and will not do. When people see you clearly, they can be close to you. They can also reveal who they are to you. Then you both know the rich experience of sharing authentic contact.

WAYS TO BE HAPPY #2: THINK LOVELY THOUGHTS

Healthy thinking offers people a second way to be happy. One views oneself and the world through a lens that is favorable. Epictetus realized this when he stated: "Men [and women] are disturbed not by things, but by the view which they take of them."[31]

I choose my lens. Through one lens the world looks lousy. People are mean and critical of me. Events are tragic, and my fault. My one mistake reveals my life to be saturated with folly. I am stuck in a handbasket, convinced of my destination.

Viewed through another lens—the same facts—but the world is okay. People are doing their best. I can act to make things better. I have intrinsic worth and am therefore loveable. I am made just right by God. I am blessed. Indeed, Peter Pan coached his friends in thinking lovely thoughts. Then, they flew!

For example, three masons are at work. When asked what he is doing, the first sourly replies, "I am staking rocks." The second, not much happier, "I am making a wall." But the third beams as he replies, "I am building a cathedral." Ministers may have mundane tasks but can view them through a lens that sees those tasks as analogous to building a cathedral.

Here are some generic helpful thoughts:

> I am a worthy and good person.
> This problem will pass, and my life will be better.
> I can solve problems.
> If others are angry with me, I can handle it.
> I love others and am loved in return.
> I trust God.
> We are in this together.

You could add to these helpful thoughts.

Optimism

Optimism is a way of thinking that helps a person rally back from life's inevitable blows.[32] Optimism assesses a bad event as temporary, local, and caused by factors other than oneself, and a good event as resulting from permanent causes that apply everywhere for which one has some responsibility. The optimistically losing team gripes about external factors, like umpire blindness. The optimistic winners gloat: "We are a great team!"

Pessimism dismisses a good event as an anomaly out of one's influence: "Our winning is a fluke." It views a bad event, losing, as permanent, pervasive, and personal: "We are not fit for the game of baseball." This team is unlikely to rally back and win the next game.

I Am Okay

Thoughts include one's view of oneself. One can judge oneself on a continuum between superhuman and worthless. At the healthy middle, one acknowledges imperfections and worth.

Someone experiencing low esteem criticizes oneself. It is as if one is performing on a stage with a critic in the balcony grousing about how inadequate one is.[33] Such criticism and the assumption "There is something wrong with me" can lead one to hide, because venturing out onto any stage would mean exposure to one's internal critic and to anyone else who would see and judge one's obvious flaws.

Having an inner critic also makes criticism from other sources difficult to handle. If Buster expresses criticism, and one's inner critic joins in the attack, one then faces two critics pummeling one's hapless sense of worth. Buster's criticism is bad enough. Adding to his criticism would be like finding his knife in one's ribs and adding another. *Ouch!*

One may not control Buster's criticism, but one can quiet one's own internal critic. Bringing that critic to light weakens it. One can bring it to light by observing its function. That critic might

> blame one when things go wrong,
> compare one to others,
> set impossible standards of perfection,
> set expectations for how one should live, criticize when
> one does not life up to those expectations,
> tell one to be the best, punish when one is not the best,
> beat one up for the smallest mistakes,
> keep an album of one's failures,
> forget strengths and accomplishments,
> call one names: "stupid," "selfish," "weak,"
> read others' minds and assume they are critical, and
> exaggerate failings with words like "always" and "never."

It helps to imagine the critic as separate from one's self. To support this externalizing, it might help to name the critic. Call him Buster.

You can talk back to the critic, saying, "No! You're not accurate." You can sum up what that critic has cost you in confidence and security and declare, "Enough!" You can affirm your worth: "I am a miracle of creation."

The critic often pounces when one makes a mistake. In response, one can develop humane ways to view mistakes. Mistakes are teachers. What one realizes in 20:20 hindsight was a mistake was the best decision one could have made based on one's awareness at the time. Mistakes are warnings that prevent something worse. They come with any spontaneity. Everyone gets an allotment of mistakes.

Humor

With the critic quieted, it is easier to take life lightly, and people need to laugh. Indeed, humor stimulates parts of the brain associated with rewards and positive emotions. In the midst of an anxious system, that is being oh-so serious, humor can save you. Victor Frankl, for example, saw humor as a way to "rise above any situation, even if for a few seconds," even in a Nazi concentration camp.[34]

Forgiveness

When one has been done wrong, forgiveness involves giving someone who hurt you the gift of good will, even when they do not deserve it, because that spares you, the forgiver, the pain of carrying ill will and resentment.[35] Indeed, to carry resentment is like drinking poison and wanting for the other person to die. Resentment floods the body with stress hormones, raises the blood pressure, and impairs the immune system.[36] And the target of your resentment may be feeling no ill effects from your wrath and instead be sipping daiquiris on a beach in the Bahamas.

Forgiveness is not forgetting or condoning harmful behavior. Our minds are not built to forget things, and we can have standards of behavior and not want to condone actions that violate those standards. Forgiveness also does not mean trusting or becoming buddies or having any contact with someone who has hurt you, just not wishing them to suffer.

The process of forgiveness begins with feeling fully the pain of the offense.[37] In response to a deep violation, these emotions can include anger, terror, and despair. A blithe dismissal of the pain leaves wounds hidden in the psyche, where they will have their unhealthy influence. Nevertheless, feeling the pain can be painful and takes some courage to go through.

To forgive, one wishes to forgive—someday.

To forgive, one validates the offending party by imagining what it is like to be in the offender's shoes. I may not like or condone the offending behavior, but I can understand why they did what they did. For example, a mugger might have grown up with substance-abusing parents, become addicted himself, and taken my money as a desperate way to support his addiction.

To forgive, one finds meaning and a lesson from this episode. For example, one who was abused as a child gains some meaning by not abusing their child, thus stopping the transmission of violence.

To forgive, one lets go of the impulse to retaliate. I may approve of my mugger landing in jail, so as to protect the public from further crimes, but hope his jail sentence goes well and that it leads to a healthy, pro-social life after prison.

I think grace is involved. Forgiveness is so difficult, I thank spiritual sources for help in softening my resentment toward someone who has hurt me. Then one forgives.

In addition to the creeps and traumatizers one has the misfortune to encounter, two central individuals to forgive would be mom and dad. No parent is perfect, and children bear pain for the times and ways their parents failed them. This pain might include anger, rage, sadness, confusion, fear, and more rage. It is scary and vulnerable to uncover this historical pain, like unearthing a tomb, revealing demons, and knowing they are inside of you. It is also difficult to view parents as having failed. Nevertheless, experiencing such pain is a step to forgiveness.

In *No One Is to Blame*,[38] Bob Hoffman describes one man's anger toward his clergyman father:

> Dad was often the center of attention at gatherings, a fine singer, a good story-teller, and knowledgeable in discussions of the world and religious affairs. Somehow, I was always excluded. The son of a ____ gave lots of attention to everybody in his congregation but me.
>
> He always seemed busy. After work he'd say hello, give a dutiful hug and kiss to my mother but usually not to me. I felt left out. I wanted a hug and a kiss too. I wanted to talk to him. He'd sit and read is newspaper until dinner, where conversation was limited to his ministry or the family, or about teaching me geography or vocabulary, or there were arguments over trivia. After dinner, either he went upstairs, closed his door, and worked on sermons (to instruct the world on how to love and have better marriages and raise children).

Expressing this history and its wrenching emotions is a good first step. The next step is to understand mom and dad in their imperfection. They had their imperfect parents and resulting pain. One individual had this sympathetic address to his father:

> Who has loved you, self-centered little boy having to pretend to be a man? You hated and mistreated us just as you were hated and mistreated by your parents. Now you are dead and this life's chance is gone. You didn't want things to be this way! I wish I could help you! I want to help you. I want things to have been different for you. Oh, Daddy! How I wish it could all have been different.

After the storm of anger, the rainbow appears. Forgiving mom and dad leaves one cleansed and at peace. Furthermore, it leaves one less reactive to people in one's congregation who echo mom or dad.

Wholeness

Each person is a whole system. To be whole involves integrating all aspects of one's identity. Indeed, the word "integrity" comes from the same root as the word "integer," which means "whole number."[39] Someone with integrity is whole.

Wholeness involves integrating one's "shadow." Carl Jung defined the shadow as the repository of the contents of one's unconscious.[40] That shadow can contain benign aspects of ourselves; a man attracted to a woman sees in her his inner femininity, a woman sees her masculinity in a man. The shadow also contains one's less-than-laudable qualities. While I am thoughtful, brave, clean, and reverent, my unconscious shadow contains my opposite qualities: thoughtless, cowardly, dirty, and profane. If as a minister you are deeply drawn to, or profoundly repelled by, someone in your congregation, he or she might represent some shadowy aspect of yourself. The shadow can also contain repressed emotions. I am happy, but could have anger in my shadow.

One's shadowed contents can erupt with ill effects. For example, during graduate school I was single, lonely, broke, and supporting myself in part by officiating weddings. One day, leading a rehearsal for a lavish wedding at a swell hotel, the delighted couple teasing and joking, I, hoping to join in the humor, blurted, "Oh, grow up!" They looked open-mouthed at me. We continued the rehearsal, but I realized my shadowed discontent with my life, as contrasted with theirs, had erupted.

Paved over, the shadow still pushes upward, creating cracks in the pavement that can trip you up. The trick is to accept and embrace the shadow.[41] I am full of features, some I may not admire. So be it. Embraced, the shadow has less of a chance to surprise me with destructive eruptions at otherwise happy wedding rehearsals.

Finally, when ministers integrate their own wholeness, shadow and all, they can appreciate and welcome their congregation's wholeness, including its shadow.

Feel the Feelings

When one is whole, one experiences the spectrum of emotions. Those feelings have a purpose: they provide information about what one is going through. Happiness occurs when facing something you like; anger when facing something you do not like. Sadness occurs with a loss; fear when facing a threat. Confusion occurs when you do not know something. Guilt occurs when you have broken a rule, and shame when some flaw in your personhood has been exposed.

Alongside these seven emotions there are three types of emotions.[42] Primary affective responses are felt in direct response to life's experiences. These emotions can be felt powerfully and viscerally. They guide behavior well. They change when one's experience changes. Standing on the edge of a cliff, one can feel fear and a tremor. That fear guides one away from the edge of the cliff, where the fear passes, and one can enjoy the view. Indeed, healthy, primary emotions flow like a river. A patch of angry water can flow by, then sadness, then relief, then something else. Conversely, just as damming a river stagnates its water, restraining emotions keeps them static where they fester. Furthermore, as a diagnostic instrument, it helps to welcome your feelings. "Hello, anger. What are you telling me about my congregation?"

A secondary emotional response is an emotion one has been socialized to feel and express. A boy told never to cry is socialized to resist sadness, so when facing a loss, instead of crying punches a wall. A girl told never to express anger is socialized to be complaint, and instead of showing anger when offended, cries. Such a secondary feeling lingers longer because the experience one is having is not being felt and processed. It also guides behavior poorly. Standing on the edge of a cliff, if one is not allowed to feel fear, one instead expresses bravado. "Hey guys, watch this ..." could be one's last words.

Thirdly, instrumental emotions are feelings that manage or manipulate others. These emotions are not linked to one's experience, do not guide behavior well, and last, with slight exaggeration, forever. Anger, for example, might be used to intimidate others, forever. Sadness and pathos might pull for ever more pity and caretaking, even after one has received the support of Mother Theresa.

Moderate Reactivity to Pain

In seeming contradiction to feeling your feelings, growth also means moderating reactivity to your pain. Going through the dark night of the soul requires exploring its painful depths and breadths, hoping for rebirth. To do this, one views pain through a lens that accepts it, like an athlete who views pain as weakness leaving the body.

Principled leadership can be painful. I imagine Abraham Lincoln bore considerable pain to move the country through a war toward the principle of rights for all her people. Any leader would do well to have the courage of one's convictions, even when that is painful.

As an unhelpful defense against past, present, or future pain, people employ *the protector*.[43] The protector can take the form of a persona, such as the one who has no flaws, and therefore cannot be judged, or an aggressive tyrant who cannot be crossed. The protector can also take the form of defensive or avoidant habits.

As the protector is busy protecting the individual from pain, the core aspect of a person, or one's spiritual center, is sitting idly by. That self is secure, and with that security is open to others, relaxed about what one feels, and guided by one's values, beliefs, or principles.

To let the self emerge, one can detect the protector, thank the protector for its service, and allow it to rest. Pain may be felt, but as noted above, emotions do not last forever, and after pain there will be another emotion. Maybe relief. If so, one can learn that life without the protector is not so bad. With that realization, the self can emerge from the background and offer its guidance.

Although I am not Lincoln, I did have my difficult year in ministry. When my self-definitions kept getting thrashed at board meetings, it hurt. Still I believed that self-definition was a more valuable principle than avoiding pain. Therefore, instead of protecting myself—by defending myself or avoiding exposure—each month I defined myself, like a boxer stepping into a ring expecting to take a hit.

Move toward Fear

Similar to accepting pain, one can face fears. Indeed, to quiet a fear, one makes gradual steps toward that fear.[44] At each step, one breathes, eases one's racing heart, and goes back to less scary activities. After many such steps, that fear eases; one's range of freedom increases.

For example, a CPE chaplain's first call to a trauma in the emergency room (ER) likely generates fear. "What am I going to face? What if I can't handle it?" But as you arrive at the ER, speak to the people involved, hold their hands, and lead them in prayer, your fear diminishes. Over time and practice, your fear of traumas in the ER fades, and you are strolling to handle ER traumas as if it's a walk in the park. Well, not quite, but the ER no longer triggers panic.

Helping one face a fear is one's desire. I think that fear and desire are opposites. When fear is strong, desire is relatively weak, and one is stopped. When desire is strong, fear is weak, and one is proceeding forward. When describing why someone took the courageous step they made, someone will often say that they wanted to do it: "I just wanted to try skydiving."

Related to wanting and self-control is the trick of acting as if, and the feelings follow. For example, the new chaplain may be gripped with fear entering the ER for the first time, but the chaplain acts calm, approaches the family like he or she does this all the time, listens to them, and prays with them, and the fear diminishes.

ASSUMPTIONS

Assumptions, like gravity, often go unnoticed, yet they are thoughts that powerfully guide one's life. Assumptions are often learned in childhood. For instance, a benign childhood that involved affectionate, responsive parents leaves the constructive assumption: I am loved.

Unfortunately, not-so-benign childhoods can leave unhelpful assumptions. A childhood marked by blame, judgment, or abuse can leave the destructive assumption: there is something wrong with me. A childhood marked by competition can leave the assumptions: this is a dangerous world of winners and losers; I have to fight hard to win. A childhood marked by neglect or scarce support, or with parents who demonstrated that they were insecure and needed approval from their children, can leave the assumptions: my needs will not be met; I have to give in order to receive. A childhood that denied one's power or voice can leave the assumption: I have no power, no voice. A childhood in which reality shifted according to parental whims, or intoxication, can leave the assumption: I can't trust my perceptions. A childhood that involved conflict, danger, and trauma can leave the assumptions: this is a dangerous world; I am not safe.

Here is a catalog of difficult assumptions:

> This is a dangerous world. I am not safe.
> There is something wrong with me.
> I am not worthy.
> I am not valued.
> Conflicts involve winners and losers.
> I have to fight hard to win.
> I will lose.
> I have no power, no voice.
> To survive, I have to be someone I am not.
> My needs will not be met.
> I have to give in order to receive.
> I have to please others.
> I have to earn my love or other rewards.
> I am alone.
> I can't handle being alone.
> I can't handle _____.
> I can't feel _____.
> Reality shifts, and I cannot count on my perceptions.
> There could be more.

THAT PUSHES MY BUTTONS

These destructive assumptions persist into adulthood, forming triggers to reactivity, known colloquially as "buttons." Buttons trigger reactivity because they are associated with threat. The criticized child who carries into adulthood the "there is something wrong with me" button may have worried as a child about being so unworthy as to be rejected by their parents and kicked out of the family, threatening that child's survival. Plus, parental judgment would have caused painful emotions: guilt and shame. That individual's childhood has left the assumption/button, "There is something wrong with me," big, ready, and easy to push. When, as an adult, one hears a complaint, the button is pushed. The childhood nightmare of banishment and pain recur. Happening again, it looks like the nightmare will persist forever.

To moderate reactivity, one first recognizes the button issues that could trigger such reactivity. One can realize: "My parents criticized me and delivered the message that there was something wrong with me, which left me insecure about my belonging and survival. Hearing a complaint now pushes that historical something-wrong-with-me button." Knowing that story, one's prefrontal cortex can reassure one's amygdala: "That was then, and this is now. I am no longer dependent on parents for my survival. As an adult who can pay rent and buy groceries, I can handle my survival. I am not so threatened by this complaint." Furthermore, one can replace difficult assumptions with helpful assumptions, or anti-buttons, such as "I am okay." One's security shrinks one's buttons, making them harder to push.

Here is a list of helpful assumptions or anti-buttons:

> I am safe.
> I am okay.
> I am worthy.
> I am valued. I am valuable.
> Conflict can result in everyone winning.
> Conflict is an opportunity for closeness and creative
> problem-solving.
> I will emerge from this conflict with some success.
> I have power and a voice.
> I can be myself.
> My needs are being met.
> I can ask and receive.
> I can do what I like and still be loved.
> I can be myself, and that is intrinsically rewarding.
> I am loved.
> I can be alone or with others as I choose.
> I can handle challenges.
> I can feel all of my feelings.
> I can trust my perceptions.

Personal development can be seen as making it harder for one's buttons to be pushed. Having made that development, one realizes that a stressor such as criticism, which before would have pushed one's button, today has little effect. Furthermore, as one manages one's own buttons, one no longer has to

seek security by trying to change other people, whom one cannot control–
Please stop pushing my buttons! Instead, unflustered by triggering behavior
and refraining from pushing others to change, one is a moderately reactive
presence.

To understand your button, you can ask yourself: What is my key button?
What in my history gave me that button?

One caveat: sometimes the intrinsic threat of a situation can trigger reactivity. If a lion walks in as you are reading this, you may not have a childhood
marked by feline trauma, but you might still find yourself believing: "I am
not safe."

ASSUMPTIONS AND CHANGE

Assumptions underlie resistance to change.[45] For instance, I have a goal: eat
healthily. It is not hard to do. I understand what is needed. Sermons and lec-
tures don't add to my understanding of this situation.

Nevertheless, I eat junk food, which blocks me from reaching my goal.
I have rationales that support that behavior: "I don't have time to prepare
healthy meals. I'll improve my diet later. I'm healthy enough." Supporting
those rationales is an assumption, such as "I am not worth it." When change
is blocked, one can dig through the contrary behaviors and their rationales to
unearth the assumption(s) blocking such change.

As with supporting moderated reactivity, to support change, one can
develop the anti-buttons or alternative assumptions listed above. To change
at the assumptive level, I choose a new assumption and test it. To eat healthily, I choose the assumption that I am worthy. I test the new assumption by
living as if it is true. If, after many such tests, I find that the new assumption
makes life better than the old assumption, that new assumption becomes
internalized.

As I practice and live by the new assumption, my mind develops the habit
of thinking it, which changes the brain. The brain is composed of neurons,
which are pathway cells along which thoughts and feelings travel. The brain
is malleable and changes to strengthen and enlarge pathways as one practices
the thoughts they carry. Practicing a healthy assumption expands the neural
pathway along which that thought can travel. It then becomes easy to have
that thought.[46]

A person has control over one's thoughts. One can entertain unhelpful
thoughts and assumptions, or helpful ones. I recommend watching one's
thoughts and choosing to entertain the more helpful ones. These helpful
thoughts support good moods, healthy functioning, and help make one a
secure leadership presence.

CONCLUSION

You are the agent of health for your congregational system. Your unmet needs or anxieties can impede your pastoral response to the congregation's needs and anxieties. Therefore, bringing the congregation health requires your security. You gain such security when your needs are met, your thoughts constructive.

QUESTIONS FOR REFLECTION

If you designed a program for your own personal health and development, what might it consist of?

What are the personal advantages and costs associated with being an agent of health for a congregation? How does it feel to bear that responsibility?

What did your childhood give you that prepared you for success in ministry? What legacies did your childhood leave that make you less effective as a minister?

NOTES

1. "Joy and insanity are woven fine" is a play on a line "joy and woe are woven fine" by William Blake in his poem "Auguries of Innocence" in *The Complete Poetry and Prose of William Blake*, ed. David Erdman (New York: Random House, 1988).

2. Tom Smith, "Job Satisfaction in the United States," Chicago: University of Chicago (2007). http://www-news.uchicago.edu/releases/07/pdf/070417.jobs.pdf.

3. Paul Vitello, "Taking a Break from the Lord's Work." *New York Times*, August 1, 2010.

4. "Clergy Self-Care Renewed: How Clergy and Congregations Can Prevent Burnout and Support Healthy Living" Mental Health Ministries. http://www.mentalhealthministries.net/resources/brochures/clergy_burnout/clergy_burnout_self-care.pdf.

5. George Barna, "Why Pastors Leave the Ministry" (Fuller Institute, and Pastoral Care, Inc., 2014) https://feic.org/wp-content/uploads/2014/10/Why-pastors-leave-the-ministry.pdf

6. Rae Jean Proeschold-Bell and Sara LeGrand, "High Rates of Obesity and Chronic Disease among United Methodist Clergy." *Obesity* 18 no. 9 (2010): 1867–70.

7. G. Jeffrey MacDonald, "Congregations Gone Wild," *New York Times*, August 7, 2010.

8. Vitello, "Taking a Break."

9. Alice Morse Earle, *Sabbath in Puritan New England* (New York: Dossier Press, 1911/2015).

10. Pew Research Center, Religion and Public Life, "America's Changing Religious Landscape" (Washington, DC: Pew Research Center, May 12, 2015). http://www.pewforum.org/2015/05/12/americas-changing-religious-landscape/

11. Gerald May, *Addiction and Grace* (New York: Harper Collins, 1988).

12. Louis Cozolino, *The Neuroscience of Psychotherapy,* 2nd edition (New York: W.W. Norton, 2010).

13. Ibid.

14. Carl Rogers, *On Becoming a Person, A Therapist's View of Psychotherapy* (New York: Houghton Mifflin, 1961/1989).

15. Frederick Buechner, *Wishful Thinking: A Seeker's ABC* (San Francisco: Harper, 1993).

16. Abraham Maslow, "A Theory of Human Motivation." *Psychological Review* 40, no. 4 (1943).

17. Roy Baumeister and John Tierney, *Willpower* (New York: Penguin, 2012).

18. Roger Walsh, "Lifestyle and Mental Health." *American Psychologist* 66, no. 7 (2011): 579–92.

19. Edmund Bourne, *Anxiety and Phobia Workbook* (New York: MJF Books, 1995).

20. Timothy J. Schoenfeld, et al. "Physical Exercise Prevents Stress-Induced Activation of Granule Neurons and Enhances Local Inhibitory Mechanisms in the Dentate Gyrus." *Journal of Neuroscience* 33, no. 18 (2013): 7770–7777.

21. Daniel Kahneman, "The Riddle of Experience vs. Memory" (TED talk, TED.com, Feb. 2010).

22. Richard Davidson and Sharon Begely, *The Emotional Life of Your Brain* (New York: Penguin, 2012).

23. Stacy Lu, "Mindfulness Holds Promise for Treating Depression." *Monitor on Psychology* 46, no. 3 (2015): 50–3.

24. Davidson and Begely, *The Emotional Life of Your Brain*.

25. Ibid.

26. Ibid.

27. James Maas, *Power Sleep* (New York: Harper Collins, 1998).

28. Daniel Goleman, *Social Intelligence* (New York: Random House, 2006).

29. Janet Maykus and Penny Long Marler, "Is the Treatment the Cure: A Study of the Effects of Participation in Pastoral Leader Peer Groups" (Austin, TX: Austin Presbyterian Seminary, 2010). http://www.austinseminary.edu/uploaded/continuing_education/pdf/SPE_Survey_Report_and_Analysis_April_2010.pdf

30. Bourne, *Anxiety and Phobia Workbook*.

31. Epictetus, *The Enchiridion* (Radford, VA: Wilder Publications, 2012).

32. Martin Seligman, *Learned Optimism* (New York: Pocket Books, 1990).

33. Matthew McKay and Patrick Fanning, *Self-Esteem* (Oakland: New Harbinger, 1992).

34. Victor Frankl, *Man's Search for Meaning* (New York: Pocket Books, 1946/1963).

35. Robert Enright, *Forgiveness Is a Choice* (Washington: American Psychological Association, 2001).

36. Goleman, *Social Intelligence*.

37. Enright, *Forgiveness Is a Choice*.

38. Robert Hoffmann, *No One Is to Blame* (Palo Alto, CA: Science and Behavior Books, Inc., 1971).

39. *Oxford English Dictionary*, 3rd edition, s.v. "integrity."

40. Carl Jung, "Aion: Phenomenology of the Self" in *The Portable Jung*, ed. Joseph Campbell (New York: Penguin, 1951/1971), 139–62.

41. Connie Zweig and Steve Wolf, *Romancing the Shadow* (Emeryville, CA: Alibris, 1998).

42. Leslie Greenburg and Jeremy Safran, *Emotion in Psychotherapy* (New York: Guilford Press, 1987).

43. Jay Earley, *Self-Therapy* (Larkspur, CA: Pattern System Books, 2009).

44. Bourne, *Anxiety and Phobia Workbook*.

45. Robert Kegan and Susan Laskow Lahey, *Immunity to Change* (Boston: Harvard Business Press, 2009).

46. Cozolino, *The Neuroscience of Psychotherapy*.

5

Church Structure

When struggles arise in your church, your diagnosis can consider, in addition to systemic anxiety, problems or gaps in your congregation's organizational structure. If Buster is misbehaving, you might notice that the church has no covenant to guide his behavior. If you and your lay leaders clash over what you are called to do, you might notice that your job description is vague. If board meetings drone into the wee hours, you might notice that its role in the church is all-encompassing, leaving it burdened. The diagnosis of a structural problem in hand, you intervene to strengthen that structure.

Your congregation's organizational structure delineates who does what and how. That structure can be informal, when everyone just knows how we make decisions and accomplish tasks. It can be formal, that formal structure including written documents, contracts, budgets, job descriptions, committee charters, policies, procedures, bylaws, and covenants.

THE BENEFITS OF A HEALTHY STRUCTURE

Church structure is the unsung, not-so-glamorous, managerial side of church life that could save your ministry. Its documents have value beyond their sleep-inducing effect at 3:00 a.m.

Structure guides action. Like the signed fire exits created and posted when there is no fire, structural policies and procedures are ideally developed at calm, maybe dull, but thoughtful meetings, rather than as a reflexive reaction to an emergency. In an emergency, when people are panicking and can't think, those pre-thought policies and procedures can guide helpful responses that resolve the emergency.

Structure supports people's trust in their community. For example, a covenant that is public, widely accepted, and applies to everyone, gives everyone a guide for how to belong to that congregation. As they adhere to that covenant, people can feel assured that their belonging cannot be withdrawn on a whim. A covenantal item, such as "Everyone here has the right to be safe and respected," assures the members that their safety is important, which further supports their sense of safety. When people feel safe, they live on the thought side of the thought-reflex continuum, where they enjoy health.

Structure helps people learn social skills. For example, a covenant that includes the behavioral standard, "Here we listen to each other," helps people learn to listen.

The congregation's structure is one form of self-definition. People can realize: "We are a formal, board-centered church" or "We are a casual, minister-led congregation."

A sound organization helps the church fulfill its tasks and meet its members' needs. The children have crayons, coffee hour has coffee, and the phones work.

A sound structure balances stability and change.[1] Structure's guidance supports a congregation's homeostasis and prevents people from having to reinvent wheels. On the other hand, that structure can flex. The bylaws include a revision clause. Members know the structure includes wiggle room within which they can influence the system.

Structure supports growth. A congregation's organization can include unfilled jobs into which new members can be included. Such a roomy structure would be like the slightly too-large clothes into which a child can grow.

Structure clarifies boundaries between committees, staff, and boards, preventing turf battles. People know their jobs and do not stray into someone else's.

Structure gives leaders a moderate response to infractions. If Buster is behaving disrespectfully, people can remind him of the covenant to which he had agreed. If a staff member is behaving irresponsibly, their contract would clarify that person's responsibilities.

Structure is like ballast that keeps a ship from capsizing in a storm. Ballast may not be an exciting spinnaker billowing in a stiff breeze, but ballast prevents shipwrecks and spares everyone grief. And so it is in one's interest to consider structure when facing a problem in the system and to develop interventions that bring healthy organization to the congregation.

FOR EXAMPLE ...

I remember the day my congregation was in peril, threatening to capsize in a gale, when its bylaws came to the rescue. We were growing in number and moving from pastoral to program size. New subgroups were organically forming, giving their members closeness among other people who shared similar interests. Naturally, I welcomed these new groups.

One day a few of our young adults approached me with an interest in forming a group interested in the pre-Christian worship of nature, otherwise known as Paganism. I knew that a pagan group would be a stretch for this still-small congregation in the Midwest, yet I wanted to support these new members. So, fine, Pagan Group it is. Let's run it by the board. The young adults made a responsible proposal to the board, which gave its imprimatur, and the Pagan Group began.

A few days later, Jane, one of the church's founding and much-beloved matriarchs, called me: "What's this about our having a pagan group at our church? If people in town heard about this, our reputation would shatter."

I informed her that the board had okayed the group, but that if she had an objection, she was welcome to bring it to the next board meeting. She did. She spoke of the church's fragile reputation as a liberal congregation in a not-so-liberal town. She worried that, just as we had begun growing and thriving, a pagan group would cast us into the realm of the fringe.

Everyone on the board knew her as a gracious and valued matriarch, and they took her and her concerns seriously. The board was in a bind between the new Pagan Group and Jane, a person they cared about who raised valid concerns.

Given this bind, with Jane present, one board member wisely suggested consulting our oracle: the bylaws. Pulled out of someone's binder, they read that one mission of the church was to support religious education. The Pagan Group, wanting to learn about earth-centered religion, fit that mission. Jane, an educator who might have even written that clause, accepted that the Pagan Group belonged in our congregation. Thank you, bylaws.

But Jane and the board further considered what to do about the church's reputation as hosts of a pagan group. They arrived at the idea of asking the Pagan Group to adopt an innocuous name for themselves. The Pagan Group agreed. The "Nature Religion Study Group" continued to meet. Jane was relieved of her anxiety. The church adhered to its mission and sailed on into calmer seas.

The bylaws rescued us. They offered clarity about what activity the church exists to support, which settled the matter of the acceptability of the "Nature Religion Study Group" and kept a kerfuffle from becoming a brouhaha.

STRUCTURAL INTERVENTIONS

A congregation's structure—its bylaws, policies, staff handbooks, procedures, covenants, and charters —is vast and provides a target-rich environment for leadership intervention.

A congregation or any subgroup can set behavioral standards, also known
as a covenant. Such standards increase the odds of constructive behavior and
guide moderate responses to problematic behavior.

Each committee can create a charter, articulating that committee's purpose,
tasks, and goals for each year; its personnel, how its members are included
and recruited, and the duration of its leaders' and members' tenure. These
charters can be reviewed and approved by the board. By clarifying the
committees' roles, such charters keep one committee from meddling with
another committee's business. When a committee charter limits duration of
its leader's tenure, that prevents someone from becoming the self-appointed
committee chair for life.

Each committee and board creates structure when it sets an agenda for
each meeting. That agenda keeps the meeting focused on its business and
prevents tangents. If people seem bent on taking tangents, those tangents
may indicate people's need to socialize. If so, the group holds a check-in at
the beginning of each meeting after which people would be ready to stick
to its agenda.[2]

Structure would include the recording of the minutes of each meeting—its
discussions, decisions, and delegated tasks. At the next meeting, people review the minutes for accuracy and check on the completion of those tasks.
Such accountability increases the odds those tasks are completed.

Structure can include job descriptions. For some staff members, the job
description is pretty evident. For ministers, there can be differences of opinion regarding what a minister does. Therefore, at the outset of a minister's
tenure at a church, I suggest that minister and the congregation's lay leaders
separately list in writing the minister's tasks, the lay leaders' tasks, and their
shared tasks. They next compare their lists, talk through any differences they
might have, and merge their lists of tasks into one for the minister, one for the
lay leaders, and one they share. Those resulting job descriptions will clarify
everyone's roles. As the church evolves and with turnover in the laity, leaders
can revisit these job descriptions.

Structure can involve planning and delegating. For example, I suggest that
once a year, representatives from each committee and program convene to
plan the church calendar and review the members' and friends' participation.
To plan the calendar, they would post on newsprint a calendar for each month
and let the committees and programs plot their events on those calendars in
coordination with each other. When everyone creates the calendar together,

that prevents the awkward surprise when the annual retreat occurs on the same weekend as the church's gala social event.

Secondly, they review the membership rolls, considering who is active and not to be pestered with more requests, and who is not and which committee or program might want to extend an invitation. We come to Buster on this list and realize he is not involved in any committee or program activity. The worship committee chair thinks Buster would be a good addition to her committee, and the meeting agrees.

The next day the worship chair calls Buster. This personal invitation from the chair of a committee will likely elicit a more positive response than the broadcast appeal for help. Maybe Buster joins and contributes to the committee, leaving both Buster and the committee happy. If Buster declines to be on the worship committee, he still has a friendly, inviting conversation, and the committee chair might learn that Buster really wants to help with building and grounds. The chair relays that information to the building and grounds committee, which welcomes Buster to its next meeting, where together they plan to replace the roof. Through this exercise, the less-involved receive a personal invitation to involvement, the already-active people continue in their roles, and activity spreads throughout the congregation.

A FEW POSSIBLE STRUCTURES

The Board-Centered Structure

Congregations tend to organize around a few types of structures.[3] First, there is the board-centered structure in which the board is the one key body, overseeing both the larger policy-setting and the smaller program issues. Its members chair the committees. Its meetings review and amend committee decisions.

This board-centered structure is common among family-sized churches. This structure is informal and so fits a smaller congregation in which there is not much to organize.

In a family church, personal relationships outweigh formal structures, meaning there can be a *de jure* board as well as a *de facto* "board" of patriarchs and matriarchs of the church. There might be overlap as the "parents" serve on the board, but any big decision is ultimately rendered by the "parents."

The downside of this board-centered model is that, as the go-to, catch-all body, the board takes up the minutiae of ministry and program. This work is time-consuming. Indeed, when the board gets tangled in minute issues and is attracted to the next shiny object of ministry decisions, its meetings can

become knockdown, drag-out marathons, leaving board members martyrs
to the cause. Plus, as a minister, sitting with a board as its meeting yawns
into the night, I lose interest in the matters being discussed and want to give
a dope slap to the next person who utters a word. Having experienced such
long meetings, some colleagues wrote new lyrics to the song, "Charlie and
the MTA"[4] about the meeting that never adjourned. One verse describes its
attention to minutiae:

> They debated the cost of the computer paper
> And the fine points of nametag use;
> They debated the length of the minister's sermons,
> And the cookies and the juice.
> But did they ever adjourn? No, they never adjourned …[5]

Furthermore, when the board makes so many decisions, that prevents others
from decision-making, from empowerment, and from making a meaningful
difference. Committees with little power and meaning look uninteresting to
people who would like to become involved and do not offer their members
ways to learn leadership and problem-solving skills.

Ideally, instead of the board, the minister and office staff discuss computer
paper; the membership committee takes up name tags; the worship committee
gets to consider the sermons; and hospitality, the cookies and the juice. The
board develops fiduciary policies and wraps it up at 9:00 p.m.

The Staff-Centered Structure

Second, there is the staff-centered model in which a charismatic, dynamic
minister leads all.[6] That pastor provides a vision for the congregation as
well as management of its organizational details. This model often occurs
in pastoral-sized churches in which the clergy is like the hub of a wheel, its
committees and groups radiating out from that ministerial hub.

In this staff-centered structure there are fewer organizational chores for
the laity, less time for them to be bogged down in deliberations, and more
programs (set up by the minister) to be involved in. Hotchkiss[7] notes one
congregation that liked this model and coined the slogan: "Fewer meetings,
more ministry!"

On the other hand, this staff-centered model creates a dependence on one
leader. When that leader departs, if no one else has practiced leadership, no
one knows how, and the congregational wheels grind to a halt. Furthermore,
there is the two-or-more-heads-are-better-than-one principle. Indeed, at its
best a meeting can be an opportunity to seek the truth and listen to the spirit,
even when considering the mundane, such as the best way to handle snacks
for the children.

The Committee-Centered Structure

Third, there is the committee-centered model, seen in larger churches. Board members liaise with the committees, but the committees run their own business. The board does less leading and more responding and reacting as it listens to committee reports and proposals. Unfortunately, in this structure no overarching body guides the minister and committees with visions or policies.

MINISTRY AND GOVERNANCE

Finally, there is the ministry and governance model, which I suggest.[8] The governance side of this structure owns and manages the human and material resources of the congregation to ensure the congregation remains in existence and is serving its mission. The ministry comprises the events, worship services, classes, service projects, and all other church programs.

The Governing Board

The congregation's governance is led by the governing board. That board makes the big decisions about capital investments, staffing, policies, program philosophy, and outreach.

The governing board attends to the mission of the church.[9] With support from the board, the congregation's members discern and articulate that mission to which they are called. The board then develops larger strategies and long-range plans to support the exercise of that mission. It also oversees the congregation's human and material resources such that they are used for the benefit of the mission.

The board develops the larger policies that support the viability of the church and the exercise of its mission. A policy is an authoritative written statement designed to guide many individual decisions over time. A good policy prevents people from hassling through case-by-case decision-making.

The board controls its agenda. It considers large questions and avoids micromanaging. Board meetings can include a friendly, personal check-in. It can take up consent agenda items: routine matters and actions that do not require discussion. It can explore discussion agenda items, two or three per meeting. From time to time the board can evaluate: How are we doing as a board? What is going well? What could we do differently?

The board works with relevant committees. Standing board committees—finance and personnel—help the board set policies. The board can appoint temporary committees to handle particular tasks, such as nominating, budget formation, or auditing. The board can convene an executive committee to handle sensitive matters efficiently.

The Minister

Ministry, all the activities and programs of the church, is led by the clergy. Although guided by the clergy, that ministry is carried out by everyone: clergy, staff, and laity.

Hotchkiss suggests a global delegation policy in which the minister makes all operational decisions not explicitly reserved to the board, assigned to someone else, or to a committee, or prohibited by other policies.[10] So there would be board decisions, defined by the board's covenant, and committee decisions, defined by committee charters, staff decisions, defined by their contracts; everything else goes to the minister.

Although the board and minister share responsibility for the effective use of staff, they hold different staff-related functions.[11] The board ensures that the congregation's human resources are used for the benefit of its mission by setting a larger staffing strategy, delegating its implementation, and evaluating that implementation. The board then delegates the job of chief of staff to the minister, with the responsibility to hire, supervise, and discharge the staff.

When hiring a senior staff member, such as a religious education director, the minister nominates a search committee to the board, who gives the committee its go-ahead. The committee finds and recommends a candidate or candidates. The minister selects the top candidate and presents that individual to the board for final approval. When hiring a non-senior staff person, the minister consults with lay leaders to whom this staff person would be important and makes a selection.

When supervising, the minister monitors the staff person's effectiveness at carrying out one's tasks and the staff person's progress toward one's professional goals.

When firing a staff member, the minister first ensures that this decision complies with applicable laws, board policies, contracts, job descriptions, and the personnel manual. Basing a firing on the violation of a contract or policy bases that action on objective criteria, thereby preventing that action from being, or appearing to be, a personal vendetta. If everyone can see the violation of contract or policy, the dismissal can be accepted, and the partisans of the dismissed person would have little grounds for objection. The minister could inform the board of the firing, or church policy could assign the final act of dismissal to the board.

Governance and ministry overlap in places. Both are involved in considering and articulating the identity, mission, and vision of the church. Both can engage together in goal-setting and evaluating progress toward those goals.

But the minister and governing board work best with some distinction from each other. The board monitors the minister's performance but does not make programmatic decisions. The minister respects the board's fiduciary responsibility and stays clear of it. Ideally, all realize they are working together, complementing each other on behalf of their shared mission.

Ultimate Power

In the ministry and governance model, the board handles governance; the minister leads the ministry. The congregation supersedes the board and minister as the final decision-making authority.[12] It decides the largest matters, such as the selection of a minister. And the congregation ultimately ministers. The minister guides, but it is the congregation that lives out its ministering mission.

Although the congregation has ultimate decision-making authority, it is beholden to its mission.[13] Its mission states the ultimate purpose of that religious community: to usher in the Kingdom of God, to save lives and souls, to worship God, to bring justice and peace, to engender love, to support people's spiritual journeys. That mission is the congregation's ultimate authority, the real owner of the congregation on behalf of which its leaders and members serve.

A congregation's religious mission has that ultimate value because the mission brings salvation. Indeed, a congregation's members find salvation when they live in accord with that which is most meaningful to them: their mission. Valuing their mission, the people of a congregation form a structure, codifying and schematizing patterns of activity, to support and preserve that salvific mission. In the end, the mission saves the people; the structure saves the mission.

CONCLUSION

Because its structure applies to the whole congregation, strengthening a congregation's structure supports the congregation's wholeness. Because structure supports the living out of a congregation's salvific mission, strengthening its structure also supports its mission.

QUESTIONS FOR REFLECTION

Considering the congregation you are closest to, how is it structured? What is the relationship of its board, committees, and minister?

What are the advantages and disadvantages of that structure?

What would be additional or different structures that could benefit this congregation?

NOTES

1. Dan Hotchkiss, *Governance and Ministry: Rethinking Board Leadership*, 2nd Edition (Lanham, MD: Rowman & Littlefield, 2016).

2. Ibid.

3. Ibid.

4. Jacqueline Steiner and Bess Lomax Hawes, "The MTA Song" (1949).

5. Robert R. Walsh, "The UU's Who Never Adjourned" (1989) permission granted with credit to author.

6. Hotchkiss, *Governance and Ministry*.

7. Ibid.

8. Ibid.

9. Ibid.

10. Ibid.

11. Ibid.

12. Ibid.

13. Ibid.

6

Calm

During a conflict or a crisis, or even chronically, a congregation's anxiety can run high. When the system is flailing about, throwing its arms in the air, and displaying symptoms of systemic anxiety, it is, of course, not a healthy place for people's spiritual journeys, nor for people's functioning in general.

So you come along to cool the fires. Diagnostically, instead of blaming one symptomatic element of the system as the culprit, you think: The system is a whole, and this system is anxious.

Given that the system is a whole, each member of the system is connected to and influencing each other, ramping up arousal or offering calm. Leaders have especial influence. People look to leaders for cues about how to feel.[1] Citizens look to a president for how to feel about their country. Employees look to their CEO for how to feel about their company. Parishioners look to their pastor for how to feel about their church.

The leader's influence on emotions likely goes back to when primal people relied on the clan's many eyes and ears to detect danger.[2] If one individual sensed a threat, their facial expression alarmed, everyone could see this and swing to reflex and arousal. They would likely turn to their leader for what to do. The leader investigates, and what had looked like a lion turns out to be a jackrabbit. The leader's face calms, and he or she goes back to reading *The New York Times*. Everyone takes this cue about how to feel from their leader and relaxes.

Leaders can work with emotions for good or ill. A leader can intentionally gin up anger and claim to be the only one who can solve this outrage, so as to hook people into following that leader. A leader can scare people

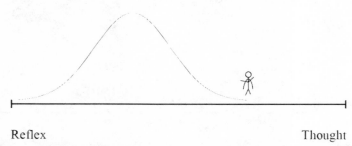

Reflex   Thought

Figure 6.1   Anxious congregation with its minister on the thought side of its bell curve.

and claim to be The Great Protector, creating a dependency on that leader. An insensitive leader can lower people's morale, as in: "The beatings will continue until morale improves." Unintentionally, a bewildered leader can leave people confused.

When parishioners are anxious and looking to you, hopefully the emotion you offer them is calm. As a minister, you may want to solve problems, support love, and journey with people; but for an anxious system, first, calm. When calm, their arousal eased, blood and oxygen flow to people's brains, and their prefrontal cortex kicks in. They can think with creativity and flexibility, solve problems, care about each other, and take their spiritual journeys.

What brings calm to an anxious system is the presence of a leader who is grounded in security and knows that jackrabbits may be approaching, but not lions. Your stance on the thought side of the thought-reflex continuum (shown in Figure 6.1) influences them, bringing them with you into thought. You are like the soothing parent in whose contact the child calms down.

THE PRESENCE OF THE LEADER: SELF-DEFINITION

Calming an anxious system involves noticing the anxiety the system evokes and behaving in ways that do not comply with that anxiety. An anxious system evokes self-protection. Some people self-protectively pressure others to merge with them, so as to erase any differences they might have with each other. Other people respond to anxiety by merging with their anxious compatriots and becoming anxious, or by becoming emotionally or physically absent. To refrain from complying with anxiety one would be oneself in relationship with others, which would calm the system. Systems theorist, Murray Bowen, labeled this ability to be oneself and be close: "differentiation of self."[3]

To be oneself in relationship, a differentiating person defines oneself to others. One speaks in "I-statements," articulating feelings, thoughts, wishes, values, beliefs, principles, goals, and what one will and will not do.[4]

The differentiating person also lets others be who they are. One listens to others and welcomes their feelings, thoughts, wishes, values, beliefs, principles, goals, and what they will and will not do.

Being oneself in contact with others who are able to be themselves, the differentiating person enjoys meaningful relationships.

A differentiating person is like a cell enclosed by a membrane. That cell membrane keeps the cell's protoplasm intact and repels other cells that would invade. Although it is containing and protective, the membrane is not a wall; it lets the cell communicate with and interact with other cells. Those contained but interacting cells maintain a body's healthy functioning.

Differentiation is a process, not an achievement, better expressed with the verb "differentiating" than an adjective "differentiated."[5] Don't expect to be done someday.

Conversely, a less differentiated person is not able to be oneself and is overly influenced by others. "He did this, so I did that" is often the formula. Decisions are made not based on principles but on what "feels right," which depends on what others are doing. Without the steady guidance of principles, one experiences hair-trigger reactions to other people. Being powerfully affected by others whom one cannot control, a less differentiated person would experience other people as threats, causing one chronic arousal and anxiety.

Less differentiated individuals fuse with others or cut off. When fused, they are hungry for approval and belonging and become chameleons, fitting in, but lacking personal convictions. Cut-off people appear aloof and isolated, displaying an exaggerated facade of independence and boasting of emancipation from other people yet living with reactive distancing.

A differentiating leader is like any differentiating person—defining oneself, while relating to others—except that the leader, having more influence than others in the system, would face out-of-the-ordinary pressure to comply with the system's anxiety. To explain with the cell analogy, a system of cells would include pathogens, cells that invade other cells, causing those cells either to fuse with the pathogens or to disintegrate. The differentiating leader would bring health to the system, making it immune to pathogens. Knowing the leader could weaken their influence, the pathogens seek to weaken the leader by invading with unusual intensity. In an anxious congregation, as in an ill body, the pathogens will be even more inflamed. The leader is then further pressured into becoming another pathogen or disintegrating.

Different congregations impose pathogenic pressures in different ways. A chaotic congregation makes it risky for a leader to take a stand. An escalating system pulls its leader to escalate. An extremist congregation pulls its leader to impose immoderate solutions to problems. A reactive congregation pulls its leader to speed up. A desperate system pulls a leader to become its autocrat. A conflicting congregation pulls its minister to take sides. A scapegoating system blames its minister for its ills. An invalidating system judges and labels its minister. A threatened system appoints its minister to be its hero and to fight its villains. A system that uses pressure pulls its minister to wage reform campaigns. A threatening system scares its leader into hiding. A rigid system causes its leader to give up on change. A dependent system pulls its leader to rescue them at the expense of the leader's principles and values. A pessimistic system defeats its minister's hope. A serious system defeats its minister's playfulness. A system ruled by obligation presses duty on its minister.

Crowded by these pressures, you, as minister and leader, may not be allowed much space to be yourself, but the more self you have, the less space you need to function.[6] This self consists of qualities and ideas you know to be true about yourself, such as your values, principles, or beliefs. With that secure self, the leader can express those values, principles, and beliefs, even when pressure from pathogens to fuse with them or disintegrate makes such self-expression perilous.

For instance, a leader guided by the principle of fairness might face pathogens whose unfair behavior could evoke unfairness by the leader, resulting in the surrender of one's principle. On the other hand, the leader who continues to demonstrate fairness in the face of unfair interactions indicates that despite the system's crowding, the leader is still being oneself, guided by one's principle of fairness. Seeing someone be who they are, and being guided by a principle rather than by reactivity, calms the system. Furthermore, if the leader, in the midst of a pathogen-generated storm, continues to live by the same principles as in calm, that offers the calming implication that conditions are not so stormy that all principles need to be heaved overboard.

The differentiating leader not only resists being invaded but does not invade the invading pathogens, such as by pressuring them to change. Instead, one stays in contact with the pathogens and listens to those who would invade, letting them be who they are and respecting their integrity. When this leader gives others, even pathogens, the experience of self and space, that limits the system-wide invasions of pathogens and frees people from the fear of invasion.

The leader who stays in contact with the system, relieves people of the fear of abandonment. An anxious system feels tense and scary, causing some leaders to leave it, either physically or by becoming a nonentity, in effect disintegrating. Instead, the differentiating leader remains connected and relating. Knowing the leader is still present calms the system.

The differentiating leader shows people the possibility of a sweet spot in which people have the space to be themselves and be connected. Finding this best of both worlds—freedom and love—calms the system.

Moderated Reactivity

Related to being differentiated, Friedman suggests leaders bring calm by adopting a "non-anxious presence."[7] Unfortunately, a leader who aspires to be non-anxious but feels anxious in an anxious system might believe one is leading poorly and feel even more anxious. Therefore, I say, you will feel anxious in an anxious system for good reason. There is anxiety all around you, and it's contagious. Also, as a diagnostic instrument, your anxiety provides information: this system is anxious.

A less anxiety-generating term might be "moderated reactivity" or the "moderately reactive presence." Within an anxious system, your anxious emotion gives valuable information about what you are going through, and, unless you are a piece of wood, it is impossible not to feel. Fortunately, managing one's behavior, especially reactive behavior, is easier on than trying to manage one's emotions. You can, for instance, pause a moment before acting. You take this moment to remember your principles, such as fairness. You choose a behavior consistent with your principle of fairness. You then feel the system's anxiety, but behave moderately in spite of that anxiety. That moderated behavior would be calming.

I think this "moderately reactive presence" is consistent with the moderated, thoughtful ministerial presence Friedman suggests. Friedman described this moderation as being like a step-down transformer.[8] The system's anxious voltage comes into you, the leader. You take it in, apply moderation and thoughtfulness, and express yourself with a lower voltage. The energy emerging from you is calmer and clearer, which calms the congregation.

Balanced Responsibility

In an anxious systems, people are dependent and pull others to assume responsibility for making them happy. "Solve my problems, now!" in response, one can accept full responsibility for others' feelings and happiness. At the other extreme, one can deny any responsibility for others' feelings. At either extreme, anxiety rules.

There is a calming medium between assumption and denial of responsibility for others' feelings and needs. One can respond with compassion and concern. There needs to be a footnote added here, footnote number.[9] One accepts responsibility for one's intentions and can attempt to be benevolent, while accepting one's limits in the ability to fix all and command happiness.

This third version of responsibility implies that others can assume responsibility for themselves, while receiving support, which is calming.

Vision

One of a minister's jobs is to offer a vision, and a leader's visioning calms people. Scripture articulates the value of visioning with the line: "Where there is no vision, the people perish" (Proverbs 29:18, KJV).

While anxiety evokes hiding, expressing a vision is a form of exposure. Watching not-hiding in front of their very eyes, people can realize, "Someone here is secure enough not to hide" and conclude they are not as much in Threatworld as they might have supposed.

Furthermore, when you express a vision, you are out of the weeds of the moment and seeing the path ahead, which is calming. The group realizes, "Life here is not just about putting out fires and handling emergencies. We are going someplace great."

Visions can take three forms. There can be bricks and mortar visions, which name something concrete to be developed, like a new sanctuary. There can be programmatic visions, naming programs you wish to see developed, like life-span religious education. There are intangible visions, such as mutual support on our spiritual journeys.

As you express your vision, you allow others to have their visions. Indeed, as you demonstrate envisioning, observers will likely start imagining their own visions. If the minister pressures people to conform to one's vision, that escalates the system's anxiety. But when others begin to state their own visions, whatever they are, those self-definitions indicate your having given them a safer, calmer system.

Furthermore, when people envision grand possibilities, they can be less reactive to pain, that pain made meaningful by the possibilities of the meaningful vision. It may be painful slogging through the Sinai, but we are going to the Holy Land.

Prioritization

Another version of self-protective hiding involves accommodating to the system's dependency by doing everything for one's dependent system. People will likely not complain that you are busy running yourself into the ground, although your body and soul will.

One way to refrain from pleasing and overfunctioning and instead define oneself, is to take the abundance of tasks forever on your plate and prioritize. To prioritize, you have criteria that help you decide what is most important.

These criteria could include the congregation's mission, your principles, your vision for the church, and your underlying motivation for ministry.

In my case, I envisioned inspirational worship, and made that a priority. If other less vital tasks were not done, maybe the church did not really need them or, if done but with mistakes, maybe the church could learn something. The clear, prioritizing presence brings greater calm than running around tackling infinite tasks.

Vulnerability

When an anxious system evokes self-protection, vulnerability shows self-protection to be unnecessary, which disrupts the anxiety. Clarissa Pinkola Estes expressed the effect of this vulnerability: "One of the most calming and powerful actions you can do to intervene in a stormy world is to stand up and show your soul."[10] Vulnerability does not have to involve publishing your darkest secrets in the newsletter, but it would involve self-definition, revealing your values, visions, and principles. Observing that vulnerability, others can trust, come out of hiding, and be vulnerable themselves. When people are openly themselves, that supports secure, intimate relating.

Slowness

An anxious system will likely evoke fast action by running around in a panic. Others see panic and start panicking themselves. Just stopping to think suggests that speed is not so necessary. If you do slow down, the system might pressure you to speed up. As the system intensifies pressure to speed you up, it would take steely nerve to remain slow. Nevertheless, unless the building is on fire, slowing down would eventually be calming.

Furthermore, in anxious system I may not be clever enough to conceive of some genius action that cools the system's anxiety, but I can do nothing. When people expect and evoke speed, and face a relaxed "Well, I don't know. Let's just think about this for a minute ..., " they would have to slow down, too. Finding that the pause does not cause their heads to explode would be calming.

Playfulness

In an anxious system people's reptile brains are in charge, and they are serious. The leader can conform to the system's anxiety by joining the system in ponderous seriousness. The alternative, joyful playfulness, emerging from the mammal brain and the thought side of the continuum, reflects your security, offers an antidote to oppressive earnestness and seriousness, and throws doubt on the system's anxiety. "If our minister is safe enough to be smiling, maybe we are not under so much threat."

Playfulness does not mean becoming a stand-up comedian or minimizing or distracting people from the seriousness of the congregation's challenges. It does mean adding a lightness to the proceedings that reveals your confidence that the issues can be resolved.[11] One can also find a humorous side to a situation that conveys a positive or redeeming aspect to the issue.

Diagnosing

A congregation behaving anxiously evokes the personality-problem diagnosis: "They are crazy." Such judgment adds anxiety to the system. Alternatively, as discussed in Chapter 2, a diagnosis that does not criticize but which understands how it is to be in the congregation's shoes, and which validates its behavior, is calming.

Neutrality

An anxious system engaging in a conflict evokes partisans. A minister's neutrality amid the partisan battle sees both sides as having validity, which de-escalates the battle and is calming.

Furthermore, a traumatized congregation benefits from a ministerial presence that is neutral about what it should do, and is thus not controlling the congregation. A trauma is the experience of being forcefully and painfully controlled. If controlled again by the "helpful" minister, that control would reenact the trauma. Instead, a leader who is neutral and personally disinterested in the outcome, and therefore does not re-traumatize, allows people to find their own calm and bearing.

Music

Your worship services likely include music, and music soothes the fearful amygdala. In a children's burn clinic, for instance, music played during painful procedures calms patients and caregivers alike.[12]

THE LEADER'S WELCOMING OF THE PEOPLE: EMPATHY

In addition to baring one's soul, thereby showing people the system is safe, the calming leader receives and accepts what the people express.

Receiving others' self-expression, the leader offers empathy. With empathy one suspends one's own agenda and temporarily enters another's world and life, understanding their words, feelings, and intentions, sensing meanings and avoiding judgments. Empathy involves listening without taking responsibility for the speaker, but with a recognition of what the speaker is experiencing. Carl Rogers, a master of empathy, defined empathy as the ability "to perceive the internal frame of reference of another with accuracy and with the emotional components and meanings which pertain thereto as if one were the person without ever losing the as if condition."[13]

Empathy is difficult, and well-intentioned people can deviate from empathy by offering corrective suggestions. For example, if someone is anxious, the correction could sound like: "Don't worry. It will be okay." Or "You should not think like that. Here is another way to think." If that corrective input works, great.

If the correction does not work, the anxious person may not be ready or interested in the oh-so-helpful new perspective. Instead, they'll keep being anxious and try to convince you of the validity of their anxiety. Plus, they will feel alone and misunderstood. Furthermore, when the non-empathic listener imposes a new perspective, that implies (a) the anxious person's feelings cannot be trusted; they are too difficult and must be avoided by jumping to a new perspective; and/or (b) the anxious person's thinking cannot be not trusted; one cannot develop one's own new perspective and so someone else has to do the thinking for them. If someone can't trust their feelings or thoughts, their anxiety will likely increase.

Although the correcting "helper" imagines themselves being helpful, their attempt to change the anxious person could be an attempt to relieve the "helper" of one's own anxiety. The "helper," could be saying, in effect, "You calm down, now, so I won't have to be anxious."

What Empathy Does for Others

Empathy calms by letting someone experience acceptance and validation.[14] One can be oneself in a safe, trusted relationship to someone else. By not judging or correcting from a superior vantage, the listener sets up equal terms with the speaker, and equality is safer than a hierarchy. By refraining from offering advice, empathy also shows trust and respect for the speaker's ability to find their own solutions to their problems. The speaker can then open up further and self-disclose with deeper vulnerability. You know empathy is working when someone unpacks more of their story.

Empathic listening supports the speaker in developing a safe relationship with oneself. Empathy holds up a validating mirror in which the speaker can see oneself more clearly. When someone can recognize one's experience and emotions, that can guide one toward constructive behavior. Furthermore, as one accepts one's emotions as valid, one does not have to use self-destructive ways to manage emotions, such as emotional repression or substance abuse; nor ways that are destructive to others, such as aggressiveness.

When one's story is told, the emotions expressed with space and acceptance, emotions do what emotions are naturally supposed to do: flow on to the next emotion. Emotions provide quick information about what one is going through.[15] As circumstances change, emotions change with them. Emotions are not supposed to be dammed up and persistent, but flow like a river. Empathy invites one to undam one's emotional river. For instance, if an anxious person is accepted and validated by their empathic listener, that reflects a change in their circumstance—"Someone is listening to me!" The new circumstance leads to a new emotion: relief. On the other hand, trying to persuade someone not to feel their anxiety dams up the anxiety where it lingers like stagnant water and adds one more reason to be anxious.

The freedom and space to express one's feelings to someone else brings comfort. Maya Angelou speaks to that comfort: "There is no greater agony than bearing an untold story inside you."[16] Empathy tells another, "You are not alone. I am witness to you and your story." The comforting that accompanies responsive emotional engagement can release oxytocin, a neurotransmitter associated with calm, joy, and trust.[17] The presence of oxytocin reduces stress hormones, such as cortisol.[18]

In response to empathy, one calms and settles back to the thought side of the thought-reflex continuum, where the ability to think returns. With thinking, one can access more adaptive, helpful, problem-solving responses that had been absent while aroused.

Types of Empathic Responses

Just being present and offering a few *uh-huhs* and *hmms* allows the other time and support with which to process what is happening.

One can name the emotion. The other may not be aware of what they are feeling and so may benefit when their emotion is named.

Parishioner: The pledge campaign has come in lower than we budgeted.

Minister: That's disappointing.

One can restate what the other has said.

Parishioner: I think we will have to cut your salary.

Minister: Cutting my salary does offer one option for balancing our budget.

One can affirm the meaning of the other's experiences, as if one is standing beside the other on a hilltop sharing a view of the situation.

Parishioner: We don't want to cut your salary, but our church is just not growing.

Minister: You face a dilemma.

Learning Empathy

Empathy is a skill one can learn through practice. It helps to bring a tentative, exploratory attitude to what another is saying, as if the conversation is a process of discovery. To do this exploring takes some imagination and effort. Your imagination can be supported by your own understandings of how life can feel.

When reflecting someone else's emotion, it helps to remember the seven emotions: anger, sadness, joy, fear, confusion, shame, and guilt. It does not require a lot of mental searching to consider which off the list they might be experiencing.

Any guess is constructive. If naming one feeling misses the mark, they might say, "I am not so much angry as confused." If so, your guess about anger landed somewhere near the target. Coming close to the target, your guess helped the speaker clarify and name their own emotion. Through this conversation, you are both collaborating in the process of focusing and clarifying someone's experience. In addition, your guessing shows your caring and desire to understand, which offers the speaker safety.

As one is trying to be empathic, it helps to offer empathy to oneself. It is difficult to listen with empathy to another's discomfort.

CONCLUSION

A leader's calming interventions would be based on that leader's security. With that security, amid an anxious system, a leader can define oneself and receive others defining who they are, which calms an anxious system.

QUESTIONS FOR REFLECTION

When trying to offer someone else empathy, what emotions or statements from them would be most difficult to hear? Instead of giving them empathy, what might be your defensive responses?

When did you last define yourself to someone else? What did you say? How did that feel? How did the other person respond?

NOTES

1. Daniel Goleman, Annie McKee and Richard Boyatzis, *Primal Leadership* (Cambridge: Harvard Business School Press, 2002).

2. Daniel Goleman, *Social Intelligence* (New York: Random House, 2006).

3. Edwin Friedman, *Generation to Generation: Family Process in Church and Synagogue* (New York: Guilford, 1985).

4. Edwin Friedman, "Bowen, Theory and Therapy" in *Handbook of Family Therapy, vol. II,* ed. A. Gurman and D. Kniskern (New York: Brunner/Mazel, 1991), 134–70.

5. Lawrence Matthews, "Theology and Family Systems Theory in Dialogue" in *Leadership in Ministry,* ed. Israel Galindo (Middletown, DE: Didache Press, 2017), 164–86.

6. Friedman, *Generation to Generation.*

7. Ibid.

8. Edwin Friedman, "Bowen Family Systems Theory Seminar for Clergy" (lecture, Offices of Edwin Friedman, Bethesda, MD, October 1990).

9. Marshall Rosenberg, *Nonviolent Communication: A Language of Life* (Encinitas, CA: PuddleDancer Press, 2003).

10. Clarissa Pinkola Estes, "Letter to a Young Activist during Troubled Times," https://www.mavenproductions.com/letter-to-a-young-activist.

11. Dan Hughes, "The Communication of Emotions and the Growth of Autonomy and Intimacy within Family Therapy" in *The Healing Power of Emotion,* ed. Diana Fosha, Daniel Siegel, and Marion Solomon (New York: Norton, 2009), 280–303.

12. Monica Brady-Myerov and George Hicks, "Music Therapists Help Ease Treatment of Children with Severe Burns" (WBUR: October 9, 2002).

13. Carl Rogers, "A Theory of Therapy, Personality, and Interpersonal Relationships, as Developed in the Client-Centered Framework" in *Psychology: A Study of Science,* ed. Sigmund Koch (New York: McGraw-Hill, 1959), 184–256.

14. Jeanne Watson, Rhonda Goldman, and Greet Vanaerschot, "Empathic: A Postmodern Way of Being?" in *Handbook of Experiential Psychotherapy,* ed. Leslie Greenberg, Jeanne Watson and Germain Lietaer (New York: Guilford Press, 1998), 61–81.

15. Leslie Greenberg, *Emotion-Focused Therapy* (Washington, DC: American Psychological Association, 2002).

16. Maya Angelou, *I Know Why the Caged Bird Sings* (New York: Random House, 1969/2015).

17. C. Sue Carter, "Neuroendocrine Perspectives on Social Attachment and Love." *Psychoneuroendrocrinology* 23 no. 8 (1998): 779–818.

18. Jolanta Gutkowaska, et al., "Oxytocin Is a Cardiovascular Hormone." *Brazilian Journal of Medical and Biological Research* 33 no. 6 (2000): 625–33.

7

Change

Ministers often envision themselves as change agents—so exciting to bring change and so gratifying. But as political philosopher Niccolò Machiavelli cautioned: "There is nothing more difficult to take in hand, more perilous to conduct, or more uncertain in its success, than to take the lead in the introduction of a new order of things."[1] If you still want to take on this challenge, systems theory provides theoretical and practical guidance.

Systems theory focuses on changing the whole system. The change agent does not divide the system and pit one side against each other, nor try to reform one aspect of the system only, as if there are good and bad parts of this whole.

Systems theory observes multiple causality: every element in a system influencing each other. Conversely, according to mechanistic theory, one party can change another: minister A changes congregation B, like the cue ball changing the location of the 8-ball—an autocrat's method of change. Systems theory offers the more complex multiple causality, in which the minister is one of the balls on a billiards table, all moving and bumping into each other. Then minister A is changed by congregation B, as congregation B is changed by minister A. For instance, the minister responds to the congregation's influences by changing one's change interventions. That minister who respects those many influences in one's congregation supports its democratic processes.

According to systems theory, when one element in the system changes, the system changes. Therefore, changing a system means changing oneself, to which the system adjusts. To change the system toward health, one interacts healthily with the system, appreciating its wholeness, supporting its safety, and offering principled, moderated leadership.

For systems theory, the process, or how one promotes change, is important. A valuable change message, conveyed via a discordant process, may well fall flat.

Ideally, a congregation changes such that it more concertedly fulfills its mission. A spiritual community becomes more spiritual; an activist community becomes more effectively active; a support community becomes more supportive. Indeed, I do not recommend waging a reform campaign against the church's mission, pushing a spiritual community to become activist, or pushing an activist community to cool its jets. Furthermore, when a minister supports a congregation in fulfilling its mission, rather than campaigning against that mission, that minister is supporting the congregation's integrity or wholeness and helping the congregation align with its source of meaning: its mission.

STASIS AND CHANGE

Systems change and stay the same. Gregory Bateson observed this yin and yang of stasis and change: "All change can be understood as the effort to maintain some constancy, and all constancy is maintained through change."[2] Like the adjustments of a tightrope walker, the system adjusts to keep balanced and moving.

Extremes of stasis and change become problems. Too much stasis becomes stale. Too much change brings upheaval and confusion. Sometimes a minister might spur change ahead, at others pull back on the reins.

So on one hand, systems maintain their homeostasis. People who resist change are speaking for their system's homeostasis.

People resist change for three reasons:

1. The status quo is familiar and predictable, despite its discomforts. The devil you know is better than the one you don't.
2. The status quo serves some function or offers some benefit.[3]
3. Attempting change will be awkward and incur mistakes, which could be viewed as failure. To avoid failure, resist change.

On the other hand, systems change and evolve in unpredictable ways. For example, who in the Cambrian Era would have ever thought fish could learn to get out of the water and walk?

WHAT MINISTERS TRY

If the congregation wants to try something new, learn something, or grow, it asks for the minister's diagnosis of its problems and for advice on what to do. Then, of course, that minister has a golden opportunity to bring change.

But if the congregation is not seeking change, and I, as minister, initiate it, the path forward is perilous. Going where angels fear to tread, I begin by diagnosing a problem with the church. "My church is too _____ (fill in the blank)." Seeing fault in the church leads to an intervention: the reform campaign.

To wage the reform campaign, I have to fight against the church in its current state. That sets up minister vs. congregation battle lines, disrupting the wholeness of the system. As I tense for battle, that infects the system with tension. As the people find themselves in the crosshairs of my reform campaign, they become anxious.

Trying to reform them causes me problems. As I ponder what is wrong with them, negativity and frustration fill my firmament, leaving me with negativity and frustration. I might remain unhappy until they change, which could mean a long spell of unhappiness. I might invest prodigious energy into changing them, which they can easily thwart by doing nothing.

Despite these cautions, I might begin the reform campaign with a common-sense intervention: an offer of insight. With insight come explanations, theories, rational arguments, advice, and promises of success if the change does occur. The message consists of "Here is the problem. Here is the solution. Go do it!" Sometimes people welcome insight, learn from it, and change.

Unfortunately, though, insight does not work unless people want to change. Furthermore, when they are living in Threatworld, people's reptile brains are not amenable to insight. I might apply the three strikes model: if three attempts at insight fail, the group might not want to receive insight, or be too reactive to receive insight. After three strikes, the insight-related interventions are out and have to slouch back to the dugout.

If insight fails, I might resort to pushing harder at reform. I might exhort people to increase their will to act. "You must do X." "We must do Y." Such impassioned rallying may not actually change people's wills. Furthermore, pushing others to change requires pressure. As I model pressure, others follow, resulting in a congregation in which people pressure and crowd each other, limiting everyone's freedom to be themselves.

Ramping up the pressure, I evoke guilt. I list their mistakes and the consequences of their failure to act. I speak louder. No results.

Then I complain of the congregation's defects in character or will. I decry sinfulness from the pulpit. Still no change. I complain that the congregation is stuck or resistant. Then—no surprise—they do not rally into action. Despite the would-be change agent's impassioned good intentions, if people are not following the leader's leadership, it is not the people's fault; the leader's leadership is faulty.

Despite vigorous applications of blame and pressure, I do not control other people, and if they do not want to be reformed, they do not change, and I join the legions of bitter, disgruntled change-agents discarded on the ash heaps of history.

All is not lost. There are ways to lead change in a system that do not require delivering insight, enlisting people's wills, or applying pressure and blame.

THE MINISTERIAL ALLIANCE

Your relationship with the congregation is the medium of change. This relationship is analogous to the relationship between therapist and client. With a secure therapeutic alliance, the client trusts the therapist and believes the therapist understands them and is on their side. That alliance, more than therapeutic techniques and theories, is the most important factor in therapeutic change.[4] Applied to ministry, the alliance you have with your congregation is itself a therapeutic instrument. Their trust in you, their belief that you understand them and are on their side, makes whatever you say or do be influential.

You form that alliance by respecting the congregation, understanding their identity, giving pastoral support, and behaving ethically. You respect the people; they trust you. In addition, the rituals attending ministry—the ordination and installation ceremonies, the wearing of vestments, times of prayer— symbolize the alliance and support the belief that ministry is important and instrumental. The ministry that is seen as instrumental is instrumental, according to the placebo effect.

On the other hand, one way to disrupt that alliance would be to start proposing changes in a way that is discordant with the system. You might do this by offering brilliant and needed suggestions before you have become integrated into the system. Offering premature suggestions, you could be perceived as telling them you are the smart one and that they have been running their church stupidly, leaving them ashamed and guilty. If you are an emitter of shame and guilt, they will move emotionally away from you. Goodbye, alliance.

You also foster a secure alliance by respecting the stage of change people are inhabiting. Not only that, but a leader's change interventions work best when they fit the followers' stage of change. Conversely, when the change agent pushes for change in ways that are discordant with people's stage of change, that change agent is pushing for change on two fronts: pushing for the desired change and pushing people to adopt a new stage of change, making change twice as difficult and disrupting one's alliance with them.

STAGES OF CHANGE

There are five stages of change.[5]

Pre-Contemplation

This first stage of change is the profound and absolute resistance to change. It looks and sounds like "No."

> "Do you want to try this new thing?"
> "No. Absolutely not. Never."

When facing the pre-contemplation stage, pushing, pleading, cajoling, or negotiating will likely run aground on the shoals of resistance. Inducing change in people occupying the pre-contemplation stage can seem futile, but you do have options.

Paradox: Lean in with Empathy

Paradox can work at this stage. With paradox, when the sensible move is to go right, you go left. You support people in going where you do not want them to do, and you go where you do not want to go, say the opposite of what you want to say. A paradox seems crazy. It is a move both the opponent of change and the change agent do not expect.

One paradoxical move would be to accept the congregation as it is. As Carl Rogers observed: "The curious paradox is that when I accept myself just as I am, then I can change."[6] As you accept someone as they are, they experience safety, which allows them to be flexible and then change. For example, someone disquietingly insists: "We want to complain about you behind your back." About to spring from your lips is an eloquent argument that will set them into a whole new universe of being, but your eloquence will fall on deaf ears. Instead, you listen and reflect back their view: "So, complaining in secret seems like a good idea." They don't expect that. You surprise yourself as you validate that which seems so far from the constructive, even though validating does not mean agreeing. That atmosphere of acceptance offers the other the safety with which to rethink their view of the world.

Not only when people are "wrong," but when people are in pain, you can feel in impulse to change them right away. You have the answer to their problem about to pour from your sympathetic heart, but at the pre-contemplation stage, they might not be ready to feel or do something different. Therefore, you listen, accepting them as they are. For example, Murray Bowen is said to have told a psychotic patient: "I am not trying to change you. I want to understand your thinking."[7] As you empathize, that gives their painful emotions space and support, which allows those emotions to do what emotions naturally do: flow to the next feeling.

Paradox: Make Things Worse

A second way paradox can work involves not just validating people as they are, but taking a difficult situation and temporarily making it worse. As you respond with, "So, complaining in secret seems like a good idea." it is as if you are making their view seem more valid, more entrenched, and then worse.

Another example of paradoxically making matters worse occurred at a high school basketball game between an Indian team from the Pine Ridge Reservation visiting a white team in Lead, South Dakota.[8] As the game was about to commence, the Indian players in the locker room heard the Lead fans making heckling calls and chants derogatory toward Indians. Nervous about facing this hostile arena, one player told her team, "I can't handle this." Another teammate, SuAnne Big Crow, offered to go first onto the court. Ian Frazier recounts:

> She came running onto the court dribbling the basketball, with her team-mates running behind. On the court the noise was deafening. SuAnne went right down the middle and suddenly stopped when she got to center court . . . SuAnne turned to Doni De Cory and tossed her the ball. Then she stepped into the jump-ball circle at center court, facing the Lead fans. She unbuttoned her warm-up jacket, took it off, draped it over her shoulders, and began to do the Lakota shawl dance. SuAnne knew all the traditional dances . . . and the dance she chose is a young woman's dance, graceful and modest and show-offy all at the same time . . . SuAnne began to sing in Lakota, swaying back and forth in the jump-ball circle, doing the shawl dance, using her warm-up jacket for a shawl. The crowd went completely silent. "All that stuff the Lead fans were yelling—it was like she reversed it somehow," a teammate says. In the sudden quiet all they could hear was her Lakota song. SuAnne dropped her jacket, took the ball from Doni De Corey, and ran a lap around the court dribbling expertly and fast. The audience began to cheer and applaud. She sprinted to the basket, went up in the air, and laid the ball through the hoop, with the fans cheering loudly now. Of course, Pine Ridge went on to win the game.

With the unfriendly Lead fans shaming the Pine Ridge team for being Indians, the Sioux players could have come out looking like they wanted to hide, giving the Lead crowd a victory. Or the Pine Ridge team could have joined in the hostility, shaking their fists at the Lead fans, which might have fed the obnoxiousness of the crowd. Or someone from Lead could have lectured the Lead fans about manners, which might have quieted them but not really changed their attitude.

Instead, as the Lead fans were attacking her Indian identity, SuAnne came out with more of her identity. Showing more of herself, she paradoxically made herself more vulnerable to their attacks, that vulnerability making her life momentarily more difficult. Then her paradoxical vulnerability moved the Lead fans from in no way changing their attitude, to changing their attitude. She did not ask the Lead fans to change their attitude, but she did not let the Lead fans change her attitude about being an Indian. The Lead fans could appreciate her vulnerable pride in her identity.

In another example, I once worked with an intern minister, who, at our supervisory meetings, complained that I was critical of him. I tried three times to say that I was not judging him, but at the pre-contemplation stage, he was not budging. So I made it worse. I leaned in to his belief by encouraging him to watch for my judgments of him and to report them. I offered him a pad of paper on which to note each time he heard me judging him. The paper remained blank. He gave up his belief that I was judging him.

As another example, when my congregation's board president did not want to change her view that people should be free to complain about me behind my back, I could have paradoxically made matters worse by encouraging her: "You are doing a brave and caring act for our members by standing up to me on behalf of people's safety. I think the congregation needs you to advocate for secret complaining. People might lose something if they did not have that protection." Ideally, her reaction to my prescribing the symptom would have been a recoil with the thought: "This is weird." That recoil is the immune system kicking in to fight the illness.

If the board president were to become amenable to change and suggest relinquishing the symptom, I could have paradoxically voiced restraint. "Maybe it's okay to people to complain to me directly, but I don't know. They might not be ready for this."

Ideally, as I resisted change, the system's push for change would increase: "I think we can do it."

"Are you sure?"
"Yeah, no problem."

Report the Effects of the Status Quo

Another version of paradox at the pre-contemplation stage involves reporting how the status quo affects you. This move is paradoxical because it involves vulnerability when common sense dictates hiding. For example, during a conflict, instead of hiding from it, you report: "This conflict is scary." As another example, I once told a parishioner, who seemed perennially irritated with me, that I was afraid of him. He looked surprised. He did not offer me a warm handshake or hug of fellowship, but I felt an ease in our tension. Furthermore, given the system's relatedness, my vulnerable and open move with him, when vulnerability and openness did not make common sense, made vulnerability and openness more normative system-wide.

There is a structure for reporting how one is affected by what is happening:

> "When X happens . . ." or "When you do Y . . ."
> "I feel . . ."
> or "I think . . ."
> or "I do . . ."
> or "I want . . ."

Making clear how one is affected gives the other information with which the other might change.

Propose, Then Wait

Another intervention at the pre-contemplation stage is to propose a change and then wait, letting the system move through the stages of change at its pace.

I did this when, after serving a church for two years, I thought I had enough credit to ask the worship committee to add to worship the sharing of joys and concerns. I did not want to spring the idea on the whole committee, or begin it unilaterally one Sunday, so I proposed it to the committee chair. Being at the pre-contemplation stage, he responded to my proposal with statements like "No way. Over my dead body!" I could see that persuasion would go nowhere, so I left it at that. But a month later, in another one-on-one moment with the chair, I proposed the joys and concerns time again. His refusals were a little softer. A month later, the same proposal. He suggested I bring it to the committee, albeit without his support. I brought it to the committee. They were dubious. Another month went by. I raised it again; they were more open. After another month, they agreed to let me introduce joys and concerns during the services I was leading, but that lay-led services would not include joys and concerns. At my next service, I introduced joys and concerns. The earth did not open up and swallow the church. After a few times watching me lead joys and concerns, the lay-led services just happened to include them too.

Expanding the scope of change, one can announce one's vision for the church, in the mode of Martin Luther King's "I Have a Dream" speech: "I have a dream that one day we will trust each other and share with each other our sorrows and celebrations." Then wait.

Express a Value

An anxious and reactive system is thrashing around in the weeds of its issues. Unfortunately, scoldings or exhortations will not lift the system out of the weeds and would instead reflect the leader's own anxious thrashing in the weeds.

Alternatively the leader could express values. Someone expressing values is standing out of the weeds and viewing the landscape from above. For example, the leader can articulate the values that emerge from one religious tradition: "We value love, guided by Jesus's love."

Hearing a leader speak from a loftier vantage reassures people: someone is out of the weeds. Expressing a lofty value invites people to be guided by that value, or find and live by their own value. As they are guided by a value, they too have emerged from the weeds.

Be the One the System Tries to Change

When encountering people at the pre-contemplation stage, inducing change in someone else is difficult because you cannot control them. Furthermore, it is easy for them to resist change by doing nothing. Alternatively, one can cease efforts to make them change and become the one they are trying to change, giving them the harder job. For example, when I brought to board meetings my visions, principles, goals, etc., I had to bear their pressure on me to change, but they had to strain to change me. When I kept not changing, the system adjusted around me.

This style of change reminds me of A. J. Muste, a peace advocate who stood a nightly candlelight vigil in front of the White House during the Vietnam War. When a reporter asked him whether he thought his lonely vigil would change the US military policy, he replied, "Oh, I don't do this to change the country. I do this so the country won't change me."[9]

Decline to Comply

To influence an anxious congregation at the pre-contemplation stage, one can discern what the system is evoking and do something different. For example, I briefly served a church after the minister quit over his conflicts with the music director, and the music director had been fired by its board. The choir, in solidarity with its director, was boycotting Sunday services. But the choir still planned to sing at a town-wide church choir concert, which outraged some in the church. I could sense how easy and politically expedient it would have been to join the outrage and scold the choir for shunning the church but still singing at this community concert.

Nevertheless, I remembered the system is a whole and did not want to deepen its divisions by villainizing the choir. I also hoped the choir would someday reconcile with the congregation and return. So I decided to support the choir. On Sundays, I announced the community concert, indicated that I would be going, and invited everyone else. Many people came, even board members still unhappy with the choir and its director. They and the choir's supporters sat together and applauded our choir, which moved the congregation a few steps from partisan division to wholeness.

The status quo and its pulls are hard to recognize, and so one could believe one is combating a problem, while ineluctably complying with a system's illness. On this regard, Adolf Hitler is supposed to have said: "The great strength of the totalitarian state is that it forces those who fear it to imitate it."[10] Using bad behavior to fight bad behavior complies with bad behavior.

Compliance with the system may "feel" right. Indeed, it will seem safe and comfortable to operate within the bowels of the system and risky to act differently than what the system is endorsing. But rather than be guided by comfort, one can be guided by one's principles or values, which have been thought through and do not simply echo the system's anxiety. Guided by thoughtful principles and values, one offers healthy change.

It takes some discernment to know what the system is pulling one to comply with. Luckily, in an anxious system, patterns recur; missed once, there will be other opportunities.

Use the System's Interconnectedness

In an interconnected system, any step a leader takes moves the whole system. One can plant seeds trusting there will be delayed and indirect effects. One can practice humane processes, trusting those processes will contribute to the system's health. One can strengthen the relationship with any member of the congregation, which would strengthen all relationships in an "act locally, think globally" effect. One can intervene with the whole system, such as in a sermon, trusting this intervention will ripple through the system in a "act globally, think locally" effect. The homeostasis of the system would induce the minister to change back, but if the minister resists the system's homeostatic pressure, and stays in that new place, the system will eventually gravitate around the minister and have changed.

Empower the Healthy

Another way to influence an anxious congregation is to empower the less anxious. Unfortunately, the more anxious elicit attention. They are so vocal about problems in the congregation, they appear motivated to address them, and so sometimes they are given power. Such empowerment would be like giving the booing critic in the bleachers the job of quarterback, where they do more damage than back in the bleachers. In addition, ministers can strain to cure the anxious, seeking to shift the congregation's bell curve by lifting the anxious end of it.

Instead of supporting change by working on the lower-functioning end of the system's bell curve, I suggest cultivating the higher functioning. These are people who are positive, calm, thoughtful, and gracious; who don't raise a big fuss or thunder with indignation; and who listen well and can be heard easily. They may be quietly attending and paying their pledges, saying little about the church because they are generally pleased.

Empowering the higher functioning helps them become visible, where they can model healthy behavior, making high functioning normative. When healthy people hold leadership, other healthy people want to join them in leadership, making them a healthy crew that can absorb a few loose cannons on deck. Healthy leaders generally move the system's bell curve toward moderation and thought.

Led by moderate people, the moderated system benefits everyone. The high functioning enjoy offering their gifts. The less functional look around, see high functioning as normal, and improve their functioning.

Furthermore, the congregation is like a family. It can attend to the misbehaving child and neglect the well-adjusted. The well-adjusted need attention, too. Neglected, they may feel unrewarded and leave.

I like to spread my ministerial energy homogenously across the congregation, but I know that energy spent to empower the people who are healthy and motivated is like spreading seeds on good earth; they sprout and grow, doing more for the church's health and indirectly for those who are less healthy, than shoring up the less healthy or installing them in power positions.

Work with Relationship Triangles

Emotional triangles can stop change. A triangle is a three-part system.[11] The points of a triangle can be populated by people, habits, beliefs, jobs, objects, gods, anything. A family composed of husband, wife, and child constitutes one triangle. A congregation is composed of hundreds or thousands of triangles.

At any given moment in a triangle there are two insiders and an outsider. The mother and child in a conversation would be an insider dyad; the dad sitting quietly by, the outsider. The insider position is preferred, unless there is a conflict, when being the outsider is safer.

In a healthy triangle, the insider and outsider positions shift. The mother turns to the father and talks, and the child is outside. The father addresses the child, and the mother is outside. Child and mother speak to each other, setting dad outside again.

In an unhealthy triangle, the insider and outsider positions are frozen. The two insiders become too close and limit each other's freedom, and the frozen-out outsider too distant and powerless. For example, two people holding a secret are too close and not free to disclose their secret to a third party. Someone not privy to the secret is powerless.

Change is stopped by the way people often act in a triangle, which is to "help." For example, a mother (B) and child (C) have a problem, with attendant stress. Discomforted by the stress, they involve, or "triangle in," a third party, the father (A), and send stress there. The "helpful" father can try to relieve the mother-child dyad of its stress, by trying to "solve their problem" for them. As stress goes to dad, there is less stress and discomfort for the mother and child, which lowers the motivation for them to solve their own problem, and the problem persists. Figure 7.1 shows this predicament.

On the other hand, if father A is savvy enough to sense the mother-child dyad pulling him into their issue and their stress, and tolerates their discomfort while staying the outsider, that unrelieved mother-child discomfort motivates them to change their relationship. The father would be a change agent. Figure 7.2 shows this dynamic.

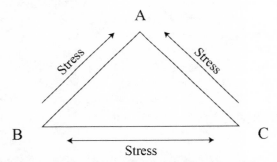

Figure 7.1   Stress given to A, no change in relationship of B and C.

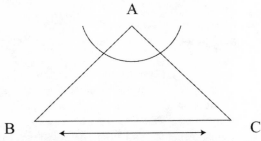

Figure 7.2   Stress between B and C can change the relationship of B and C.

In general, when there is an issue between the B and C corners of a triangle, corner A has no power to change that B and C relationship. For example, a woman married to an alcohol-abusing husband forms the triangle of husband B, alcohol C, and wife A. Wife A can try to intervene and change the dyad of husband and alcohol, throwing away alcohol, begging and pleading, threatening and fighting, and covering for the husband when he is hungover, all of which is stressful. But the relationship of husband and alcohol persists. Spouse A bears the stress of the husband-alcohol relationship but has no power to change it. With stress and no power, it is lose-lose for spouse A. Figure 7.3 shows this situation.

Ideally, A understands the limits of her power. She can be kind and sympathetic to the husband, but she ceases her futile and stressful campaign to change the relationship between husband and alcohol. Hopefully the stress of the relationship between husband and alcohol causes a change in the form of sobriety. If so, the wife has been a change agent.

As another example, congregation B is struggling to raise sufficient pledge money to meet its budget C. The "helpful" minister A tries to manage the relationship between the congregation and its budget. The minister proposes changes to the budget, volunteers to solicit pledges, and offers to accept a cut in pay. This activity is stressful for the minister and does not change the troublesome relationship of the congregation and its budget.

On the other hand, the minister/change agent could empathize with the congregation about its predicament and allow the congregation to relate to its budget in a way that changes the B-C dyad such that budgeting and pledging are balanced. The minister serves as an actually helpful outsider in the triangle of congregation B, budget C, and minister A.

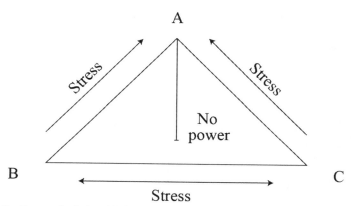

Figure 7.3   Stress of relationship between B and C is delivered to A, but A has no power to change that relationship.

In the triangle between you, another person, and their pain, the more you let the person encounter their pain while staying in relationship with them, the better that person will function. Restated, person B has been restricted by their avoidance of pain C, but if person A can tolerate person B's discomfort, person B can better tolerate their own discomfort, thus becoming less restricted in their functioning.

Such de-triangling requires moderating reactivity to others' discomfort. For example, when my board president accused me of "making this so hard for us!" I did not reply, "Oh, so sorry. You can talk about me behind my back with my blessings." I said nothing. To move the congregation toward greater openness and security, I had to tolerate my board president's discomfort. (Again, I think I would have done better still by responding pastorally to the board president and validating her predicament, while remaining true to my vision of open communication.)

Contemplation

After the pre-contemplation stage follows contemplation. Here people are considering a change, with what looks and sounds like "Maybe." "Do you want to make this change?" "Maybe." As with pre-contemplation, pushing and pleading will not hasten change along.

Weigh the Pros and Cons

At the contemplation stage, people are weighing the pros and cons of the change. The change agent can support this pro-ing and con-ing by making the process more explicit, such as by listing those pros and cons in writing. To make the decision-making process even more explicit and thorough, one can also list the pros and cons of the status quo. Then you would have clarified the pros and cons of change and of not-change, supporting useful thinking about the possible change.

As my worship committee weighed the possibility of including joys and concerns in worship, they voiced the concerns that individuals would talk too long, or raise awkward issues, or that the service could devolve into a little chaos. On the other hand, they acknowledged that the support of the congregation could be valuable and that they wanted to support their friends.

Supporting the process of weighing pros and cons, the change agent remains neutral, although one can interject important considerations. With my committee, I added to the cons regarding joys and concerns, while also planting what to me was a crucial pro: the ministry of the congregation is shared by all of its members, and hearing each other's stories lets them fulfill that ministry. After that, it remained their decision.

Let Them Speak for Change

As people are contemplating whether or not to change, they have an internal conflict, one side in favor, the other, opposed. At this point the change-agent minister can weigh in on pro-change side. Unfortunately, with the pro-change side spoken for, people will speak for the opposed-to-change side. Their internal conflict will have shifted to an external conflict, with the minister on the yes side, the people on the no side. As they speak against change, their resistance increases.[12]

Here the minister pushes for change and evokes the resistance:

Lay leader: Our membership is not growing, and maybe we should do something to help our congregation grow.

Minister: We definitely should grow. I suggest an outreach program into our neighborhood.

Lay leader: Yeah, but we are comfortable with who we are. We are small, but intimate.

Minister: We can reach out to our community, where people would find with us a supportive home.

Lay leader: But we are a quiet church. We don't evangelize.

Minister: Many of us are doing too much work. More hands would lighten our loads.

Lay leader: We are good at what we do. New people wouldn't understand how we operate.

As this minister advocates for change, the minister unintentionally elicits the no-change arguments from the ambivalent lay leaders, who hear the no-change arguments coming from their own lips, dig in their heels, and talk themselves out of change.

Instead of counterproductively advocating for change, the minister can support weighing of the pros and cons to change and elicit from the people their arguments for change. When the people speak for change, they hear the arguments for change coming from themselves, which is more convincing than to hear the advocacy from someone else. For example, the lay leader observes: "Our membership is not growing, and I am not sure, but maybe we should do something to help our congregation grow."

Minister: Yes, our attendance has gone from 100 to 60 on Sundays. How do you feel about that?

Lay leader: I feel mixed about that.

Minister: I see. What are the plusses and what are the minuses involved in this trend?

Lay leader: Well, we are more intimate. We don't really have to change. I am comfortable with how we run things. All mainline churches are declining.

Minister: I see, greater intimacy, no need to change. You're pretty comfortable with how we run things. And we're on par with other mainline churches. Good. Any other plusses? No? Any minuses?

Lay leader: I suppose we can't keep expecting the same people to keep doing all the work. I find it a little disheartening to see the attendance slip.

Minister: Risk of burnout, loss of morale. Any other minuses?

Lay leader: I suppose we could stagnate.

Minister: You mean, not growing and instead doing things as we always have could stagnate us?

Lay leader: I guess.

Minister: Okay. On the minus side: risk of burnout, loss of morale, and stagnation. Am I characterizing these accurately?

Lay leader: Yeah, that's about it.

Minister: Let's look at growth. What are the plusses and minuses?

Lay leader: Growth brings people here we do not know. It will change us. And we're a quiet congregation. We don't evangelize.

Minister: Okay, strangers in our midst, a change in who we are, and a challenge to be other than a quiet, reserved congregation.

Lay leader: Yes.

Minister: What might be the benefits to growth?

Lay leader: New ideas. New help with projects. I had to run the bake sale all by myself last month. I was baking brownies until midnight. We had a new member join last month, and it felt good to see her enjoying the congregation. She said she was really benefiting from our ministry.

(Here the lay leader is advocating for change. The lay leader may not be totally behind the change, but at least he or she is not the voice of no-change.)

Minister: So to sum up: with new people, we would have new ideas, and help with projects. You might not have to bake into the wee hours. And we could share our ministry and support for people.

Lay leader: Hmmm. I guess we do have a problem with our membership declining. What do we do? How about an outreach program into our neighborhood?

Minister: What a great idea.

A similar process involves contrasting people's pain alongside optimal possibilities. Exploring problems with the status quo evokes pain.[13] Exploring the good news to come if the change occurred would evoke hope for what could be. Enough pain contrasted with enough hope tips the system into change.

Modeling

As someone is contemplating change but has not committed to it, they are ripe for observing a model. For example, if one is contemplating being less shy and sees someone else make an announcement in church, one could conclude, "I could do that."

Address Assumptions

One version of contemplation occurs when people profess wanting to change but do not. They earnestly declare their intention: "We want to grow our membership," but that growth mysteriously fails to materialize. The overt pros for change bump up against covert cons against change, and change is thwarted. These covert cons of change consist of assumptions.[14]

To uncover the assumptions blocking change, the leader begins by noting the stated goal: membership growth. Then one lists the actions that get in the way of that goal: "We ignore visitors." "We hide the guest book." "We wear buttons that say: 'Go away!'" After listing the actions that block the goal, there would be rationales for those actions: "We do not know how to attract and retain visitors." "They might be unpleasant people." "Growth and change are difficult." Underneath these rationales would be assumptions. This non-growing church might assume: "There is something unworthy about us, so we hide so as not to expose our flaws." Furthermore, "We do not have the power to do something different or new." These assumptions back the rationales that justify the behaviors that block the stated goal.

It takes self-examination to unearth these assumptions, but with some excavation, the blocking assumptions can be discovered and examined. A group can then consider whether it wants to keep its assumptions or not. If not, they can adopt new assumptions, replacing the "We are not worthy" assumption with "We are okay." It can replace the assumption that it lacks power with "We can and we will."

People then test their new assumptions to see how they work. The people act as if they are worthy, or they take some action. As they live out these experiments and find they go well, the new assumptions become internalized and do not block, but actually support, achievement of the stated goal. Indeed, the congregational system can alter its assumptions just like its minister, as described in Chapter 4, "Working on Yourself."

Two Sides Representing the Contemplation Stage

Sometimes a congregation can be divided regarding change: one side wants a change; the other does not. Some people want to grow the membership; others do not. It can look like you have two stages of change represented: pre-contemplation and preparation.

But viewed through the systems theory lens, this apparently divided church is actually a whole system at the contemplation stage. The whole congregation regards growth with a maybe. One group is speaking for the pros—sharing the church's ministry, gaining dynamism—the other speaks for the cons—strangers in our midst, changes in our culture. To support the contemplating congregation, the minister stays neutral, guides discussions of the pros and cons, and waits for consensus to form.

Preparation

The next stage of change is preparation. This stage looks and sounds like "Yes, I want to make this change, but not yet. I need to prepare."

Develop the Ability to Change

As people are preparing for change, they are working on believing they are able to change. They are doing the "I think I can; I think I can . . ." speech to themselves. Standing for the first time on the high diving board, wanting to take that leap, one is working on believing one is able. Someone already in the pool can calls up, "You can do it!" And so, one step into midair, a moment of terror, then *ker-splash!*

At this stage people welcome insight and advice. The change agent gets to coach and advise people in the skills they need to succeed at the change for which they are preparing. The leader can also review changes the people have made in the past and reinforce the skills that helped them succeed with these previous changes. A caveat: if they ask for advice and then resist it, you have the pre-contemplation or contemplation stages disguised as preparation.

Preparing to make a change, people might also want to know how others have handled that change. When my worship committee was not sure about joys and concerns, they asked me how this ritual went in other churches. When I reported how the practice worked successfully in those churches, the committee could trust that joys and concerns could go well in our church.

When preparing, people craft a plan, which reassures them that they can accomplish the change. The plan can include a goal, objectives, a start date, actions to take, accountability, and reinforcement.

Train the Leaders

New lay leaders preparing for their jobs would be open to learning how to do those jobs. You can offer training. Elementary training could teach leaders how to set an agenda, stick to it, and run a meeting. Advanced training could teach them how to handle conflicts. Furthermore, as discussed earlier, a minister can ask each lay leader how they might want to grow personally in their lay position and how that minister might best support that development.

Articulate Norms

A system preparing for change would welcome guiding norms. A community's norms are powerfully influential. If the norm in an anxious system is to hide, people will hide. If the norm is to wear hats to church, those not wearing a hat will feel awkward and make a mental note to find a hat in the closet for next Sunday.

A minister has a bully pulpit from which to articulate norms. For example, I begin every Sunday by restating the norm: "We are a support community for people on various journeys toward ultimate goals, such as love, or peace, or liberation." In their state of preparatory openness as the service is about to commence, people are influenced by the articulation of this norm. Furthermore, if someone intended to be other than supportive, I want that person to feel awkward and out of place, like a hatless individual where everyone is wearing hats.

The best time to articulate a community norm is when people are preparing to become a community. John Winthrop timed it well by setting the norms "to doe Justly, to love mercy, to walke humbly with our God," on a ship bound for the New World.[15] While you may not be able to set norms at your congregation's founding, you still have beginnings: the beginning of a church year, a new board, or the charging of new volunteers.

Action

The next stage of change is action. This stage looks and sounds like "Yes! And now." People try the new thing.

Positive Reinforcement

Here the change agent offers positive reinforcement, like an enthusiastic coach: "Good job. You did it." This reinforcement helps people reflect on and internalize what worked and then be able to repeat their success.

Such encouragement tells the people they do not have to be perfect. The goalpost of perfection dispirits the group and lowers their motivation and morale. Instead, one appreciates their efforts and their improvement. One says, "You worked hard, and you did something you were not able to do before." Tasting success, they'll want more. Even if their action was not a slam-dunk victory, but a baby step in the hoped-for direction, positive reinforcement supports morale and motivation, setting up another try.

Positive reinforcement can even be used at other stages of change. If someone at the pre-contemplation stage accidentally acts in a new and constructive way, one can catch them in the act and applaud.

Maintenance

The final stage of change is maintenance in which the new behavior keeps happening.

Guidance

At this stage, further reinforcement keeps the momentum going. People might also welcome tips and guidance to refine the new behavior.

Leadership Development

For lay leaders now into and maintaining their roles, a minister can support their development. When the lay leaders are just embarking on their jobs, the minister tells them what to do and how to do it.[16] As they learn the job, the minister shifts to coaching, which involves an emotional component, "You're getting the hang of it!" while still teaching them how: "And next time, try telling the committee what time it is meeting." As the followers gain further skill, they no longer need to be told how to do their jobs but still want you around for emotional support. Then you are participating, as if you were one of the group, or cheerleading, not telling them what to do but offering emotional support. When the followers are very skilled and do not need you around anymore, you can delegate: "Can you handle the flowers for next week's memorial service?" They say, "Yes, we're on it." You say, "Great! Thanks." And off they go.

To support lay leaders' development, you can shift your interaction to match their next stage of development and see if they can handle it. With a skilled committee, you try backing off from coaching to see if they can make decisions with only your cheerleading. You are then unobtrusively supporting the committee's maintenance of change and development.

A group's development may not be linear. If there is a crisis, or if the group is declining in function, it is time for the leader to shift from delegating to telling or coaching. I observed this nonlinear development each program year. In the fall, the committees and board, composed of new members, and rusty over the summer break, had the starting-from-scratch feel. I was telling and coaching. By the end of the program year, the committees seasoned and capable, I could relax, sit back, and delegate.

ADDITIONAL STRATEGIES ON BEHALF OF CHANGE

Get in Front of Development

Human development is powerful, and a change agent does well to discern where that development is going and lead people in that direction. If the congregation is developing greater openness and trust, one can support greater openness and trust. If humanity is developing greater peace and harmony, one can support that peace and harmony. Then one is riding the wave of development, which can take you as change agent, and the system you are changing, far.

The Least Intrusive Intervention First

As noted in Chapter 2, "Diagnosis," to solve a problem, one begins with the least-intrusive intervention. Guided by this logic, your physician treats your cough with advice to try tea or a throat lozenge. If the least-intrusive intervention works, great. If not, ratchet up the intrusiveness. Try an antibiotic. If that fails, take an X-ray. If all else fails: a lung transplant. But your physician would not begin with the lung transplant suggestion.

In a church, as they struggle with a problem, you can begin with a mildly intrusive intervention: "Let's talk about it." If random conversations fail: "Let's bring it to the appropriate committee." If the committee can't solve it: "Let's take it to the board." If the board is flummoxed: "Let's bring in an outside consultant." If nothing works: "Lung transplants all around."

Vet the Proposal

You have a great idea, and propose it at a congregational meeting. They shoot it right down. You might have hoped that the congregation would have run through all the stages of change over the course of one meeting to embrace your new idea. Likely they would not. When you have a big, brainy idea, dropping the proposal like a bomb out of the blue onto the larger congregation would likely result in a dud.

Alternatively, you run the new idea by key players, committees, and stake-holders.[17] You field their input, make changes in the idea, and obtain their buy-in. You give people time to weigh the new idea and to go through the stages of change. When the congregational meeting occurs, people having digested the new idea, you have counted the votes and know it will pass. You propose the idea, and everyone says, "Yes."

Respect the Symptom

Any congregation, or any system, lives with behavioral patterns developed in response to historical situations and carried on into the present. Some of those patterns, some of the time, no longer work and indeed cause problems and symptoms. Nevertheless, the patterns helped people cope in the past and are still serving some function in the present.[18] For example, my church had a symptom: some people wanted to complain about me behind my back. This impulse to complain in secret may have reflected an underlying distrust of male authority figures. Maybe in the past, people were treated poorly by male authority figures. To protect themselves from another such male authority figure, they advocated for being able to talk about me behind my back.

Curiously, they told me they wanted to do this secret complaining. It was as if they were hiding from me and telling me they were hiding from me; like someone playing hide-and-seek and calling out: "Ha, ha! You can't find me." They wanted to continue to hide and be protected from me, while also want-ing to grow so as not to have to hide.

As their minister and change agent, I did well to indicate that the system was safer than they might have guessed, by being open and self-disclosive in the face of hostility and pressure. When I did not hide, other people could emerge from hiding into leadership. I did not do well, though, at respecting the symp-tom's function: to protect people from a potentially threatening authority figure.

Removing a symptom results in the loss of a coping mechanism. Asking people to speak directly to their minister, without their fear of authority fig-ures fully settled, caused a loss for the people who feared such directness. They then left the church, hurt and frustrated. So much for making the system safe for everyone.

The responsible change agent considers the losses resulting from the elimi-nation of a symptom. One asks:

What function does this symptom serve?
How does the congregation stabilize the symptom?
What would be the consequences and who would lose as a result of chang-
    ing this symptom?

Had I considered these questions, when advocating for direct feedback, I could have developed these answers:

The function of the symptom was to protect people.

The congregation stabilized the symptom by empowering protective people into leadership.

As a consequence of eliminating this symptom, the most vulnerable people would have no means of protection, would feel unsafe and disregarded, and leave.

In retrospect, I wish I had respected the protective function of the secret complaining symptom. As noted earlier, I could even have validated the symptom to my board president as an understandable protection from a male authority figure. My friendly validation of the impulse to protect people against male authorities would have called into question the assumption that male authorities are to be feared. My board president might then have seen me as less a threat and more an ally. We could have allied with each other to support safety in the system and could have brainstormed how to do that, together supporting the openness I envisioned.

CONCLUSION

People go through stages on their way to change. The minister, influenced by the congregation, adapts one's change interventions to fit the people's stage of change. That adaptive change agent then both respects the congregation and is effective in leading it into change.

QUESTIONS FOR REFLECTION

The last time you tried to change someone else into thinking or behaving in a new way, what did you do? How were your interventions received? Did the person change?

Considering the last time someone else tried to change your thinking and/or behavior, what did that person do? How did their interventions feel to you? Did you change?

The next time you are participating in a meeting, observe the stages of change being expressed at that meeting.

NOTES

1. Niccolò Machiavelli, *The Prince* (New York: HarperCollins, 1532/2012).
2. Gregory Bateson, *Steps toward an Ecology of Mind* (New York: Dutton, 1972).
3. Ronald Heifitz, Marty Linsky, and Alexander Grashow, *The Practice of Adaptive Leadership: Tools and Tactics for Changing Your Organization and the World* (Cambridge, MA: Harvard Business Press, 2009).
4. John Norcross, "The Therapeutic Relationship" in *The Heart and Soul of Change*, 2nd edition, ed. Barry Duncan, Scott Miller, Bruce Wampold, and Mark Hubble (Washington, DC: American Psychological Association 2010), 113–141.
5. J. O. Prochaska and W. F. Velicer, "The Transtheoretical Model of Health Behavior Change." *American Journal of Health Promotion* 12, no. 1 (1997): 38–48.
6. Carl Rogers, *On Becoming a Person: A Therapist's View of Psychotherapy* (New York: Houghton Mifflin, 1961/1987).
7. Edwin Friedman, "Bowen Family Systems Theory Seminar for Clergy" (lecture, Offices of Edwin Friedman, Bethesda, MD, October 1990).
8. Ian Frazier, "On the Rez." *Atlantic Monthly* 284, no. 6 (December 1999).
9. Andrea Ayvizian [free-standing quotation], *The Sun*, no. 227 (November 1994).
10. Mfonobong Nsehe, *The Adolf Hitler Book* (CreateSpace Independent Publishing Platform, 2008).
11. Philip J. Guerin Jr., Leo F. Fay, Thomas F. Fogarty, and Judith G. Kautto, *Working with Relationship Triangles: The One-Two-Three of Psychotherapy* (New York: Guilford Press, 1996).
12. William Miller and Stephen Rollnick, *Motivational Interviewing* (New York: Guilford, 2002).
13. Ibid.
14. Robert Kegan and Lisa Laskow Lahey, *Immunity to Change* (Boston: Harvard Business Press, 2009).
15. John Winthrop, "A Modell of Christian Charity," a sermon written in 1630 on board *The Arbella* on the Atlantic Ocean (Boston: Collections of the Massachusetts Historical Society, 1838).
16. Paul Hersey and Ken Blanchard, *Management of Organizational Behavior 3rd Edition—Utilizing Human Resources* (Upper Saddle River, NJ: Prentice Hall, 1977).
17. Lyle Schaller, *The Change Agent* (Nashville: Abingdon, 1972).
18. Peggy Papp, *The Process of Change* (New York: Guilford Press, 1983).

8

Conflict

A conflict occurs when people are troubled by their differences with each other. We are not clones; our differences make conflicts likely. People disagree about some issue. They want different outcomes. Conflict ensues.

Common sense advises approaching a conflict as a quest to erase differences, or as a me vs. you, or us vs. them, competition with the goal of dominating and silencing one's opponent. Uncommon sense tells me that human differences make relationships interesting and are not so troublesome. I remember that my conflicting partner and I both belong to the same system, be it a family, congregation, nation, or world. Guided by systems theory, I choose not to let our conflict break the wholeness of the system. Furthermore, because I share the same system as my partner, what affects them affects me. Therefore, it is in my interest to consider how to meet their needs, as well as mine, and otherwise ease our mutual pain by mending our conflict. I propose ministers apply this uncommon sense to view conflict as a pastoral opportunity to appreciate differences between people, to support the system's wholeness, and to meet people's needs. (Not just ministers, this is a good idea for everyone.)

EMOTIONS DURING CONFLICT

Who out there enjoys conflict? I don't see many hands. This is not surprising. A conflict is painful. War is hell. Emotions get dramatic, if not operatic.

During a conflict, I want something that I am not receiving from my opponent in conflict, which triggers anger. Anger occurs when facing something one does not like. We have a disagreement, my needs are not met, someone is unhappy with me—much to dislike.

I cannot control my opponent, and cannot successfully demand compliance, so I also experience futility. I try harder to get what I want. Taking to
the warpath, my anger escalates. Consumed by a righteous wrath and manic
fever, I can't sleep, plotting how to win and force my opponent to slink away
defeated—as they deserve! Nevertheless, my partner in conflict does not simply surrender, rendering all my passionate plotting futile.

In our conflict, the other wants me to stop my application of pressure and
pain, pressuring me to change. We both feel anger, futility, and pain.

Conflicts expose human differences. Our differences are threatening
because, in the hierarchical, survival-of-the-fittest world, resources, such as
love, attention, money, time, power, professional advancement, or turf, go to
the most fit. If someone else is different from me, that person might be fitter
than me, which would demote me on the hierarchy and threaten my access to
needed resources, triggering fear.

Furthermore, a competition to claim superiority threatens to expose all
the ways I am not superior: my flaws. I have flaws, oh so many, but having
them exposed is painful, that painful emotion being shame. Unfortunately,
flaws accompany human imperfection. I can strive to be perfect and blameless, but that requires enormous, killing labor and still is doomed to failure.
Since I cannot act to un-flaw myself, I feel helpless. Helpless, ashamed, and
doomed to lose needed resources, I can feel despair and contemplate not
existing, or I could withdraw from relationships that expose my flaws and go
live under a rock. But people like to live, belong, and be free, so people hide
flaws and avoid shame by seeking to win conflicts. Although I think no one
has actually died of shame, I think plenty of people have escalated conflicts;
killed to say: "Those nasty people are flawed, not me"; or died in the process
of killing, all to win conflicts, to appear without flaw, and to gain a superior
position in the survival-of-the-fittest hierarchy.

During a conflict, people also feel guilt, the emotion that follows breaking
a rule. I might have rules in my head, such as "I should not make mistakes"
or "I should not be a party to problems." Someone unhappy with me could
imply that I broke one of these rules. Being guilty, I am not free. Indeed, guilt
means they slap on the handcuffs and trundle me off to jail.

STYLES OF CONFLICT

People exhibit five styles of conflict, most of us defaulting to one or two.[1]

Competition or dominance: One works to win and make someone else lose.
Accommodation or appeasement: One accepts defeat. Oh well …

Avoidance: One views conflict as perilous and avoids it.

Compromise: One seeks to split a quantifiable difference.

Collaboration: One seeks to meet the difficult-to-quantify needs of both parties. If someone needs warmth and affection, and the other needs space and autonomy, they negotiate how to have both.

Sometimes people's conflict styles are complementary (spelling). The dominator and the appeaser do the dance of winner and loser. At other times, styles might clash, such as when two parties seek to dominate. Or if one party is trying to dominate and win, while the other is trying to collaborate, they would face a problem reconciling their differing processes.

These conflict styles relate to the four ways people handle differences, as shown in Figure 8.1.

1. A claims superiority. B gives in

2. A and B compete to win

3. A and B stop talking about their differences, or stop talking at all

4. A and B recognize they differ, but keep talking

Figure 8.1 Four ways of handling differences.

Someone can claim to be right, and the other gives in. Two parties can compete to win. Two parties can avoid discussing their differences. Two parties can speak of their differences with the goal of mutual understanding.

CONTENTS OF CONFLICT, OR WHAT WE ARE FIGHTING ABOUT

At the surface, there are a bazillion issues people fight about. Under the surface there are a few.

Symbols

People often fight over symbols. Such conflicts become intense because symbols, when handled correctly, bring ultimate rewards: salvation, union, and peace. Used incorrectly, they are useless. Therefore, they have to be handled just right, and everyone is an expert about the right way to handle a symbol. Symbols further intensify conflicts because people can't compromise about a symbol or cut a symbol in half. When people whip up a frenzy over seemingly trivial matters—whether to plant daffodils or tulips in the church yard—the flowers symbolize something.

Sometimes new ministers imagine their church will be a placid, harmonious community of loving people and are shocked when blistering conflicts erupt. But what do churches deal in? Symbols.

Power, Control, Turf

Power struggles address who controls what turf. Turf can include a physical space, money, time, another person, or oneself. If someone hauls off and hits me, that person is invading the turf that is me. If you change some aspect of the church, and an irritated parishioner tells you, "You should have checked with me first," you have invaded their turf.

Proximity

People jockey for closeness or distance. Someone might push: "Back off!" Someone else might explode: "Get closer!" the wish in seeming contradiction with the angry tone.

Expectations

People fight about expectations. "I expected X. I got Y. I'm not happy."

Worth

In a conflict someone might assert and defend one's worth, while diminishing their opponent's worth.

To Test Trust

During a conflict, people might test whether they can trust each other. For example, if you follow a pastor who was critical of the congregation, at some point the congregation unconsciously might raise an issue in which they will be testing whether you will slip into criticism. They might start a conflict, or criticize you, or in other ways evoke criticism. If you do not criticize, you will have passed the test and earned their trust.

Identity

Not everyone will agree about every aspect of the congregation's identity. Some might want it to be more evangelical, others more activist. When my two lay leaders told me not to attend committee meetings, they asserted a family congregation perspective in which only they, as long-tenured members, had the authority to make decisions. I, in conflict with them, held a community congregation perspective and saw my ministerial presence as a useful guide for the committees' decision-making process.[2]

One Key Underlying Issue

At root, conflict is a competition, the goal of which is to win, be up in the survival-of-the-fittest hierarchy, and then, for the moment, secure. Figure 8.2 depicts these contents of conflict.

CONFLICTS CAN ESCALATE

When people face a problem, they can solve the problem or escalate tensions. When they escalate, people assume it is a win-lose world, that to win is essential, and so "cry 'Havoc!' and let slip the dogs of war."[3]

A conflict can escalate as follows:

1. A problem to solve
2. A disagreement
3. A point of tension
4. An argument
5. A battle
6. A war
7. A cutoff, and we're never talking to each other ever again!

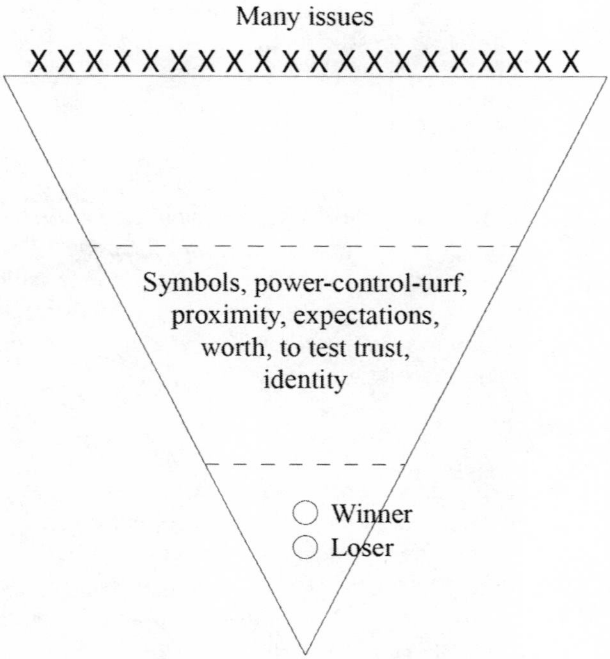

Many issues

X X X X X X X X X X X X X X X X X X X X X X X X

Symbols, power-control-turf,
proximity, expectations,
worth, to test trust,
identity

○ Winner
○ Loser

Figure 8.2   What people fight about.

STAGES OF CONFLICT

Some conflicts go on for hours, years, or centuries, marked by furious walks into the night, alcohol, and talk radio. But a rift does not have to persist forever. Ideally, a conflict runs a course through four stages from harmony, to rift, to return to harmony.

Stage One: The Honeymoon

At the honeymoon stage, there is no conflict. It is lovely and pleasant, and people enjoy the harmony. They can drag out the honeymoon, though, with a "peace at any price" attitude, and avoid reckoning with their differences. That "price" can be depression, boredom, anxiety, and physical illness.

Stage Two: Pressure

The honeymoon eventually breaks down. Differences surface and cause discomfort, moving matters to the second stage at which one participant pressures the other to change. The message is "I'm uncomfortable; you change."

Or "I am in pain; you fix it." Or "You are wrong. Here are the facts." The one receiving this message responds in kind: "Now I'm in pain; you change."

As the conflict escalates, people play the game of the-one-who-applies-the-most-pressure-wins. I do not want to work out our differences in a way both of us can be content. I want my opponent to agree with me, or hide their differences with me, or cease to exist. I apply the devastating argument, the furious retort, the raised voice, the put-down, escalating to lawsuits, violence, war, and political campaigns, all stage two moves, all saying: "I am superior and refuse to change; I will make you, who are inferior, do the changing." At stage two, people use aggression and defensive, as if they are hiding behind castle walls lobbing bombs at their opponents, who hide behind their walls lobbing bombs back. Here are stage two processes in detail:

Seek to Win

In a conflict, ruthlessness drives each party to win, no matter what.

Pressure

One can attempt to make someone else change by applying pressure on that person. One is then being guided by mechanistic theory in which person A pressures person B to change.

Pressure can take various forms, including:

> "Do like I say."
> "Adopt my opinion."
> "Have this thought."
> "Change in this way."
> "You are wrong. I am right."

Pressure has a wide spectrum. At one end: my wife's suggestion on a cloudy day to take my raincoat. At the other end: war. My wife cares for me; at war, no such caring. But across the spectrum, pressure is applied to cause others to do something they would not do, such as bring a raincoat, or be someone they do not want to be, such as dead.

Pressure can be overt: "You must do X, now!" It can be covert. When you feel pushed to do something you do not want to do, and feel unable to be freely yourself, your congregation might be applying pressure on you. As a diagnostic instrument, when you feel pressured, you can surmise that others do too in your pressure-filled system.

Even ministers have been known to apply pressure. Historically, ministers threatened eternal punishment on their flocks to gain their obedience. These days I hear pressure in the form of sermons that say: "Here is the right thing to do, so do it." Friedman adds an almost poetic list of ways a minister might apply pressure. One can "push, pull, tug, kick, shove, threaten, convince, arm-twist, charm, entice, cajole, seduce, induce guilt, shout louder, or be more eloquent."[4]

Pressure crowds people making it difficult for them to be themselves. Despite this problem, pressure is common, and not even noticed, like gravity. Under pressure, people have three unhappy options: exit, accommodate, or pressure back.

As an exit, one can leave the relationship. The problem: one is then alone. Furthermore, exiting prevents one from learning how to deal with pressure, and when pressure recurs, one exits again, setting up a life of escaping. If people leave the congregation, bothered that they cannot be themselves, they could be experiencing pressure in the system. By the same token, if you want to leave, you could be detecting pressure.

One can give in to the pressure. One finds a brief relief, but accommodation rewards pressure—it will be back. The other problem with accommodation is that as one contorts oneself to please, one loses one's identity. Enough such contortions, and one becomes unhealthy. If you sense yourself forgoing your values, beliefs, and principles, or becoming depressed or anxious, you could be accommodating to pressure.

Third, one can pressure the pressurer. "You pressure me. I pressure you." The mutual applications of pressure escalate conflict. The higher the tensions escalate, the more threat in the air, the more reactive the system, the less effective our thinking, not to mention the wider the rift between us. As you conceive of ways to pressure others in your system to change, you could realize you've got a real pressure cooker goin' on here.

Speak in a Way That Is Difficult to Hear

When I am trying to win a conflict, I use argument, criticism, name-calling, profanity, screams, all difficult to hear.

Drown Them Out

More words wins. I interrupt and keep others from speaking by flooding my opponent in a tsunami of verbiage.

Claim Superiority

To justify triumph, I claim superiority: "I am good. You are evil." "I have the truth. You are wrong." "My motives and actions are virtuous. Yours are destructive." One can escalate into the *Wizard of Oz* head, flaming with virtue and heaping scorn on Dorothy and her friends, all to protect the little man behind the curtain.

Blame

I escalate, while avoiding any responsibility for a problem, by blaming: "It's all your fault."

Complain

I deliver pain in the form of guilt and shame by complaining: "You did X (a bad thing)." "You didn't do Y (a good thing)."

Draw a Line

I place myself on the good, true, and virtuous side of some line, my opponent on the evil, false, and bizarre side. On the bad side of the line, all manner of ills can befall my opponent, but they are bad, so who cares?

Lie

To quote Aeschylus, "In war, truth is the first casualty."[5] So, to win a conflict one hides the truth, spins the facts to one's benefit, or lies outright.

Stake a Position and Refuse to Budge

I insist on one and only one idea for how to handle a problem and dismiss all other proposals before they have even been offered.

State Belief as Fact

"You are doing this to hurt me" is a belief expressed as a fact. Not only would the content be difficult to hear, but the declaration of the belief as fact makes it difficult to express alternative views.

Retrospectively Assign Guilt

When someone confronts a problem, they often wonder why that problem occurred. They ask the likely culprit: "Why did you do X?" Such a question delivers guilt to the other person, and puts them on the defensive. The other launches into explanations for why they did X. The person who raised the problem has two problems: the initial problem has yet to be solved, and they have to hear the defensive explanation. The accused also has a problem: guilt. The problem has multiplied. The two can then go around the block a few times with accusations and defenses regarding the motivations, good or ill, for doing X. During that drama, the initial problem sits there unsolved.

Hear Inaccurately

Alongside speaking in a way that is difficult to hear, I can hear inaccurately. I distort what I am hearing to find some advantage. I listen not to learn but to find an error I can exploit. I twist words and meanings to cast my opponent in a bad light, filter their words to my advantage, and look for "gotcha" opportunities.

Take Distracting Tangents

Another version of listening inaccurately involves picking up one sub-point my opponent is making and getting into a tangle about that. For example, someone at a finance meeting states: "If we do not have a clear budgetary process for handling small items, we will have problems with big items, like a new roof someday." Instead of working on solving the budgetary process, I fly into the roof: "We can't have another slate roof. We have to have shingles." Then people begin wrangling about the roof.

I do not even have to follow some sub-point someone else made but can grab any non sequitur distracting issue from the ether: "How 'bout those Red Sox?"

Assume Motives

I guess the other's motives based on my fears. I fear X. I leap to assume my opponent wants X, and so I defend against X by attacking my opponent.

Seek Revenge

Another way to win is to feel hurt in a conflict and use victimhood to legitimize retaliation. In one breath, the hurt party utters a cry of anguish, and in the next shouts for revenge. Because the other supposedly hit first, they are morally inferior, which justifies an attack against them. When such reprisals are carried out, the other, now hurt, seeks their revenge, and the conflict escalates.

Make an Attributional Error

A system's interrelatedness means that if I share a problem with someone else, my actions have contributed to that problem. But to win a conflict, I deny any culpability and defend my innocence by claiming my actions were caused by the situation, or by my opponent, for which I am not responsible. I further claim that my opponent is guilty because they freely chose to do the bad thing they did due to flaws in their character. "I had to do X, but they *chose* to do Y."

Sulk, Shun

I can passively escalate and prolong a conflict by retreating in a sulk, or by shunning my opponent, delivering them guilt and shame, albeit quietly and with an air of pained innocence.

Stage Three: Vulnerability

People can assume conflict consists only of stage two and stay there for a long time, sometimes centuries. But ideally stage two becomes tiring. Stage two is hell. Neither side is winning, and matters do not improve despite vigorous applications of pressure. Participants who care about each other, spouses for instance, can feel agony. They might remember Jesus's admonition: "You have heard that it was said, you shall love your neighbor and hate your enemy. But I say to you, love your enemies, and pray for those who persecute you" (Matthew 5:43–44, ESV). So, after attempts to pressure the other have failed, and recalling the value of love, people do something they fear: become open and vulnerable and move to stage three.

If stage two involves two parties within their castles lobbing bombs at each other, stage three involves coming out from behind the stone walls, open and vulnerable. I take a risk to be myself and be close to someone else, which requires letting myself be known, vulnerable, and exposed. Such vulnerability is difficult enough during harmony, but perilous during a conflict. Nevertheless, if one participant ventures into stage three, that makes it safe for the other to join them there. The participants can feel uncomfortable with vulnerability but relieved to end the back-and-forth attacks.

There are many stage three processes.

Wish to Mend the Conflict

The misery of conflict makes peace attractive.

Offer Humility

Superiority offers personal aggrandizement and protection against the exposure of one's flaws, but stokes the flames of conflict. To bring peace, one acknowledges one's flaws and mistakes.

Define Oneself

Rather than castigate the other, one speaks openly about oneself.

Disclose

Honesty signals one's shift from dishonesty on behalf of victory, to transparency on behalf of peace.

Express a Vision

Consistent with defining oneself and disclosure would be the clear expression of what one wants and why. Such an expression is not intended to persuade but reveal. For example, "I envision open communication in this congregation because I believe it would allow us all to be honest and feel safe with each other."

Validate One's Opponent

In a conflict, it seems normal to criticize one's evil opponent. To resolve the conflict, despite not liking what one's opponent is doing, one can understand that opponent. To validate during a conflict means saying: "I hate what you are doing, but still I will understand it."

Distinguish Fact from Belief

It is easier to hear a belief expressed not with the definitiveness of a fact, but with the subjectivity of a belief.

Consider the Future

When faced with a problem, instead of the retrospective allocation of guilt, one can consider how to respond. Instead of "Why did you do this?" one goes right into "How do we solve this?" This consideration of the future generates optimistic, constructive thinking.[6]

Share a Goal

When feuding parties are presented with a shared enemy or a common problem, they often become allies.

When Facing Pressure, Use Curiosity and Self-Definition

As noted above, under pressure, people can exit the relationship, accommodate, or pressure back, all of which comply with and feed pressure. Two other options, curiosity and self-definition, require some nerve but do not comply with pressure.

In the face of pressure, one gathers more information about that which one is being pushed to do. "You want me to do X. What would that do for you?"

In the face of pressure, one can also respond with who one is. One can report how one is being affected by the pressure. One can state one's principles, policies, values, beliefs, emotions, thoughts, opinions, what one will and will not do, what one likes and does not like, what one wants, or whom one loves, all of which indicate: "You can pressure me all you want, but I will still be myself."

Comment on the Process

In a conflict, people can become stuck on a point of content and go round and round about what was said. But shifting the conversation from contents to process can free it up. For example, a process observation during an argument could be: "It seems we are not hearing each other" or "It seems like we are in a power struggle." Addressing the process can move people out of a locking-of-antlers stuckness into a more productive conversation, such as about how to improve the process.

Apologize and Forgive

To end the cycle of attack, pain, retaliation, and more pain, the conflicting parties can apologize and forgive each other.

There are two kinds of apologies. One involves the admission that one did something egregiously harmful. "I apologize for lobbing bombs at you." The second apology acknowledges that someone was not happy with something one did, even though that act was done with good intentions and would not be generally seen as harmful. You might preach a sermon that brought enlightenment to multitudes, its words to be carved in stone when they erect a temple in your honor, but which one person found offensive. Then an apology would be in order: "I am sorry my sermon offended you."

As a complementary act, people forgive. As previously discussed, forgiveness involves giving an offender the gift of good will because that spares the forgiver further pain. Although apologies make forgiveness easier, one can forgive without the apology. One can absorb hurt without retaliation, which stops the cycle of hurt and revenge.

See the Conflict as a Mutual Predicament

Common sense views a conflict as resolving with one happy winner and one unhappy loser. But belonging to a marriage, a family, a congregation, a country, or a world binds people into a network of mutuality in which "we are in this together," what affects one affects all. Therefore, if one loses, all lose. With that realization, the parties in a conflict see each other's problems as shared predicaments. They are pained by the other's suffering.

Set Behavioral Standards

Destructive misbehavior can be prevented by jointly agreed-upon standards in the form of laws, contracts, policies, marriage vows, bylaws, or covenants. Those standards support cooperative behavior and prevent conflicts from escalating.

If needed, people can create a covenant addressing conflict, using a form like this:

> During a conflict, it is okay for us to ...
> During a conflict, it is not okay for us to ...

People find the process of creating their own standards empowering. Having crafted their own standards, people care about them and uphold them. On the other hand, if the minister were to dictate what was "appropriate" or "not appropriate," those dictated standards could be rejected or evaded. Furthermore, a standard applies equally and impartially to everyone, and so if such a standard had to be enforced, that enforcement would be seen as unbiased and therefore accepted.

Solve the Problem

When faced with a problem, instead of escalating, people can move through the five steps of the problem-solving process.

Step one: Name the problem. Here people define the problem to be solved. The better the understanding of the problem, the more accurate the diagnosis, the more effective the cure.

Defining the problem works well when people name it in a way both sides of the issue agree. People sometimes try to name the problem by labeling their partner in conflict as the problem. They begin with "You ..." followed by a criticism. The one being criticized does not agree with this naming of the problem, defends oneself, attacks the other, and the solution to the problem recedes into the distance.

Instead of "You ...", the word "We ..." sets up a naming to which both could agree, as in: "We disagree about X." Furthermore, when the parties define the problem as a mutual predicament, they could become allies against the problem, rather than opponents of each other.

Naming a problem can be difficult. When people believe they should not have problems in the first place, it's embarrassing. When people can't immediately imagine solutions, it is confusing. To avoid embarrassment and confusion, people can skip away from naming, into the easier talk of solutions. Rushing anxiously away from such discomfort would (a) maintain the system's anxiety and (b) result in less-than-helpful solutions. For example, the church that is not growing can brainstorm how to grow, before exploring what keeps them from growing. Without digging somewhere near the root of the problem, hacking at its branches would prove ineffective. To help, the moderately reactive minister, tolerating the anxiety that comes with exploring and defining a problem, could guide a thorough naming of the problem while simultaneously demonstrating moderated reactivity.

Step two: Brainstorm. When brainstorming, people list solutions to their problem, seeking what they all could feel good about.

The key to brainstorming: If you do not like one idea, rather than critique it, offer an amendment or propose another idea. Critiquing makes proposing further ideas risky. Indeed, if a person's lovely dove of an idea is scorned and blasted out of the sky, one would be less likely to take the risk of watching the obliteration of another precious idea. Furthermore, criticism causes people to feel threatened. They then swing to the reflex end of the thought-reflex continuum and fight by blasting anyone else's ideas or take flight by ceasing to propose new ideas.

As an example, I practiced brainstorming while conducting family therapy with two brothers who arrived each week reporting on their latest brawl. After we had all agreed on the problem of fighting, I'd ask what they thought would help. Little Joey might propose: "Send Billy to the moon." I'd write it down as a valid proposal and then ask for other ideas. Billy followed with, "Send Joey to Mars." Okay, second idea noted. I did not argue that there was no launch vehicle in their backyard pointed skyward and venting steam. I just asked for more ideas. Then the kids came up with actually useful proposals, such as "We take a break from playing together when a fight is about to begin."

Step three: Everyone votes for the ideas they like. Those ideas that lack support are discarded. In this family therapy, after brainstorming, I asked: "How many for: send Billy to the moon? I see one hand raised. How many for: send Joey to Mars? I see one hand. How many for: take a break from playing when a fight is about to begin? I see two votes. That's is a winning idea. Let's try it." The space-shot ideas fade away as the actually useful idea gains assent.

Step four: Implement. People enact the proposals they like.

Step five: Evaluate. If the brainstormed ideas solve the problem, declare victory. If trouble persists, the problem may not have been named accurately in the first place or more brainstormed ideas may be needed.

Take Responsibility for One's Problem

Instead of blame, one acknowledges one's role in one's predicament. Instead of complaint, one acknowledges one's contribution to that about which one is unhappy. This task requires self-discipline and self-awareness. For example, "I may contribute to your difficulty with giving me direct feedback. I'd like to change to make direct dialogue easier."

Use Anger to Solve the Problem

As noted above, anger occurs when facing something one does not like. Despite anger being an empowering response to a problem, people can experience difficulty with anger. Anger can be seen as hurtful or wrong, a view developed during childhood. If a child is punished for expressing anger, that teaches the child that one's parents cannot handle one's anger, and furthermore teaches the child to associate anger with pain. To protect the parent from one's anger and to protect oneself from further punishment, the child internalizes the message that anger is bad and holds their anger inside. As an adult, one can still view anger as a taboo emotion. Without anger though, one has to like everything or be a doormat. Furthermore, when repressed, anger emerges anyway as cynicism, depression, or anxiety.

At the other extreme, someone can be freely and chronically angry. Chronic anger maintains high arousal as one lives on the reflex side of the thought-reflex continuum. High arousal releases stress hormones, which, when chronically in one's body, can cause heart disease or other illness. Interpersonally, chronic anger can intimidate and thereby manipulate others or simply drive people away.

Anger can be expressed as hostility, which defeats anger's effectiveness in solving problems. Hostility says, "I am suffering, and now you will, too, as you deserve." Hostility sets up a moral hierarchy, one-upping oneself and one-downing the other. If I am up and superior and my opponent is down, shameful, and inferior, that opponent can suffer, and who cares?

Hostility also exempts one from self-reflection, self-awareness, and personal responsibility.

Furthermore, hostility can push someone else's buttons, triggering their reactivity. They might retaliate with their own hostility. The hostility-retaliation process persists and escalates. In the end, hostility is mutually hurtful, destructive to a relationship, and leaves problem-solving long forgotten.

In contrast, healthy anger has a place in one's emotional spectrum because it energizes and empowers one to solve a problem. Ideally, one defines oneself with genuine, passionate feeling, and some vulnerability: "I don't like this chair." One makes an authentic contact with someone else without put-down or manipulation.

Problem-solving anger requires self-management and personal responsibility. When solving a problem, one is focused on the problem and not veering off into tangents. One treats one's "opponent" as one's respected equal and partner in solving the problem. So managed, problem-solving anger is safe, allowing the two sides to think clearly as they collaborate to solve the problem.

If in a conflict, you are being put down, you can apply anger to that as well, but not with a revolution that elevates you and puts the other down, instead with insistence on equality.

When using anger to invite someone into collaborative problem-solving one can do the following:

Prepare the other. Warn. Reassure. "I care about you, and I want to bring up a problem."

Define the problem in question. "I do not like this new office chair."

Describe your feelings. "When I sit in it, I am uncomfortable."

Define one's share of responsibility for the problem, as noted above. One might have only a small share of responsibility, but one does have some somewhere: "I realize I asked for this kind of chair, which you found and gave me in good faith, and so I am somewhat responsible for my problem with it."

State what you want. "Nevertheless, I would like us to find a new chair."

State the bottom line: what you will do if the problem does or does not change. The person with anger might want their partner to join in solving the problem in question, but if the other refuses, the person has a fall-back action which they can take. "If we find a more comfortable chair, I will accomplish more work and be happier. If we do not find a new chair together, I will find one by myself."

Negotiate

To resolve conflicts, people negotiate. They seek an agreement both sides can feel good about. Fisher and Ury add that a successful negotiation arrives at a wise agreement that is developed efficiently and results in a strengthened relationship.[7]

A negotiation begins with a conflict. Let's say you have not had a raise or cost-of-living increase in ten years. You propose a 15 percent raise to the finance committee, which offers a 5 percent raise. You have a conflict.

When participants debate their positions, a negotiation can reach an impasse. You argue for 15 percent, and the committee argues for 5 percent. You lock horns and go nowhere. To unlock this impasse, negotiators look beneath their positions to the needs or interests of both parties.[8] You need to break even financially and support your family. The finance committee needs to be prudent with church monies. Needs appear more valid than positions. The finance committee can understand your financial needs, and you can appreciate the committee's need for prudence.

As individuals negotiate, they often represent the constituency they want to please. Your constituency is your family; the finance committee's is the congregation. Negotiators ask: What can we offer our constituents that they would appreciate? Would your family like to be able to afford a vacation? Might the congregation like a balanced budget?

To keep negotiations on track, it helps to avoid taking the differences personally.[9] Negotiators separate people from the problem, realizing that one's partner in negotiation is not some evil menace. They merely represent differing interests that understandably need to be considered.

It is difficult not to take matters personally if the other party is making wild claims such as: "You just want to destroy the church!" A helpful response to this type of claim would be to accept it as venting steam rather than viewing it as an authoritative statement that requires a rebuttal. Passions run high under the pressured circumstances of conflict. Given space and time, tensions will likely ease. If you offer face-saving gestures and de-escalating moves, everyone can return to negotiating.

Ideally, negotiators avoid another pitfall: deducing the other's intentions based on one's fears.[10] You might fear that the finance committee does not care about your personal finances. If this fear is expressed as an accusation, the conversation will likely devolve around claims of malicious intentions and exclaimed defenses. To keep the conversation on track, keep this fear to yourself and work toward a mutually agreeable outcome.

When negotiators differ about facts or perceptions, they turn to objective measures.[11] You and the finance committee could have differing perceptions regarding inflation. You offer an objective measure: Bureau of Labor Statistics cost-of-living increases. The finance committee agrees. You find that across the United States, the cost of living has indeed grown by 15 percent over the past ten years. Other standards could include: expert opinion, law, precedent, tape measures, or any mutually agreed-upon standard independent of either side's will.

It helps to set up humane physical arrangements for the negotiation. You could face the ten big guns of the finance committee looking like Ebenezer Scrooges sitting on thrones on one side of a table, while you are given a kid's chair from the kindergarten classroom. It is time to propose a more equal seating arrangement.

It helps when both sides actually negotiate. If the other side refuses to negotiate, it is a power-grabbing ploy. You can respond with a comment on the process: "Refusing to negotiate will not help us arrive at a solution. How about if we with begin me discussing this over lunch with the finance committee chair?"

If they try pressure: "You have to agree to these terms, or else," you can call for principles: "What is the principle behind this proposal?" In addition, you can name a principle: "I suggest we be guided by the principle of fairness." If they make personal attacks: "You are just being greedy," you can affirm that you are being guided by the principle of fairness. If they offer threats, such as of a congregation-wide fight or a move to fire you, you can offer the principle of seeking a win-win solution. If they escalate, you can respond as though they are using reasoning even when they are not.[12] You can ask for reasoning with statements such as: "I am having trouble following your reasoning." The ball is in their court to demonstrate actual reasoning.

In any negotiation, you are stronger when you have a fallback if the negotiation breaks down.[13] If you do not receive the requested raise, you have Plan B in your back pocket. Your Plan B might include reduced responsibilities in light of low compensation, other forms of compensation, or a second part-time job. You might even be open to leaving the First Church of Scrooge for greener pastures.

Ideally though, you and the finance committee arrive at a compromise all can appreciate, such as a 10 percent raise this year, and another 10 percent increase the following year. Your income increases, and the church spreads its expense over two years. Everyone shakes hands and smiles.

Hold Listening Circles

When the congregation is mired in an impasse, when it has a difficult decision to make, when it is in transition, when it is lost and confused, when its identity is unclear, at such times listening circles provide a forum for a deep, exploratory, system-wide conversation.[14]

Listening circles are guided, structured forums comprised of eight or so members to which the entire congregation is invited. At these forums, participants can air issues in safety and therefore with openness and thought. When people may well be discussing such issues anyway, although in less structured forums such as in the parking lot, listening circles are useful. A listening circle is not a chance to debate, persuade, or pressure each other, nor a brainstorming and problem-solving session. Nevertheless, as people are given a safe, supportive context in which to express their thoughts and feelings and be heard, that could reveal a way forward.

The governing board initiates listening circles when it acknowledges a problem afoot about which they want guidance in its deliberations. For example, a board wants input from the congregation regarding the question of going to two services.

The listening circle agenda consists of three or four questions formed by the board and minister. Ideally, these questions generate energy and provoke reflection on both the situation at hand, as well as on the larger mission of the congregation.[15]

Effective questions are open-ended, in that they would be answered with a paragraph, rather than closed-ended, which are answered with one word. "What do you like about this church?" would be open-ended. Generally, open-ended questions use words such as "what," "how," and "why," although "why" can seem interrogative.

Effective questions use conditional verbs, so "how can" is replaced by "how could" or "how might." The conditional verb "could" implies more possibilities than the limited "can."

Effective questions pose a large and inclusive scope that invites people to reach beyond themselves and consider ever-larger parameters of possibility. "How can we serve each other?" could be replaced by "How could we serve the world?"

Effective questions are worded with constructive assumptions. "What is wrong with us?" has a limiting assumption. "What are our obstacles as we strive to live out our mission?" might approach the same diagnostic information but assumes people are striving toward a mission.

A church considering going to two services could ask:

1. How might worship best support our spiritual journeys?
2. How might going to two services affect our mission?
3. What is your vision of a congregation that meets your needs and the needs of the world?
4. How could we best serve ourselves as well as the people who would love to join us?

Having prepared the questions, the leadership, lay, and minister, select listening circle facilitators. The forums will seem trustworthy and safe if the facilitators are not partisans in the matter, but are well-respected, moderate people.

The minister trains the facilitators in the purpose and structure of the meetings and their role in them. The facilitators' job is to keep the meeting on track; to support open listening; to listen, clarify, and confirm; to reflect and record what people say without linking people to comments; and to review with the group what was recorded. Training could also cover how to handle personal attacks or someone taking too much air time.

Once the facilitators are trained and the questions developed, a letter goes out to the congregation announcing the listening circles, describing their purpose and structure and welcoming all to participate. Groups are organized, with facilitators assigned, to convene at the church or in members' homes.

Then they meet. After a welcome and instructions, the group crafts its covenant. The covenant's behavioral standards give people the safety with which they can trust the group and express themselves with openness and vulnerability. The covenant might include the following:

> We speak honestly.
> We speak for ourselves and not for others.
> We avoid assigning intentions, beliefs, or motives to others.
> We speak one at a time.
> We stay on the topic.
> We listen to understand, not to prepare a response.
> Listening to understand does not require agreement.

With the covenant established, the facilitator invites the participants to answer each successive question. What people say is paraphrased and noted, the notes to be given to the board to inform it of the members' perspectives.

In addition to guiding to the board, listening circles support respectful contact amid differences. As individuals speak with clarity, differences will inevitably emerge. Understanding each other's differences supports contact beyond sound bites and instead with increasing complexity and depth.

In terms of stages of conflict, listening circles foster a stage three conversation, characterized by vulnerable self-disclosure, openness, and listening without pressuring others to change.

Furthermore, listening circles allow for a shift from the usual taking of positions to a disclosure of people's interests and needs, which supports negotiation toward mutual satisfaction.

Deepen the Discussion

Sometimes in a conflict people make pronouncements which can be taken as the final word, but not necessarily. Such pronouncements could instead be seen as opening salvos into which one inquires further. "You say you want X and not Y. What is the advantage of X? What is it about Y that you do not like?" The conversation can unpack the sound bites.

Diving yet deeper, opponents can explore each other's values or beliefs. "How are our theologies involved in this conflict?" "It seems like matters of ultimate concern are at stake. What might they be?" Amid deeper themes, mundane differences lose significance, and people might find values and interests they share.

Change One's Self

At stage two of a conflict, pressuring one's opponent, whom one cannot control, requires huge effort and ends with frustration. The alternative involves reforming one's self, which makes success contingent on one's self rather than on someone else. Consistent with systems theory, changing oneself in the system, such as by practicing stage three responses to conflict, changes the system. Seeing the minister at stage three, the congregation could follow.

Take a Time Out

During conflict, people can experience such a flood of tension that their brains no longer work. Indeed, when triggered and reactive, the body sends its resources to the muscles needed for the fight-or-flight response and less to maintenance organs, such as the brain. People experience clouded thinking or might realize that the next thing they say will be too combative. At such a moment, a truce is called for. It can help to announce the pause and indicate its duration. People can table the discussion and retreat to neutral corners where they cool off and calm down. The body returns its resources to the brain, which begins to think again. People can return to the conversation with their brains in gear.

Learn

In any conflict, people choose to protect themselves or to learn. The contents of a conflict—symbols, power, proximity, expectations, worth, trust, and identity—all present opportunities to learn about each other. If it is a power struggle, for instance, the participants can explore what that power means to them and what each wants to do with it.

Learning does not mean agreeing but understanding. Understanding can contribute to naming the problem accurately and problem-solving. Furthermore, learning about our differences leads to a deeper understanding of our human complexities, which enriches our lives.

Stage Four: Peace

Stage three leads to stage four, which is peace. Generally, at stage three people speak in a way that is easy to hear, listen accurately, and seek mutual gain. As people speak the truth that lives in their hearts, listen to understand, and consider each other's needs, the walls that separate them disappear, a bridge spans their rift, and they meet. After the raging storm of conflict, peace feels like heaven.

When a conflict is resolved, the participants can relax in the peace that comes when all parties are content with the outcome. Their needs are met. They are safe. No one has to fear further tensions or revenge.

This peace differs from the honeymoon of stage one because the participants, having spoken vulnerably and listened to each other openly, know each other more deeply.

The resolution not only settles the immediate conflict, it also chips away at destructive assumptions, such as: there has to be a winner and a loser. It also replaces the dominant-subordinate hierarchical structure with the we're-in-this-together structure.

Indeed, included in every conflict is a second conflict between the survival-of-the-fittest and its logic, and we're-in-this-together and its logic. I suspect these two themes have characterized life since its creation. Protoplasm competed with protoplasm for survival, and protoplasm congregated and worked together. Tonight's living room conflict over who holds the remote echoes the dance of winning, losing, and working together that began at the origin of life.

Stages one and its avoidance, and two and its pressure, assume the survival-of-the-fittest organization of the world. Stage one assumes there has to be a winner and a loser and avoids the ordeal of a battle, opting for peace at any price. Stage two plays on that winner-loser logic with a vengeance: I am going to win at any price.

But stages three and four are based on the other way the world is organized: we are in this together and we survive by cooperating and collaborating. In this logic, we find win-win solutions. Our solutions could include mutually agreeable policies and plans. We also win by relating as one unique self in a close relationship to another unique self.

Spiritual experience supports the we're-in-this-together organization with the concept of redemption, the antidote to shame. Redemption teaches that in spite of imperfections, you are okay. In Christian terms, God loves you. Hindus say that at the inner human core, Atman, you are God, Brahman. Universalists teach that everyone is saved; all are redeemed.

Furthermore, a whole system contains differences, even opposites: yin and yang, secular and sacred. The encounter with differences is interesting. Indeed, opposites interacting can create something beautiful. In the interaction of sin and grace, human imperfection and divine perfection, redemption occurs.

In time though the stage four harmony is clung to, differences smoothed over, and the participants cycle back to the stage one. Differences can then surface, conflict returns. So it goes. Healthy relationships do not presume constant harmony but move with some grace through a cycle of harmony, to tension, to return to harmony. Each time people mend rifts, they learn to trust that cycle.

A Zen Story Narrates the Four Stages

A big fierce samurai once addressed a little monk. "Monk," he bellowed, accustomed to instant obedience, "teach me about heaven and hell!"

The monk looked up at this warrior with disdain, "Teach you about heaven and hell? I can't teach you anything. You're filthy. You smell. Your blade is rusty. You're an embarrassment to the samurai class."

The samurai shook with fury. Red in the face, speechless with rage, he unsheathed his sword and raised it above him, preparing to smite the monk.

"This is hell," the monk said softly.

The samurai stopped and looked down at the little monk, touched by the compassion and surrender of this man who had offered to give his life to teach about hell. The samurai lowered his sword, filled with gratitude and peace.

"And this is heaven," said the monk.[16]

In this story, the samurai expects stage one. The monk should bow and scrape to the samurai, offer meek little homily about heaven and hell, and hope the samurai goes away.

Our monk did not and moved things to stage two. The monk pressures the samurai by saying, in effect: "I am uncomfortable with your smell, your armor. You change." The samurai does stage two as he prepares to smite the monk. "I am uncomfortable with your effrontery. You change by ceasing to live."

The monk shows himself at stage three by sitting, exposed and vulnerable, as the samurai raises his sword, and by telling the samurai, "This is hell." Our monk has great faith in stage three. The samurai shows himself at stage three when he views the monk with compassion and lowers his sword. They both enjoy stage four: "This is heaven."

WORLD PEACE

As ministers support peacemaking in their congregations, they move the world toward peace. By the same token, as the world has moved toward peace, that makes it easier for ministers to support peace in their congregations. Indeed, despite today's grim headlines, over the centuries humanity has grown more peaceful. Today you and I are less likely to die by violence than people have ever been through history.[17]

During our distant past, primal humans lived in such violent conditions that Thomas Hobbes described their lives as "nasty, brutish, and short."[18] Interclan warfare was common, and on average one in seven people died by violence.[19] Yet over the centuries three factors have trended humanity toward peace: our need for order, our interdependence, and our developing ability to think.

As human associations grew from kinship-based clans of about 50 members to cities of 5,000, those cities needed order and so developed laws.[20] One such law, though often broken, was, "Thou shalt not kill" (Exodus 20:13, KJV). Creating order through laws saved lives. Indeed, when people developed cities, the rate of violent death dropped from one in seven to one in fifty. These laws were so lifesaving and valuable, people saw them as coming from the gods.

In addition to laws, in those larger societies, people developed reciprocity, the practice of helping someone to whom one is not a relative, expecting that individual someday to return the favor.

Related to laws was the development of norms of self-control. Medieval people were ill-mannered, picking teeth with their knives, and worse. Leading thinkers of the day, such as Erasmus, wrote serious and best-selling books of etiquette, with tips such as: "Don't pick your teeth with your knife."[21] More self-control contributed to less impulsive violence.

Ever larger societies developed greater order. When stronger warlords conquered territories to become even stronger, they became kings. Within their now-larger kingdoms, these kings imposed order, resulting in less violence within their kingdoms.[22]

Agriculture supported human interdependence. As farmers grew surpluses of one commodity but not another, it cost less to trade than to steal someone else's food in a war, so they traded.[23] As they both benefited from trading, they realized they needed each other. In their trading relationship, they also wondered, "What other commodities could I grow that my trading partner would like?" Wondering what one's trading partner might like developed empathy, which contributed to peace.

Over the centuries, people's intelligence has also increased.[24] When people developed language, that required intelligence. Centuries later, printed books stimulated more thinking. As people pondered and exchanged ideas on how things can be better, those ideas took hold and became enacted. As people solved complex problems, they grew smarter. Even over the last century, IQ test scores have been rising. A superior test performance in 1914 would be average today. This rising IQ reflects human development from concrete to scientific thinking. For example, one-hundred years ago the question: "What do dogs and rabbits have in common?" might have been answered concretely: "Dogs hunt rabbits." Now it would be answered with an abstraction: "Both are mammals." Abstract thinking doubts the animal logic of war and helps us understand the complex tasks of peace.

As a result of order, interdependence, and thought, war and violence have declined. The rate of death in war or homicide has dropped from one in seven people, to one in fifty,[25] to one in 7,143 people today, according to the World Health Organization.[26] Each death by violence is a waste that carries suffering and loss, but such tragedies are less common.

These human developments will persist and continue to support peace. I think we ministers can support this developmental trend. Whenever we create covenants, policies, and other structures—our versions of laws—that supports order within our congregational systems, which supports everyone's safety. When we work together, that continues the development of interdependence. When we reflect, such as in our sermons, that supports thought. With order, interdependence, and thought, we all continue working out how to live together in peace.

CONCLUSION

Guided by systems theory, we, ministers, can teach people how to work through conflict. We can view a conflict as triggered not by one errant player but by multiple influences in a whole system. We can view the system in its conflict, not as two camps but as a whole. We can practice constructive processes that de-escalate conflict and support its resolution. As we do, we foster a congregation, as well as a world, that lives by the values of love and peace.

QUESTIONS FOR REFLECTION

In your own conflicts, what would be one stage two behavior you want to do less often, and one stage three behavior you want to do more of?
Imagine being eighteen years old and being asked what you have learned from your childhood about conflict. What would have been your answer?
At your current age and development, what do you know about conflict?

NOTES

1. Kenneth Thomas and Ralph Kilmann, "Thomas-Kilmann Conflict Mode Instrument" (Palo Alto, CA: Consulting Psychologists Press, 1971).
2. Penny Becker, *Congregations in Conflict* (New York: Cambridge University Press, 1999).

3. William Shakespeare, "Julius Caesar" in *The Oxford Shakespeare: The Complete Works,* 2nd edition, ed. John Jowett, William Montgomery, Gary Taylor, and Stanley Wells (Oxford: Oxford University Press, 2005).

4. Edwin Friedman, *Generation to Generation: Family Process in Church and Synagogue* (New York: Guilford, 1985).

5. Aeschylus, "Agamemnon" ed. John Harrison (Cambridge, UK: Cambridge University Press, 2013).

6. Jay Heinrichs, *Thank You for Arguing* (New York: Three Rivers Press, 2013).

7. Robert Fisher, William Ury, and Bruce Patton, *Getting to Yes* (New York: Penguin, 1991).

8. Ibid.

9. Ibid.

10. Ibid.

11. Ibid.

12. Ibid.

13. Ibid.

14. Sandra Gamet, "Listening Circles Integrative Project Paper," A Paper Submitted to Community of Christ Seminary in Candidacy for the Degree Master of Arts in Religion (Independence, MO: Graceland University, 2005).

15. Eric Vogt, Juanita Brown, and David Isaacs, "The Art of Powerful Questions" (Mill Valley, CA: Whole Systems Associates, 2003).

16. Anonymous. in *Peace: A Dream Unfolding*, ed. Penny Kome and Patrick Crean (San Francisco: Sierra Club Books, 1986), 73.

17. Steven Pinker, *The Better Angels of Our Nature* (New York: Viking, 2011).

18. Thomas Hobbes, *The Leviathan* (London: Penguin Books, 1651/1982).

19. Pinker, *The Better Angels of Our Nature.*

20. Ibid.

21. Ibid.

22. Ibid.

23. Ibid.

24. Ibid.

25. Ibid.

26. World Health Organization, "World Report on Violence and Health," Ed. Etienne G. Krug et al. (Geneva, Switzerland: 2002).

9

Difficult Behavior

Discussing ministry in Steinbeck's *The Grapes of Wrath*, Tom Joad observed to the preacher Jim Casey the following: "Preachin's a kinda tone of voice, an' preachin's a way a lookin' at things. Preachin's bein' good to folks when they wanna kill ya for it."[1] Usually when you and your congregation are "good to folks," that warms their hearts, and they join in the cooperative behavior. Unfortunately though, sometimes people respond to care and support with confusing and disagreeable behavior. Be warned. If you believe your congregation is immune to human destructiveness, you can be blindsided when it emerges or be trapped like a deer in the headlights. To keep it from derailing your ministry, it behooves you to understand and respond effectively to that behavior. I suggest handling difficult behavior guided by systems theory; that could save your ministerial life.

THE PERSONALITY-PROBLEM DIAGNOSIS

I define difficult behavior as behavior that appears threatening, triggering reactivity. This is a subjective definition with the belief that what threatens one person might not threaten another. But behavior I perceive as a threat is difficult, at least for me.

As discussed in Chapter 2, "Diagnosis," when faced with a problem, such as difficult behavior, I begin by diagnosing. If I use the systems diagnosis, I would see the behavior as a symptom expressing the illness of the whole system. On the other hand, if I use the personality-problem diagnosis, I would view one element of the system, Buster, as being the problem due to his problematic personality.

There are a few reasons the personality-problem diagnosis is often used. It is simple and makes common sense, especially when I see Buster right there in plain sight behaving like Moe of the Three Stooges.

When threatened by difficult behavior and then reactive, I swing to the reflex side of the thought-reflex continuum, where I am alarmed and act but do not think.[2] My reactive behavior takes the quickest route to protect myself from the threat, such as by fighting or fleeing. I simultaneously fight Buster and protect myself from him by using the personality-problem diagnosis.

The personality-problem diagnosis protects me from responsibility for a problem. If we are all factors in creating the illness, then I am a factor contributing to Buster's difficult behavior, and so I am doing something that is not altogether helpful. I have to handle the implications that I have erred and am flawed. Assuming such responsibility, and related guilt and shame, is painful. To protect myself, I hide my mistakes and flaws by blaming Buster as an autonomous bad agent.

Though enticing, the personality-problem diagnosis applied to difficult behavior carries problems. When I conclude that the person displaying the difficult behavior is a separate entity, I forget that the system is a whole and instead draw a line between good people and bad people. The bad is then bad all by itself and of a wholly other order than me and everyone else. Divided by a line, the system is broken.

Line-drawing expresses a wish for unattainable purity. Given human imperfection and diversity, there will always be an impurity that people will want to line out. People can then fight to be on the pure side of the line and look for someone else's impurity to justify casting them onto the impure side. As everyone inspects each other's eyes for motes, no one can relax and trust their belonging.

Line-drawing becomes contagious. Following my lead, others draw lines. The congregation polarizes. Some could even view me on the bad side of their line and send me a pink slip.

I can further forget to follow humane processes. Judging Buster as nefarious, I relate poorly to him, which hurts him and weakens all relationships in the system.

My labeling judgment becomes a wish-fulfilling prophesy. If I diagnose someone as, say, "crazy," that orients my radar dish to locate other craziness, and I do, seeing craziness around me. Furthermore, I can worry that someone might judge me as crazy, that worry making me a little crazy.

If I condemn Buster rather than seek to understand him, my system has just that much more condemnation in its midst. I have introduced toxic criticality into my congregation, which raises the system's anxiety.

If I use the personality-problem diagnosis and blame Buster, I am being guided by feelings and the avoidance of painful ones—guilt and shame—

rather than guided by my mission to support everyone on their spiritual journeys and the congregation on its mission. My mission in ministry is not to avoid discomfort but to care for the grateful as well as the ungrateful. If, to avoid discomfort, I blame Buster for his difficult behavior and withdraw my caring for him, my ministry has left the tracks of its mission and crashed into a ditch, steam hissing from its cracked boiler. Furthermore, I model for the congregation someone who abandons their mission to avoid discomfort.

The personality-problem diagnosis invites one obvious but not helpful cure: the reform campaign. As with trying to reform the congregation, the reform campaign against Buster carries problems. It requires pressure, which increases the system's anxiety. It gives Buster power. He occupies my thoughts, impedes my happiness, and can thwart my success easily by doing nothing.

As an example of a reform campaign, I had a parishioner, Joe, who went from being a friendly supporter during my first year to a grumpy opponent in my second. He was chair of the church's worship committee, so I had to meet with him and hear him praise the guests he had invited as delivering the best preaching he had ever heard. My preaching? *Meh.*

His grumpiness bothered me, and I tried to win him over by writing sermons for him. I strained to make them what he would like or to sell myself in them so he would see me as a good guy. But he never came to church when I preached.

Eventually, I realized my reform efforts were for naught. I also noticed that in my focus on the absent Joe, I was neglecting the people who were coming on Sundays. I decided to give Joe's opinion of me less importance and to give up swaying that opinion. This move liberated me from Joe and freed me to write the sermons I wanted to write for people who were coming to hear them, which made preaching more fun.

Despite its problems, the personality-problem diagnosis is attractive and often used. Maybe I would rather apply the personality-problem diagnosis, blame someone else for a problem, and watch that problem persist in perpetuity, than assume a piece of responsibility for it, experience related discomfort, and solve it.

GUIDED BY MISSION

Not being derailed by difficult behavior means maintaining the central mission of my ministry: to support my congregation. To fulfill that mission, I use the systems diagnosis and interpret Buster's difficult behavior as reflecting an illness in the system. If Buster's dramas trigger fear and anger in me,

I glimpse the system's fear and anger. His use of pressure could entice me into waging a pressure-based reform campaign against him. I recognize the system's reliance on pressure.

I also want to fulfill my second mission: to support the individuals in my congregation. Therefore, I have a pastoral concern for Buster. I see him as having needs to belong, to have a voice, and to be understood, which he expresses clumsily. I further guess that during his childhood his needs for belonging, a voice, and understanding were not well met, and he was not shown how to meet those needs. Fortunately, the congregation and I could now meet Buster's needs and show him how to meet those needs more successfully. This sounds good in theory, but there goes Buster, making life difficult.

DIFFICULT BEHAVIOR AT THE MACRO LEVEL

The systems view of difficult behavior sees any human system as a whole, and when organized as a survival-of-the-fittest hierarchy, that system becomes a host for difficult behavior. Diagnosing the system as having a difficult-o-genic structure places the focus on the system and thus avoids the personality-problem diagnosis.

The survival-of-the-fittest hierarchy generates difficult behavior by making competition the route to success. In nature, predators compete against prey. Pups within a litter push each other aside competing for mother's milk. Human hierarchies can produce effective leaders and winning ideas, but the survival of the fittest also compels people to employ difficult behavior as they compete to win. To win and become dominant, one would judge, control, have power, make the rules, and use pressure, aggression, violence, and war, all difficult behavior that causes subordinates to suffer.

Lacking access to power, if the subordinates want something, they are left with subterranean means to meet their needs, which can be difficult in their own way. They can manipulate, be passive-aggressive, or ally with other victims.

The dominant-subordinate system can be stable or unstable. When stable, the dominants freely dominate, and the subordinates suffer and have only subterranean recourse. When unstable, the discontented subordinates stage a revolution, storm the Bastille, and guillotine the aristocracy. Now they are dominant. A revolution is often followed by a counterrevolution. The former dominants rise back up saying, "Not so fast, Buster!" Then there is revolution, counterrevolution, and carnage in the streets, all difficult behavior.

Ministers can moderate hierarchy-caused difficult behavior by supporting the equal valuing of all their congregations' members.

DIFFICULT BEHAVIOR AT THE MICRO LEVEL

At the micro level, individuals learn difficult behavior from difficult childhoods. An individual's difficult behavior can begin in infancy. At birth, our brains contain a fully formed amygdala, which is good at detecting threats and triggering fear.[3] It takes two decades for the brain's prefrontal cortex, the part of the brain that handles executive functioning, flexibility, problem-solving, reality testing, and self-soothing, to finish development. When the upset baby meets the calming parent, that parental calming supports the development of the child's cortex. Non-soothing parents, stress, and trauma impede cortical development and reinforce the amygdala. That amygdala can run the individual who perceives threats that are not there or who makes the environment threatening.

Following infancy, the child optimally learns from one's parents how to negotiate for their needs, learning to give a little to get a little. Not so optimally, a bossy parent might override the child's needs and forbid negotiation, teaching their child aggression, passive-aggression, or manipulation. An absent parent might have neglected the child's needs, teaching one the resigned abandonment of those needs.

A parent who overly caters to a child's demands[4] or lacks empathy for their child[5] can teach the child to cope by demanding their needs be met, otherwise known as narcissism. People high in narcissism have a primitive need to be catered to, expressed primitively with a child's tantrums and demands. Trying to meet those expectations and demands is like trying to hit a small, moving target. When someone misses the target, the narcissist, loudly disgruntled, complains, "You failed. I'm not pleased, and it is your fault. I am, after all, the center of the universe." I might believe the narcissist's criticism and work harder to please. Even if I succeed in giving the narcissistic person what they want, they move the goalposts and demand something else. As with a minister, a congregation can strive to please the narcissist, working hard, but still ending up with disappointment all around.

To handle such difficult behavior successfully, ministers can whisper calm to people's amygdalae and guide people in successful ways to meet their needs.

Psychopathology

Difficult behavior can also originate in the interaction of an individual's neurological system and a difficult childhood. Regarding neurology, a neuroscientist, Dr. Jim Fallon, looking at PET scans of murderers, found the presence of MAOA, or the "warrior gene," and a low level of "orbital hypofrontality."[6] These brain structures occur in people who do not emotionally engage with others. The criminals he studied also had experienced difficult or traumatic childhoods.

Dr. Fallon analyzed his own brain and found he had inherited the MAOA and other aggression and violence-related genes. "I'm the one who looks most like a serial killer," he says. This brain structure did run in his family—he had killers in his lineage—but Dr. Fallon's charmed childhood prevented his errant brain structures from leading him into violence. There but for the grace of God go I.

Pastors cannot perform PET scans or brain surgery—no, you can't lobotomize Buster—but they can limit destructiveness in their congregations.

DIFFICULT BEHAVIOR INTERACTS WITH THE MINISTER: BUTTONS AND REACTIVITY

Difficult behavior triggers reactivity. A person waving an ax when there is no wood to split, such as at coffee hour, would trigger in observers the thought, "We are not safe," prompting them to swing to the reflexive fight-or-flight response. A difficult person wielding not an ax but a complaint could also trigger reactivity in the receiver of the complaint. That complaint could be said to push the complainee's "button."

As discussed in Chapter 4, "Working on Yourself," historical threats can leave triggers to reactivity or "buttons." To moderate reactivity, one recognizes the button issues that could trigger such reactivity. One discerns that one is not so threatened. One develops anti-buttons. Then the complaint, or any trigger, is just an interesting event. More secure and less reactive, one is a moderately reactive presence.

THE CHURCH CAN SET UP DIFFICULT BEHAVIOR

To develop a systems diagnosis of difficult behavior, one considers how the church could trigger or reinforce difficult behavior.

The Church Has Buttons

A system, such as a congregation, can have its own buttons, and difficult behavior can push them, threatening the system and triggering system-wide reactivity. For example, a church that formed in opposition to something could live by the assumption: "It is a win-lose world, and we have to fight hard to win." The fight-hard-to-win button is big, fat, and ready, so when any difference emerges, the button is pushed and people fight hard to win. Similarly, a congregation that was scolded in their history could have the button, or assumption, "There is something wrong with us." Fearing further criticism, the congregation hides its identity behind a pleasing, all-things-to-all-people facade.

The Church Has a Power Hierarchy

Although you develop a fair, equitable church community, the church will still allocate more power to some—committee chairs, you—and less to others. As such, it recapitulates the survival-of-the-fittest hierarchy. In this organization, some will overlook the we're-in-this-together team you have supported, instead see the hierarchy, and play by its rules. Aggressive individuals can aggrandize their power, and the underpowered settle for indirect ways to obtain power.

Church Can Be Unsatisfying, and People's Needs Not Met

People can be disgruntled consumers of congregational and ministerial services. "No one talks to me at coffee hour," for example. The church does provide services, such as worship and pastoral care. Any service provider will be imperfect and at times fail its consumers.

This failure can be intensified by people who as children did not learn to negotiate for their needs. Not knowing how to assert themselves directly, they confer with other malcontents. Not asserted, their needs remain unmet. Their discontent grows, fueled by more subterranean grumbling, all gathering momentum for a revolution.

Ministers Try to Serve, Exhausting Themselves in the Process

As discussed in Chapter 4, "Working on Yourself," clergy can find themselves in a subordinate, servant role in which they overwork to serve and please. The subordinate, servant role is stressful, and the church, demanding service, is difficult.

During a Conflict, People Are Difficult

At stage one of conflict, people may not be battling, but the atmosphere of a system at this stage can feel mildly tense or boring, quietly difficult. At stage two, the pressure stage, people waging war display dramatically difficult behavior.

Stress Diminishes Trust

The hormone, oxytocin, is released when someone does something nice for you. It is the love hormone. It generates trust and feels good.[7] But stress is poison to oxytocin. Stress in our nation's system is currently high, linked to economic challenges and low trust in institutions such as government or the church. That systemic stress and resulting low oxytocin could leave people in less of a mood to trust when they come to church.

Churches Deal in Symbols

Because symbols have salvific power, and because it is difficult to compromise about a symbol, when people deal with symbols, which happens often in church life, people can display difficult behavior in the forms of passionate scrupulosity and resistance to negotiation.

Systems Can Lack Standards

Without standards, people misbehave. Winston Churchill lamented the absence of standards, which allowed Nazi Germany to run amok: "The malice of the wicked was reinforced by the weakness of the virtuous."[8] In a congregation, the virtuous might lack the standards and strength to check their fellow parishioners' destructive behavior.

WHAT HELPS IN THEORY: SECURITY AND SYSTEMIC IMMUNITY

Your security is the curative agent in your congregation. You show security with your transparency, vulnerability, and self-definition. In contact with your security, the difficult, amygdala-guided Buster calms down. Furthermore, when the leader remains secure in the face of difficult behavior, the system will gravitate around that leader into security. That secure system further influences Buster. It defies common sense, but I think it is easier to work on one's own security, which calms the system, than to try to reform one person in the system.

The secure system influences Buster by becoming immune to his difficult behavior. A difficult person is like a toxic cell in a body, invading other cells, causing those cells to fuse with the toxin, becoming toxic and difficult themselves, or to disintegrate, letting the toxin win, becoming silent, or going away.

You help the system become immune by demonstrating your own immunity. As discussed in Chapter 6, "Calm," you demonstrate immunity by not letting a toxin cause you to become toxic yourself or silent. Instead you resist the toxin's invasion by defining yourself, your principles, values, and beliefs. Your self-definition gives you a little space, analogous to a cell membrane within which you are secure from invading toxins. Plus, by not defining Buster, you are not invading him. You claim your space and allow others, even toxins, their space. Making the system safer for Buster makes the system safer for everyone.

Furthermore, holding your space and giving others space shows everyone how to define themselves and hold their space while letting others have space. The system in which people resist invasion and refrain from invading others has developed immunity from toxic invasions. Without the threat of invasion, people can make meaningful contact with each other while free to be who they are.

WHAT HELPS IN PRACTICE

Shrink the Congregation's Buttons

If difficult behavior pushes the congregation's buttons, a minister can shrink those buttons. To assess your congregation's buttons, you might review the list of button themes in Chapter 4, "Working on Yourself," and see which, if any, might apply. If you guess one might apply to your congregation, you could dig into the congregation's history for that button's origin. Placing that button in the context of an understandable story will leave you calmer about that button and guide you in addressing it.

For example, you guess your congregation's button or assumption is, "It is a win-lose world, and we have to fight hard to win," which leaves them prickly and ready to fight. You then learn that the congregation was founded in opposition to the Church of Pure Evil. Your understanding of the fight that founded the church calms you. As you understand the congregation's win-lose theme, you can address it by remaining neutral and refraining from joining in its win-lose debates. Furthermore, you can set up win-win processes, such as by guiding the partisans in productive negotiations. As the partisans negotiate successfully, they would experience the benefit of the win-win assumption and internalize it.

You can also articulate healthy assumptions, such as:

> We are reasonably safe.
> We are okay.
> We are in this together.
> We survive by survive by cooperating and collaborating, and we can find
>   win-win solutions.
> We share power, and all have a voice.
> We can be ourselves.
> We can meet our needs.
> We can ask and receive.
> We can handle challenges.

As you shrink the congregation's button and reinforce an anti-button, you lead the congregation in a macro version of your own process of understanding and shrinking a button.

Offer Standards and Values

Humane norms or standards prevent difficult behavior. As a minister, I promote a norm by describing the congregation as a support community. Mutual support becomes the norm. A congregational covenant would articulate additional norms.

Just expressing norms can guide behavior. This worked for me at a summer camp where I directed the oldest campers, fourteen-year-old boys, who every summer were the goon squad of the camp. At our first assembly, after some welcoming remarks, I said that we were here to create a community of mutual respect and love. No one smirked. They actually accepted that standard and behaved with mutual respect and love.

When misbehavior does occur, standards can rein it in. If Buster is calling others unflattering names, instead of calling him a name, which would join with the difficult behavior, the minister responds: "Buster, this congregation has a covenant that affirms mutual support. Name-calling is not consistent with mutual support."

Similar to norms, difficult behavior can be addressed by the articulation of values. For example, to address Buster's name-calling a leader can state: "In this congregation, we value love and support." Buster, in his name-calling, is confused about how to belong to a community. Offering him a value, or a standard, would guide him in successful belonging. Furthermore, standards, or values, apply to everyone, so calling Buster on his violation of those standards or values would not be seen as some personal vendetta against him.

The articulation of a value could also have a positive effect on everyone else. As they observe their minister articulate a lofty value, rather than thrashing in the weeds of difficult behavior, that reassures them that their leader is thinking rather than reactive and guiding them toward living in the humane manner to which they aspire. Guided by a humane value, they refrain from reinforcing Buster's misbehavior. They may even look surprised when Buster calls someone else a name. If he continues name-calling, after a while, he will feel lonely and awkward as the only one doing this and stop.

When the minister expresses the value of mutual support, the people would also see in their leader someone who, stressed by Buster, could have rejected the congregation's standards and denigrated into name-calling.

Instead, as they see a leader continue to hold humane, thought-through values, despite being under stress, they would realize those values are important.

For instance, under intense stress, Martin Luther King once prevented a possible riot by asserting humane values.[9] A few weeks into the 1955–56 Montgomery bus boycott, one evening while King was at a meeting at his church, his wife and daughter at home, someone bombed his house. King rushed home to find his family unharmed, his house damaged, and a crowd of his African American neighbors outside, along with police, the mayor, and the chief of police. Policemen began pushing the crowd to disperse, and tempers flared.

King stepped onto his damaged porch and addressed the crowd: "Don't do anything panicky. Don't get your weapons. He who lives by the sword shall perish by the sword." The crowd quieted. King continued: "We must love our white brothers, no matter what they do to us. We must make them know that we love them. Jesus still cries out in words that echo across the centuries: 'Love your enemies, bless them that curse you; pray for those that despitefully use you.' We must meet hate with love." King spoke further, and when he concluded, the people quietly dispersed.

In the face of very difficult behavior, violence directed at him and his family, King offered his neighbors the humane value of love. Meeting hate with love at this threat-filled moment strengthened the value of love he reiterated throughout the civil rights movement. If I could generalize from this anecdote, when people are aroused by threats or their buttons pushed, if they are reminded of their standards and values, as Rev. King managed to do, their behavior will remain moderate.

WHEN PUSH COMES TO SHOVE

So you understand the sources of difficult behavior. You offer individuals calming, understanding diagnoses, and pastoral and spiritual support. You value the wholeness of the congregation. You have shrunk your buttons. You are defining yourself and letting others define themselves. Your congregation has established humane norms and values. Nevertheless, you are the target of difficult behavior. Why?

Someone's fury could be directed at you because you are a safe target— you won't hit back. You could have pushed the furious parishioner's buttons. You might be targeted because you are a change agent, and the system's homeostasis is pushing back. You might be targeted because someone has a history of hostility toward authority figures, or you are not an individual's choice to be their minister. You might remind someone of their parent or some difficult person in their history.

Unless you have violated ethical codes or broken the law, the anger you receive is likely bigger than you deserve. If you are the target of anger, it always makes sense to examine your behavior for mistakes, but you probably do not have to walk on your knees through the desert repenting.

So you are targeted. Now what?

Control What You Can Control

Situations are stressful when they defy one's control of them. Difficult behavior is difficult partly because it is not regulated and out of your control. You watch Buster helplessly and wince.

Trying to control Buster (whom you cannot control) through a reform campaign increases your experience of being without control. Attempting and failing at a reform campaign would compound your stress related to the difficult behavior.

Instead, as discussed earlier, you can focus on what you can control. You can control your reactive behavior. You can choose to be guided by your principles. You can support congregational norms.

You control your interpretive lens. When difficult behavior occurs, the problem is intensified by the belief that it is wrong. "I can't believe what Buster just said!" A less pain-inducing lens would view difficult behavior as understandable because it is caused by difficult childhoods and brain aberrations, intensified by congregational dynamics and the world's stress. "Of course, Buster just said …"

Furthermore, one can remember everyone can be difficult. I was once introduced to lead a workshop on handling difficult people, with "When I thought about difficult people, I thought of Ken Reeves." We all chuckled, but the double meaning does apply. I was qualified to lead a program helping clergy handle difficult people, and I can be rotten, or at least can push people's buttons (as can all of us).

Balance Serving with Journeying

As mentioned earlier, the subordinate, serving role can burn out clergy. Serving has to happen in any relationship, but one can balance serving with guiding people on a journey. You may be the guide, but you also share the journey as one among equals. You and everyone else are exploring who you are and how you work together as a community, leading to deeper understandings and chosen covenants and policies. Furthermore, you can invite people to take a pilgrimage together into the unknowns of spiritual life. You can guide people to their spiritual sources, where they are most vulnerable and most nourished and where imperfect services are rendered moot by people's salvation.

Support Equality

Difficult behavior can hook us into the hierarchical, survival-of-the-fittest organization of the world and its assumption that there has to be a winner and a loser. Instead, one opts not to comply with hierarchical, win-lose assumptions. One acts as if we're in this together, seeking win-win outcomes. Even if everyone in the system assumes win-lose, the one outlier who assumes win-win throws a wrench in its win-lose assumption.

Offer Empathy Followed by Problem-Solving

When someone has been triggered into reactivity and displaying difficult behavior, it helps first to bring calm then offer problem-solving. As discussed in Chapter 6, "Calm," to bring calm, one listens to understand the reactive person's perspective. Understanding and validating the reactive person's feelings, needs, and thoughts offers them safety.[10] Safety moves one to the thought side of the reflex–thought continuum, where one can think again.

When the other is thinking, you can explore their needs.[11] As noted above, Buster may not know what he needs or how to meet those needs, and so he seeks to meet those needs in clumsy, misguided ways. Nevertheless, with empathy, you unearth what he needs, setting you both up to negotiate how to meet them.

For example, the notorious Buster sounds off to you about how rotten the church is. You begin with empathy: "Sounds like you are unhappy and angry about the church."

"Damn right I am. This place is a mess."
"Wow, you seem disappointed as well as angry." You reflect Buster's story such that he says, "Yes, you get it," which calms him.

Then you segue to his needs. "Given your anger and disappointment, Buster, what do you need?" Let's say he needs to have a voice in congregational life. Having a voice is a good thing and, in theory and principle, you want to meet that need. You then consider how. You are wary of ceding power to Buster, because his suggestions run counter to the direction of the congregation. You want ideas that would meet Buster's needs and that you could accept and that you both could observe when enacted.

So you and Buster brainstorm: "Buster writes a column for the newsletter." "Buster preaches one sermon per year." "Buster chairs the Board of Trustees." You might not like these ideas, but you avoid dismissing and critiquing them and keep brainstorming. Maybe you offer: "I will meet with Buster three times a year for an hour at a time. To these meetings Buster brings his complaints and suggestions. I will listen to all Buster has to offer." If Buster likes your idea of having an audience with you one hour a time, three times per year, you and he shake on it.

This is pastoral support for Buster. Your empathy followed by problem-solving not only calmed him and helped him meet a need but also showed him how to express a need constructively and collaboratively. His behavior improves. You are both happy campers.

Define Yourself

While others are defining you as unworthy, you could define them as unworthy, which would add fuel to the flames of this difficult behavior. It would be contrary and unexpectedly vulnerable to define yourself. Furthermore, vulnerably defining oneself does not comply with the practice of labeling others. Like a duck in a shooting gallery, you say, "This is what I believe to be most true. Here is my credo. Here is my vision. Fire away!".

Address the Process

When people are stuck on a point of content, that focus on content can fuel feed the fire of the debate. Alternatively, one can shift attention to the process with: "It seems like we are in a power struggle, and both of us are trying to win." You can also comment on the system's process: "This church seems to engage in debates in which each side pushes hard to win." Shifting attention to the process frees up the discussion and moves it into setting healthy process norms, such as active listening or using I-statements.

Forgive

Resenting a difficult person disrupts one's peace of mind. Alternatively, as discussed in Chapter 8, "Conflict," there is forgiveness, which gives someone a gift of good will, even if they do not deserve it.[12] That gift frees the forgiver from resentment.

Place the Ball in Their Court

Difficult people are skilled at making others squirm. For example, they complain and pronounce: "It all your fault," giving you guilt as well as responsibility for fixing the problem. The ball is in your court. The response, volley it back. This volley is not a return of guilt, a defense, or an argument, but a question that could generate constructive thought. For example, one can volley back to the complaining person: "What would it take for you to forgive me?" The ball is now in their court. They may then think and actually come up with useful ideas for forgiveness. If so, great. Or they could reply: "I can never forgive you," placing the ball back in your court. You can volley the ball back with another question: "What Christian (or fill in your tradition) principle supports never forgiving someone?" Ball back to them.

Be Skeptical about Their Emotionality

Emotions are often seen as authentic and authoritative and so are given credibility and influence. Sometimes emotions are indeed authentic. But instrumental emotions, described in Chapter 4, "Working on Yourself," manage and manipulate others.[13] These instrumental and manipulative emotions are rackets and do not reflect the person's life experiences. Therefore, you may listen to and try to please the angry person, but they remain angry. You comfort the sad person, but they remain sad for years. If you are being managed by someone's emotional racket, you can give these instrumental emotions less authority.

Don't Give Them Power

Difficult people can be loud and complaining, but Buster on the sidelines is less destructive than in the role of quarterback. One can try to appease Buster by appointing him quarterback, hoping he would benefit from power and use it responsibly, but more likely he would continue to be difficult, only now with greater destructive effect.

I recommend instead empowering healthy, cooperative people who function at the thought end of the congregation's thought-reflex bell curve. Empowering the high functioning trends the whole congregation around these thoughtful people. The healthier environment benefits everyone, including the difficult people.

Surround the Difficult Person with Health

The difficult person can be embraced in a healthy context. As you respond moderately to difficult behavior, as you articulate and reinforce values of love and respect, and as you support people's safety, that moves the system to the thought side of the thought–reflex continuum. Within that thoughtful system, Buster feels safer and becomes more thoughtful and moderate. His thoughtfulness is successful in this thoughtful system, which reinforces it. He sees thoughtful models and follows them. Finally, seeing thoughtful, moderate behavior as the norm and only option, Buster joins the system in moderation.

Set Protective Policies

When someone has hurt or taken advantage of you or others, you and the church can set policies that protect everyone from future offenses. Background checks for people working with children is an example of a policy or procedure that protects children. A policy is thought-through, not a reflexive, reaction. It applies to everyone. It is something I or the church can control that does not depend on the compliance of a difficult person.

The Nuclear Option

If someone refuses to join with the covenant and norms of the church, and seeks instead to attack the community, there is a nuclear option. I hope this option is never needed, but I have seen an individual who, despite being listened to and respected, threatened to sue his own church. Abraham Lincoln, in his Cooper Union address of 1860, commented on a situation like this. Speaking to the destructive single-mindedness of the South, he declared: "Your purpose, then, plainly stated, is that you will destroy the Government, unless you be allowed to construe and enforce the Constitution as you please, on all points in dispute between you and us. You will rule or ruin in all events."[14]

If someone wishes to rule or ruin, the nuclear option begins with reminding the difficult person that the church has a covenant that calls for mutual support. One can then ask: "Despite your apparently non-supportive actions, do you want to share with us our covenant of mutual support?" The ball is in their court.

If the person chooses and declares, "No!" they could be encouraged to find a better fit elsewhere. If they respond with "Yes," but the difficult behavior continues, one can return to "If you continue to violate our covenant, we will understand that, despite your words, you really do not want to be part of this community."

If the person continues to act in ways that show he or she is opting out of the covenant, one can advise committees and boards not to include or listen to this person. The individual may come to church and be a toxic cell in the system, but the rest of the cells are protected by cell membranes that resist the individual's invasion. One might also inform the individual: "When you're ready to behave within our covenant, we will include you in our proceedings. Until then, you may still attend church, but we will limit your influence in our community."

TYPES OF DIFFICULT BEHAVIOR: PASSIVITY

Difficult behavior can be passive. Buster does not do what he volunteered to do and does not reply to calls, e-mails, or other communications. Dealing with passivity is like pushing smoke; there is no substance to contact.

You can put the ball in the court of the passive person by indicating how you will interpret their nonaction. For example, when someone has not acted on a committee matter, communicate through a medium you know they would receive, such as a letter sent via postal mail. The letter can read: "Dear Buster, The finance committee is waiting for your input on our budget for the upcoming fiscal year. If the committee does not receive your input by its meeting on Monday, October 26, we will understand you will not be adding your input, and we will proceed." If Buster does not like this interpretation, he has to act, which solves the problem of his inaction. If he does not act, the committee can still proceed.

TYPES OF DIFFICULT BEHAVIOR: NARCISSISM

As discussed above, narcissistic people can be difficult. One can try to comply with the narcissist's demands, a Sisyphean task. Instead, to keep one from being captured by the narcissist, one accepts that one will fail to please: "Buster will not be happy with me. I do not please everyone all the time. I'm still okay and will continue doing my best." Furthermore, rather than making their satisfaction your priority, you can make your values and principles your priority. Then you are being consistent with your identity. As an additional benefit, showing it is okay to be imperfect throws a helpful wrench in the narcissistic person's belief that they have to be perfect to be loved.

In practice, you do not comply with all the narcissist demands. Then you are offering something likely missing from their childhood: optimal frustration.[15] The optimal part involves meeting their needs, such as to belong, to have a voice, and to be understood. The frustration part involves not giving in to their particular demands. You tell Buster: "You want the church to give you a new car. Interesting. We won't provide the new car, but we will give you belonging in a spiritual community." Not catering to every demand, but meeting needs, supports the development of Buster's ability to handle life's inevitable frustrations while still having his needs met. As he learns to handle the juxtaposition of frustration and needs met, Buster matures and joins the community of adults.

TYPES OF DIFFICULT BEHAVIOR: COMPLAINT AND CRITICISM

One common difficult behavior is the complaint. When making a complaint, an underpowered subordinate tells a dominant party that the dominant has failed to meet the subordinate's needs. Being subordinate and without power, they believe they cannot assert and negotiate for their needs. They have little recourse but to complain.

A complaint creates a little revolution from subordinate to dominant, then back to subordinate. It starts: "I am a subordinate and powerless victim, with little recourse except to offer this passive-aggressive complaint." The complainer next becomes briefly dominant by making a judgment: "You failed." This brief revolution gives the receiver of the complaint a taste of what it is like to be in the complainer's world: powerless, stuck, helpless, desperate, afraid, and ashamed. The complainer returns to being subordinate with the implication that all the power lies in the again-dominant receiver of the complaint to conceive of a solution and then implement it. The receiver now holds the hot potato of pressure to solve the complainer's problem.

Furthermore, receiving criticism is difficult when:

> One does not expect it or want it.
> One has little skill in how to deal with it, making one helpless.
> It comes from someone important.
> It is valid.
> It is invalid.
> It offends one's sense of justice.
> It means someone is different from us, which triggers anxiety.
> It means someone is not happy with something we have done,
>   which triggers guilt.
> It means someone is not happy with who we are, which triggers shame.

Complaints test boundaries. A mature boundary is like a sifter, allowing in truths one needs to hear and sifting out big irrelevant chunks. A poor boundary lets in too much, treating everything said as true. Another poor boundary lets in nothing, a wall to protect one's fragility.

Complaints also test personal security and self-esteem. With mature self-esteem one realizes, "I'm imperfect, but okay." With less mature self-esteem, at one extreme, one grovels with worthlessness, at the other, one struts with arrogance. Eleanor Roosevelt expressed one's control of one's esteem: "No one can make you feel inferior without your consent."[16]

HOW TO HANDLE A COMPLAINT

Seek It out Preemptively

Instead of being surprised by it, ask for it. Performance reviews also invite such feedback.

Listen

When the complaint occurs, listen. Even if you have the best intentions and are the nicest person, you still have to listen to something that is difficult to hear. Indicating that you cannot hear a complaint suggests that you can't handle the truth. The complainer can then either complain louder, escalating tensions, or give up, deadening the relationship.

Manage Discomfort

Complaints trigger painful emotions, particularly shame. Shame hurts but does not kill. On the other hand, one's attempts to avoid shame can be destructive to oneself and others. Use positive self-talk: "Buster is not happy with me, but I am okay."

Put on Hold the Impulse to Defend

When hearing a complaint or criticism, people often reflexively employ defenses, which as noted above suggest that you cannot handle the truth. You might recognize your default defense(s) from the five listed below.

DEFENSES

Superiority

One insists the complaints are unjustified and unfounded. "You have no right to complain to me." "Who are you to tell me X, when I know Y?" "What about you and all your failings?" "You are wrong, here are the facts." Then we have defensive bluster attempting to squelch the irritated complainer.

I Need You to See My Perspective

If made afraid by the irritated complainer, one can try to ease one's anxiety by changing the complainer's irritated feelings by justifying the actions being complained about. "But here is why I did what I did …" Unfortunately, saying a defensive "but …" to an angry person tends to escalate tensions. They are not ready to hear your side, and as you say "but" and start explaining your side, they will feel unheard themselves. It is like waving a red flag in front of a bull. Inside them, the pressure to be heard builds. They will come at you harder.

Withdrawal, Stonewalling

One is so guilt-stricken and ashamed in the face of the complaint that one stops communicating or leaves the scene. Communication dies.

Resentful Compliance

Compelled to submit to the complainer, one agrees to solve the complainer's problem but resents doing so. That resentment becomes channeled into revenge.

Confusion

One displays confusion: "I don't get it." Or one sows confusion by taking up some tangential topic. Bafflement ensues.

As you review these defenses, you might notice one or two you often use when handling a complaint. It would help you to note which is your default and refrain from using it automatically when receiving a complaint.

Furthermore, the complaint contains two stories, one about the complainee and one about the complainer. If you focus on the story about yourself, the complainee, the natural response would be a defense. If you focus on the story about the complainer, and their problem, the natural response would be compassion.

Restate the Problem

When hearing the complaint, you may disagree with its validity and hold as true a story that departs radically from the complainer's. But the complainer insists on having their story understood. To move toward resolution, you show the complainer you understand that story. Sometimes hearing the person out for a minute or two is not enough. Hang in there. If you restate the problem accurately, their energy will eventually cool, and they will say, "Yes, that's it. That's what I am unhappy about."

Sympathize, Apologize

If Buster complains that he was not listened to at a meeting, you offer: "Yes, I can see how that would have hurt your feelings. I am sorry about that." He adds more about feeling powerless and humiliated. Maybe he adds that as a child he was not listened to. You don't have to say, "It's all my fault." But you care about Buster and regret that he is hurting.

Invite Suggestions

When your listening and restating the problem have calmed the complainer, they can think again. Now you both can brainstorm solutions: "What could we do about this that we could both feel good about?"

Requests are easier to hear and work with than complaints. Inviting someone to shift from complaint to request gives them some responsibility for thinking through how to solve their problem, sparing you that chore. The shift from complaint to request also shifts the individual from being an unempowered subordinate staging a brief revolution, to being an empowered equal asserting oneself with the complainee.

As requests are expressed, you do not have to accede to these suggestions, but they are good information. Ideally you find a solution that you both feel good about. Maybe you both agree that when you, the minister, are attending a meeting with Buster present, you invite anyone who has not spoken to speak.

Shift the Conversation from the Personal to an Abstraction

A complaint can look personal, sound personal, and feel personal but is expressing an issue that transcends you. Returning to the meeting in which the complainer did not speak: "It sounds like you felt left out of the conversation at yesterday's meeting. I guess I talked too much. I am sorry. What can we do about this? Maybe at meetings we could go around the table and make sure everyone has commented before we make a decision." This proposal moves the conversation from the minister's volubility to a procedure for meetings. Indeed, a conversation about what could help the church develop, and thereby meet the complainer's need, is more fruitful than a discussion of the flaws in the minister's character.

Even underneath very personal complaints, abstractions can be found. Responding to a complaint about the color of his car, a minister offers: "It sounds like you don't like the color of my car. Indeed, it is very red. Maybe the church needs a policy about ministers' cars." The discussion of motor vehicle paint moves away from you and your wacky choices to something abstract, not about you, and that could lead to a policy for the congregation. No red cars for ministers!

The complainer wants his or her complaint resolved, and until that resolution, the complaint festers and rots the supporting timbers of one's ministry. Even a trivial complaint such as "You didn't cross this *t* or dot this *i*," if left unresolved, could lead to a minister's dismissal. Handled well and successfully resolved, a substantive complaint, "That sermon could have been uttered by Satan himself!" can be followed by a long and happy tenure.

CONCLUSION

When faced with difficult behavior, systems theory suggests that the whole congregation is involved in generating the difficult behavior and in the cure. Difficult behavior invites ministers to grow into health and personal security so as to keep ourselves adherent to our mission in spite of such behavior. Difficult behavior also invites congregations to grow into health through developing immunity to difficult behavior and through remaining adherent to their missions. The difficult behavior also invites ministers and congregations to respond pastorally to the needs of a difficult person and to guide Buster toward more successful ways to meet his needs. You then give Buster a supportive, safe spiritual home, maybe a better home than he has ever known.

QUESTIONS FOR REFLECTION

Considering the last time you were triggered into reactivity, what button, or buttons, might have been pushed at that moment?
What in your history could have developed that button in you?
What do you need for you to shrink that button?
Given that values moderate reactivity and guide behavior, what is the key value you would want to express to your congregation?

NOTES

1. John Steinbeck, *The Grapes of Wrath* (New York: Penguin, 1939/2006).

2. Robert Sapolsky, *Why Zebras Don't Get Ulcers,* 3rd edition (New York: Henry Holt, 2004).

3. Louis Cozolino, *The Neuroscience of Psychotherapy* (New York: Norton, 2010).

4. Theodore Millon, *Disorders of Personality* (New York: John Wiley & Sons, 1981).

5. Heinz Kohut, *The Restoration of the Self* (New York: International Universities Press, 1977).

6. Jim Fallon, *The Psychopath Inside: A Neuroscientist's Personal Journey into the Dark Side of the Brain* (New York: Penguin, 2013).

7. Richard Davidson and Sharon Begley, *The Emotional Life of Your Brain* (New York: Penguin, 2012).

8. Winston Churchill, *The Gathering Storm* (New York: Houghton Mifflin, 1948).

9. Roger Bruns, *Martin Luther King, Jr: A Biography* (Greenwood Publishing Group, 2006).

10. Jeanne Watson, Rhonda Goldman, and Greet Vanaerschot, "Empathic: A Postmodern Way of Being?" In *Handbook of Experiential Psychotherapy*, ed. Leslie Greenberg, Jeanne Watson and Germain Lietaer (New York: Guilford Press, 1998), 61–81.

11. Leslie Greenberg, *Emotion-Focused Therapy* (Washington, DC: American Psychological Association, 2002).

12. Robert Enright, *Forgiveness Is a Choice* (Washington: American Psychological Association, 2001).

13. Leslie Greenburg and Jeremy Safran, *Emotion in Psychotherapy* (New York: Guilford Press, 1987).

14. Abraham Lincoln, "Cooper Union Address" in *Abraham Lincoln: Speeches and Writings Vol. 2 1859–1865*, ed. Don Fehrenbacher (New York, NY: Literary Classics of the United States, 1989).

15. Heinz Kohut, *The Analysis of the Self* (New York: International Universities 1971).

16. Eleanor Roosevelt [Free-standing quotation] *The Reader's Digest*, Volume 37, September, 1940.

10

The Unconscious

People will sometimes have a more dramatic reaction to you as their minister than you might expect. Sometimes it is a surprisingly positive reaction. They want to be close to you, or something you said changed their lives. At other times people can have a surprisingly negative reaction. You might interject into a sermon a clumsy but otherwise benign remark and receive an anonymous outraged letter. The intensity of these responses may be fueled by people's unconscious. Indeed, unconscious material inflames passions—passionate love and passionate hate.

The unconscious is simply the contents of people's psyches of which they are not aware.[1] A system, be it an individual or a community, is a whole and includes both conscious and unconscious material. That unconscious material influences people, but without their awareness.

People's passionate displays, generated by the unconscious, can upset a minister's moderated reactivity. To remain moderate amid a system passionately charged by unconscious material, it helps to understand the unconscious. With that understanding, a minister can work with the unconscious to care for individuals and for the congregation without becoming caught up in the intense love, or intense anger, generated by that unconscious. Indeed, one does not view the love as some great new thing, at least not on the job. One also does not view the anger as meaning you and your ministry are doomed. Instead, they are matters to handle pastorally.

TRANSFERENCE

One way the unconscious can surface in the relationship between minister and parishioner involves transference. Glenn Gabbard defined transference in psychotherapy as occurring when "The patient experiences the doctor as a significant figure from the patient's past. Qualities of that past figure will be attributed to that doctor, and feelings associated with that figure will be attributed to that doctor."[2] Transference occurs not only with therapists but with spouses, friends, innocent bystanders, and ministers.

With transference, an expectation developed during a past relationship recurs in a similar contemporary relationship.[3] One is not consciously remembering that past relationship, but is unconsciously reenacting it. In a church, the parishioner might hear and see something in one's minister that relates more to the parishioner's past than to the minister. Perhaps, for example, I learned from my critical father to expect authorities, such as my minister, to be critical of me. Even when my minister is as bland as oatmeal, I expect criticism. I relate to that perceived critical person as I did to my father, with caution. Or to recapitulate familiar criticism, I might evoke harshness from the otherwise gentle minister. Or perhaps I learned from my placating mother not to expect women to take stands. I may not have admired my mother; I may have wished she had taken stands, but it still rattles me to see a woman, such as my minister, behave differently from my mom and take a stand.

Although transference applies historical expectations that do not quite belong in to a current relationship, according to Gabbard, transference is the "basis for all meaningful relationships."[4] One's transferential, or historically based, expectation of what another will do or how they will treat one may not fit this current relationship, yet one invests energy and meaning into this current relationship because one wants something from it.

What one wants harkens back to one's childhood relationships with parents. Speaking to this point, Franz Basch states that a child wants to be "understood, comforted, admired, stimulated, and forgiven."[5] When a parent meets those desires, that completes a successful transaction with the parent, which supports the child's development. But probably mom or dad did not always fulfill these desires. When the child's desire was not met, and when support that would have helped the child's development was absent, a piece of development was arrested. The desires and the development they would have supported do not disappear, but retreat into the unconscious.

Those childhood desires to be understood, comforted, admired, stimulated, and forgiven emerge again, acted out in transference. The adult is looking for a more successful transaction than he or she experienced in childhood, so as to complete an arrested piece of development. Rare for one to say: "I just want to be understood and admired right now so my development can proceed." But that desire is there. When the desire is met, a successful transaction occurs, and development can move along.

Personal development is so important, it is pushed forward by considerable energy. When an aspect of development has been arrested, energetic passion pushes to complete it. One is not aware of the incomplete development, nor of the passion pushing to complete it, so this internal drama is unconscious. Nevertheless, it is played out in transference relationships. With one's development on the line, the stakes are high, charging these transferential relationships with meaning and passion.

So someone enters a church wondering: "Will I be understood? Will I be comforted? Might I even be admired? Will this be interesting, and will I be stimulated? If I make a mistake here, will I be forgiven?" To some degree, these questions and related hopes and fears linger from childhood, and are addressed to God, to Jesus, to other spiritual sources, to the congregation, and to you as minister and representative of the spirit and of the community. If the answers are "yes," one experiences successful transactions involving understanding, comfort, admiration, stimulation, or forgiveness, and development can proceed.

Transference can be positive or negative.[6] Positive transference occurs when the parishioner sees you as an ally in their development, idealizing you and hanging on your every word. Children naturally idealize their parents because those parents are doing something wonderful: giving the child meals, a place to live, and the bonding the child needs to survive and develop. When you are idealized as someone's minister, you too are unconsciously seen as giving something wonderfully parental that helps the person develop.

Negative transference occurs when the parishioner sees you as an obstacle in their development. To further one's development, the parishioner pushes against you with surprising fury. When someone is angry with you, it would be responsible to consider the mistakes you might have made, but the parishioner's own history could likely be surfacing, especially when the anger seems more intense than you might deserve. The person's unconscious could be saying, "I want to develop through opposing you, like I wanted to oppose my abusive father." Or "All right, you seem to be able to understand me. Now I'll show you how horrible I am, and why I am so unhappy." Or "I'll show you how badly other people have treated me." Aside: unhappy people are not always going to be nice and lovable. Even with negative transference, though the person wants something from you, and a relationship occurs.

As a minister, you are not doing psychodynamic psychotherapy, but you will be the object of transference. Rather than be surprised, one can be curious about it. If people love you too deeply, what's that about? If people come at you with negative transference, complaining about your having the wrong age, gender, car, haircut, habits, theology, or storming out of meetings, or cutting off from you, that's interesting. Beneath their conscious awareness, they may want to be understood, comforted, admired, stimulated, or forgiven, which would help them complete a piece of their unfinished development. If you and your congregation can moderate your reactivity to their behavior, you both might offer the pastoral and spiritual support needed for that development to proceed.

COUNTERTRANSFERENCE

Along with transference, there are two types of countertransference.[7] With the first type, the minister is seeking to be "understood, comforted, admired, stimulated, and forgiven" by the congregation with which to complete a piece of that minister's development. Working out one's issues with the congregation is human but unethical. The minister does well to monitor this countertransference and to complete one's development elsewhere, such as in one's own therapy.

The second countertransference involves the minister's actions, reactions, thoughts, behaviors, feelings, and fantasies that are evoked by a parishioner's transference. For example, Buster, expecting to be treated with hostility, defends himself with aggression, evoking countertransferential fear in his minister.

An entire congregation could evoke countertransference. A congregation that expects their minister to be partisan might egg that minister into taking sides in their conflicts. A congregation that expects to be rescued becomes dependent and evokes codependence. A depressed congregation evokes helplessness. You could follow a minister who did everything, whom people appreciated for his or her labors, yet resented for doing too much. From you, people could expect the same labor and feel the same resentment. In your countertransference response, you labor mightily yet feel resentment over being resented.

To handle this countertransference successfully, one first discerns what is being evoked. Interesting that I keep feeling afraid of Buster. Interesting that I keep being pulled into taking sides in my congregation's conflicts. It takes discernment to notice what is being evoked. The good news: it is a pattern and will recur. If you miss it the first time, or the tenth, it will happen again; you might catch it then.

After discerning what is being evoked, to change a dysfunctional pattern, one chooses to do something other than what is being evoked—ideally a response based on one's principles, values, and mission. What if other than run away or give in to Buster, I adhered to my mission to support people and responded to him with empathy? What if I held to my value for systemic wholeness and steered a neutral course in my congregation's conflicts? It can seem normal to do what is evoked by transference and recapitulate people's maladaptive patterns, and it takes discipline to respond in an unexpected way, but departing from what is being evoked and adhering to thought-through principles, values, and mission throws a wrench into the gears of Buster's, or the congregation's, unsuccessful patterns of functioning, inviting new patterns.

PROJECTION OF THE SHADOW

People project their shadows.[8] Projection occurs when someone unconsciously recognizes in someone else an aspect of themselves of which they are unconscious, and then relates to that person as if that unconscious material actually applied to that person.

One projects the contents of one's shadow.[9] As noted in Chapter 4, "Working on Yourself," your conscious self consists of all the aspects of yourself of which you are aware. Aspects of yourself of which you are not aware—character flaws, disowned emotions, or other unrecognized personality qualities—reside in your shadow.

As an example of projecting the shadow, if I deny my capacity for violence, it resides in my shadow. I might see myself as kind but, as a projection, see a murderer as violent and wish for them to suffer the death penalty. I do not acknowledge my shadowy capacity for violence, but see that capacity in the violent criminal and then allow violence to befall the criminal. As a more benign projection, a man can project his unconscious femininity onto a woman and launch into writing poetry for her. A woman can project her masculinity onto a man and swoon over him. Off they go into wedded bliss.

Strong emotions accompany projections. The emotions might be passionately positive as one sees in someone else a desirable aspect of oneself—the man writing sonnets, the woman swooning. The emotions might be passionately negative when one sees in someone else a disowned aspect of oneself. A nice person is furious when someone shows them their shadowed hostility.

You could be the target of projections. A parishioner could have strong feelings about you because you exhibit something in that parishioner's shadow. You could make a mistake and show the "perfect" parishioner their own error-prone shadow, who excoriates you. You could accomplish a difficult task and show the self-doubting parishioner something of that parishioner's competence, who is in awe of you. You could take a vacation, which angers the overworking parishioner who would never dream of taking time off.

Entire systems can project shadows. Nazi Germany in the 1930s and 1940s viewed themselves as pure, the Jews as rapacious. Justified by this view, millions of Jews were exterminated, while the "pure" Nazis looted the wealth of Europe. The Nazis did not see their own rapaciousness, but perceived that rapaciousness in other people, and perpetrated violence against those others, while being rapacious themselves.

Closer to home, if members of a congregation have repressed their differences, believing they are one happy family, those differences wait in the shadow. When a conflict of some magnitude forces those differences into the open, strong emotions come along, such as fear of differences, embarrassment about having differences exposed after proclaiming homogeneity, anger that others have the nerve to upset that homogeneity, or anxiety about having to learn to handle differences.

The minister does well to let people's shadows emerge.[10] Attempting to stuff the congregation's issues back into its shadow would kick that explosive material down the road, fueling an even bigger explosion later. Instead, one witnesses heretofore unexpressed thoughts and feelings, welcomes secrets, and validates people's stories. While listening to people's explosive stories, one can still apply covenantal standards, such as "We speak respectfully, and listen openly." The minister can frame the formerly shadowed material as needing to be expressed and understood to help the congregation know itself better and become more whole.

One can try to make the projection process more explicit. I once worked with a conflicting congregation in which the two sides played with projection by declaring their opponents' motives: "He just wants to destroy the church!" I proposed that before anyone pronounced anything about their opponents, they begin with the phrase, "Just like me ..." What surprised me was that they did. Someone might say, "Just like me, he wants to destroy the church." After stating their projections out loud a few times, they eased back on those projections.

EXPECTATIONS AND THE UNCONSCIOUS

Chapter 8, "Conflict," notes that people engage in conflict over unmet expectations. At times these unmet expectations are clear and conscious, other times unconscious. There are three types of unconscious expectations: parental, messianic, and expectations related to love.

Parental

I think everyone has some unfinished emotional business with one's parents. The parents punished, got angry, were scary, were absent when needed; in many ways they failed to understand, comfort, admire, stimulate, and forgive.

As a child, it is difficult to address these failures with one's looming, intimidating parents. When one is adult, one can repress or in other ways sweep parental issues under the rug, leaving such business unfinished. Adults recapitulate unprocessed parental issues in transference relationships, such as with their minister.

As minister, you are a parent figure. Even if you are the youngest person in the church, your role gives you parental authority and power, with the potential for parental beneficence as well as danger.

These parental expectations offer a double-edged sword. On one hand, they help you form a bond with people. Unconsciously wanting the parental understanding, comfort, admiration, stimulation, and forgiveness that could help them develop, they look to you for these supportive transactions and hang on your every word. Roman Catholics acknowledge these parental expectations as they call priests "Father." I exercise my parental role when I welcome people to church on Sundays, express joy in their presence, offer encouragement, or appreciate their effort and improvement.

On the other hand, unconscious parental expectations set the stage for challenging moments for you. You innocently say something that reminds someone of their judgmental parent; they see you as judgmental and react with stormy drama. Or you might be expected to recapitulate one's mean parent and be regarded with wariness. Or someone could harbor unprocessed anger at their own parent and take it out on you. Or you could be different from a parent in some important way, and they could be angry about that. You might not have realized you were strolling through a minefield until you tread on someone's unprocessed tensions with a parent and *KABAM!*

You then have a conflict involving unconscious parental expectations. In this conflict, you will be looking at a parishioner who is a chronologically adult but emotionally a child still hungering for understanding, comfort, admiration, stimulation, and forgiveness.

It helps to be prepared for this inevitable conflict over parental expectations. You can offer empathy and with that the understanding, comfort, admiration, stimulation, and forgiveness they need. You can hope that your empathy will support the completion of a bit of development after which they will see you more as a professional and a human being and less as mom or dad.

Messianic

A congregation that calls you will likely have messianic expectations of you. If nothing else, they expect you to solve the congregation's problems.

These messianic expectations offer another double-edged sword. They form a bond between you and the congregation. For most jobs, people get a desk, some business cards, and a phone. As a pastor, you receive rituals, installation ceremonies, prayers, and vestments, which symbolize the bond between you and your congregation. The bond deepens during the year or so of your honeymoon during which it looks like you could indeed be the messiah. You are wonderful in their eyes—a goddess or a god. With that bond, you will find yourself having more power that you may think you want. Your words are remembered, mistakes well remembered. You are a salvific vehicle. Working well, people are saved. So much rides on you, oh messiah.

Every honeymoon wanes though. It turns out you are human and do not solve all their problems. You probably help with some problems but fail to meet all their unconscious messianic expectations. They feel disenchanted. They have conflicts with you, maybe over trivial issues, but expressing anger over your failing to be the proper messiah. You are being pressured to return to the honeymoon and to live up to their messianic expectations.

You may want to be the messiah. That would assuage all self-doubt. As a non-messiah, one might come away from a meeting or sermon with the self-doubting thought: "Why am I putting people through this?" Or things are going slowly, and one might think, "I am not solving all their problems. I'm not doing enough, or not doing it right." Underneath these concerns lurk one's own unconscious expectation: "I should be the messiah." So one works harder and harder. But unfortunately, one will fail at being the messiah, leaving one with increased self-doubt and guilt.

As the congregation is disenchanted with you, their only so-so savior, and you are wondering why anyone puts up with you, ideally the bond that formed between you and the congregation during the honeymoon is secure enough to bear this buffeting. They saw so much promise in you then, they still want you around. And ideally all the good wishes they expressed during the honeymoon gave you enough self-trust to keep you going. You continue relating to the congregation, moderating your reactivity, respecting their complaints and your limitations. Thusly you both move through this turbulent stage of your relationship.

On the other side of the disenchantment stage, you know each other more realistically. The congregation trusts your humanness. You remain ever so human. And you can still work on solving problems and making things better.

Expectations Related to Love

As with parental and messianic expectations, expectations related to love pose another double-edged sword. On one edge, these expectations cement a bond between the minister and the people. Ministers work with these expectations by offering people asymmetrical care. You give more that you receive; you attend to their emotions and care about their needs, without drawing attention to your own emotions and needs. This asymmetry of care makes you the perfect lover: all-giving, all-loving, all-understanding, and asking for little in return.

Hoping to meet their love expectations, every Sunday in my opening words I am explicit about caring for them: "I offer this service out of my caring for you and my desire to support you on your spiritual journeys. I hope that as you journey you find freedom and love and live the full richness of being alive."

To be cared about feels good. When loved, people feel buoyant and confident. They love others. They engage in spiritual journeys. And they don't earn this love from their minister. It is a gift, which bonds the people to that minister.

Your honeymoon with them deepens that bond. It is a love fest. Enjoying the warm feelings of the honeymoon, people like you and want to keep you around. Within that bonded relationship, they can receive your love and support.

Yet dangers lurk. With you so loving, someone might want to be even closer to you. You're the perfect lover; who wouldn't want that? If a congregation member is smitten by your generous care, and you are smitten back, you might think: "I can be the perfect lover that person wants." Of course, this wish sets up a potential ethical infraction that can run the ship of your ministry onto the rocks. Hopefully, Odysseus-like you steer past these siren temptations.

Even when successfully ethical, and caring generously for the entire congregation, the honeymoon will break down. Indeed, I will fail at being perfectly loving. I will take a day off, say something that hurts, fail to listen as closely as is desired, or be in a hurry. People will respond with disenchantment, hurt, and anger. When people are disappointed, it makes sense to take stock and discern what there is to learn. But people could also be reacting to the unmet unconscious expectation that you would be perfectly loving.

When people are disenchanted and disappointed, it helps again to offer empathy and support. Their unconscious desire for a perfectly loving person is understandable, as is their disappointment with your imperfection.

Ideally, having bonded securely with your congregation during the honeymoon, and as you continue to support them, your ministry will weather the storms of disappointment. You and your congregation will settle into a more realistic relationship in which they appreciate your care, trust you, and understand your human limitations.

CONCLUSION

The unconscious will play a part in your ministry. Brace yourself. When it emerges, emotions will run hot, made urgent by the importance of completing unfinished development, or by the complication of integrating that which had been repressed. Rather than further dividing people from their unconscious, one can validate it, which supports its push for development and helps an individual or a congregation become whole.

QUESTIONS FOR REFLECTION

Consider the people to whom you are strongly repelled by or to whom you are strongly attracted. What might they represent to your unconscious?

Given that your emotional involvement with these people indicates some personal development being called for, what might that development be?

NOTES

1. Matt Ffytche, *The Foundation of the Unconscious: Schelling, Freud, and the Birth of the Modern Psyche* (Cambridge, UK: Cambridge University Press, 2011).

2. Glenn Gabbard, *Psychodynamic Psychotherapy in Clinical Practice* (Arlington, VA: American Psychiatric Publishing, 1990).

3. Ibid.

4. Ibid.

5. Michael Franz Basch, *Doing Psychotherapy* (New York: Basic Books, 1980).

6. Gabbard, *Psychodynamic Psychotherapy.*

7. Basch, *Doing Psychotherapy.*

8. Carl Jung, "Aion: Phenomenology of the Self" in *The Portable Jung*, ed. Joseph Campbell (New York: Penguin, 1951/1971), 139–162.

9. Ibid.

10. Connie Zweig and Steve Wolf, *Romancing the Shadow* (Emeryville, CA: Alibris, 1998).

11

Preaching

As a parish minister, you grasp a bully pulpit from which to teach, inspire, and encourage people. The systems-guided preacher also endeavors to lower the congregation's anxiety, thereby supporting its health by preaching from the thought side of the thought-reflex continuum (see Figure 11.1), which shows the people in the pews that the preacher is safe, which indicates to the people that they, too, are safe.

DEFINE ONESELF

Unfortunately, a sermon can reinforce systemic anxiety by shielding and protecting the preacher. Indeed, even though the preacher stands in full view, talking away, one can hide behind a sermon. People watching their leader for cues about threats can detect the preacher's self-protection, guess there is a threat, and huddle in anxiety around the preacher.

To hide, one can preach from behind a persona. The persona is one's idea of whom one is supposed to be presented to the world,[1] an idea developed in childhood.[2] A child suffering with parental criticism could develop a persona that protects that child from further criticism, such as the earnest and good persona. This good persona, expressed now by the adult preacher is of course blameless and therefore safe, but boring. Emerson complained of such a preacher: "He had no one word intimating that he had laughed or wept, was married or in love, had been commended, or cheated, or chagrined."[3] *Yawn.* The people in the pews see this same self-protective image Sunday after Sunday and wonder where the real preacher is. The real preacher is hidden, suggesting it is not safe to be real and that others should hide behind their per-

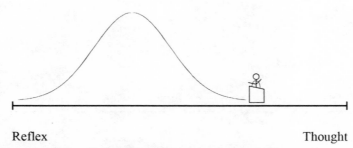

Reflex   Thought

Figure 11.1   Preaching from the thought side of the thought–reflex continuum.

sonas as well. An anxious congregation can exacerbate the preacher's anxiety, causing the preacher to cling further to one's protective persona.

The preacher comes out of hiding by defining oneself. Self-definition suggests that it is safe enough here to be exposed and vulnerable and that therefore everyone is safe. Furthermore, when self-definition consists of a principle or value that has been thought through, rather than raw and reflexive, that shows the preacher to be on the thought side of the thought-reflex continuum, which also calms the system.

One self-definition is your key sermon. I believe each minister has one sermon that can be distilled into one sentence that one preaches over and over again. This is not so bad; people need repetition to learn. Furthermore, to the preacher, their one-sentence sermon means the world. My one-sentence sermon goes: "We belong to a mysterious oneness, from which we draw life and love." I arrived at that sermon through my religious experiences, and so it is sacred to me. In hundreds of forms, with different emphases and shadings, I offer that sermon every time I preach. And as I do, I am defining myself and being vulnerable.

A similar self-definition involves one's testimony. To tell people what has saved you is a reaching in to where you are most alive, or where your deepest brokenness has been healed, and an offer of that brokenness, healing, and spiritual gift to others. One hoped-for effect is that people in the pews see your openness, and trust that they too can be open, and so would open themselves to their spiritual sources and receive salvation.

Another self-definition involves stating your vision for the church. When you offer a vision, you are exposing what you yearn for. Your yearning is a sensitive matter, and to express it is risky and vulnerable. So here I go: "I envision our congregations supporting all of their members on their spiritual journeys."

Another way to be self-defining and vulnerable involves admitting human flaws and foibles. Such acknowledgment models vulnerability, and when people are vulnerable with each other, they know each other well and are close. I suggest not telling painful stories that pull the congregation to rescue you, nor juicy tales that place you at the center stage of gossip. But recounting a foible parishioners can relate to supports systemic safety, while keeping the focus not on the preacher but on the spiritual message of the sermon. So, for example, a preacher recalls:

> I once took a week-long retreat, and I liked everyone there, except Buster. While everyone else was open and spiritually blessing each other with their warmth, he was mopey, such a downer to be around. I felt a glow being around everyone else, but Buster threw a wet blanket on my spiritual glow.
>
> Then I was paired with Buster for a trust walk. I dreaded the exercise. An hour with Buster! *Ugh!* But during the walk he revealed that his wife of thirty years had recently died. He told the story, crying softly the whole time. I could not help but warm to him and hug him when we concluded. I learned from walking with Buster that blessings can come from unexpected sources.

This story expresses a human foible—the quick dislike and the second opinion—making the preacher vulnerable, without immersing the congregation in the sordid details of that preacher's life.

TAKE A STAND

Another form of hiding is to exhort, which pressures other people into action. I hear sermons that exhort: "To work for peace and justice is the right thing. You need to march for peace, write letters for justice." The preacher can further pressure the whole congregation to become something it is not, such as exhorting a sanctuary congregation to become activist. Members of that sanctuary congregation might, over time, find Sunday services to be an ordeal, rather than spiritually supportive.

If the preacher is not called to change or act, the sermon is saying, in effect, "You all go do what I tell you to do, but I am too scared to take that action myself. Instead, I will sit on the sidelines, watch, and judge." Witnessing such self-protective exhortation reinforces the congregation's anxiety.

Pressure also reinforces systemic anxiety by invading, like a toxin, people's heads and tinkering with people choices. A pressured-filled sermon says, "You want what I want you to want, and that is X." My wanting occurs inside my head, which makes it my business. When I hear a sermon telling me what I should want, thereby invading my head, that is threatening. It also suggests, "I know what you should do better than you do," which, unless someone is asking for advice, could spark resistance.

When the preacher makes frequent use of exhortation and pressure, pressure becomes common and accepted as normative in the congregation. As discussed earlier, pressure crowds people's space and results in a less free, more anxious system.

Exhortation extracts these costs with little benefit. Exhortation is the least effective route to change; positive reinforcement and modeling work better. Furthermore, although exhortation seems to be a common sense sermonic intervention for change, it would fall with a thud before a congregation occupying the pre-contemplation stage of change. Telling a congregation of sourpusses to be more loving is wasted breath. When preaching for change to people at the pre-contemplation stage, instead of exhorting, one can speak paradoxically: "I understand that it is difficult to love. Being vulnerable with someone else is risky." Validating the opposite of what you wish to happen could paradoxically allow the listeners to change.

Instead of trying to change people at the pre-contemplation stage, one could also take a stand in a sermon and let the people try to change you. Here is an example of a sermonic stand:

> I believe that using the criminal justice system to eradicate drug use does not work. With every increase in interdiction efforts, has come an increase in drug importation. Our prisons are crowded with drug offenders, their lives and potential contributions, wasted. The costs of the drug war have gone from millions to billions, and the nation's addiction rates have not budged. Therefore, I support decriminalizing all drug use, treating addiction not as a crime, but as an illness, and shifting the interdiction and imprisonment moneys to fund drug treatment on demand.

As a stand, this passage states a clear belief without insisting everyone agree.

Such a stand would probably receive three types of responses. Some people will agree with you. Fine. Some will define themselves in disagreement with you but not push you to change. Fine.

But some will pressure you to change. They are outraged by your temerity, and so forth. As you listen and absorb their pressure without pressuring back, you allow them to occupy stage two of a conflict, while you offer stage three in return. You respond: "I understand you are worried that legalizing drugs would allow more people to become addicted. You want the more robust action of making drug use illegal. Nevertheless, I still hold the opinion I expressed in my sermon." You are listening and reflecting their opposing view without pressuring them to change, while not succumbing to their pressure on you. They watch you at stage three and possibly join you there. If they do, you might hear: "Well, I appreciate your challenging perspective." From stage three you can both go to stage four and share together a cup of coffee. They have changed.

As discussed in Chapter 9, "Difficult Behavior," as you let people try to invade your space to change or silence you, yet you prevent their invasions, and as you do not invade their space in return, they would experience you claiming the space to be yourself, while they retain the space to be themselves. You are yourself, they are who they are, and although holding different views, you are still relating to each other. You both find yourselves in that sweet spot in which they are being who they are with you, while you are being who you are with them. You share autonomy and closeness, freedom and love. Furthermore, the space you offer gives the other person the experience of tolerating a difference and living to tell the tale. For someone who assumes there must be uniform agreement or else, they will have the unnerving but healthy experience of surviving an encounter with someone different from them.

In my experience, you don't have to tee up a controversial sermon. After a honeymoon year, there will probably be something you say or do that will stir things up. There will be pressure on you, which gives you an opportunity to show people how to be themselves, handle a difference, and still be together.

When preaching to people who are contemplating the pros and cons of a change, if the preacher advocates for one side of this question, the people will likely swing to the other and resist the preacher's perspective. To avoid this resistance, the preacher can explore the pros and cons of both sides of a question.[4] "On the one hand, love brings warmth and meaning. On the other, it is risky." Your unpacking the pros and cons of a question supports people's clear thinking on the issue, which supports change.

After reviewing the pros and cons, you can show how you have settled your internal conflict on the issue. For example, here is the beginning of a sermon on peace in which I worked through my ambivalence before arriving at my stance.

Like many red-blooded American boys, I grew up interested in war. I read history books and focused on the battles. I played war with my friends, and any stick could become a gun. I noted on the evening news the Vietnam War body count, with about a hundred American soldiers killed each week, and many hundreds of enemy Vietnamese. It seemed like keeping score, and that we were winning.

As I grew up, my attitude shifted. I recall a conversation with my dad, a veteran of the peacetime Navy, who stated that no war in history had ever been justified. "What about World War II?"

"It could have been prevented."

I had to ponder that for a while, and as I did, war lost its thrill. I began to doubt the wisdom of the Vietnam War. I attended church as a youth and heard its message of peace. I had spiritual moments of closeness with other people, and, caring for others, I did not want anyone to suffer in a war.

Ideally, people in the pews can observe the preacher's progress through the pros and cons of an issue and make such progress themselves.

Unlike preaching to people at the pre-contemplation and contemplation stages of change, addressing people at the preparation, action, and maintenance stages of change follows common sense prescriptions. One can suggest action, coach how to take that action, and reinforce action being taken. Reinforcement supports change by telling people they have succeeded, which makes it safe for them to try again. So for example, the minister who wants to see political action appreciates the political action already occurring in the congregation, as if speaking to them at the maintenance stage, which encourages people to do more of it.

As a caveat about exhortation, when it is not about making people change, but encouraging them to be who they are, or to keep doing the action they are already taking, that can rally people. This exhortation is akin to cheering a runner in a race. The runner's identity is to be a runner, and as she continues running, she is in the maintenance stage of change. Exhortation calls the runner to fulfill her identity and maintain the maintenance, by saying, in effect: "Keep being yourself! Maintain your action!" The runner smiles and gives a thumbs-up as she strides by.

If the congregation is activist, preaching the good news of activism, and rooting them on to further activist activity, fits that congregation, and they might grin, race out the door, and start doing good all around the neighborhood. Mindful of this constructive exhortation, I exhort you to be the preacher you most want to be. As you type your manuscript and grasp your pulpit, I am cheering: "Preach your most vital truth! Tell it to the people!"

FACE UNKNOWNS

Another way a preacher could increase systemic anxiety is by claiming to be right. Granted, it is gratifying to be right and to know. I suppose that sermons asserting righteousness emerge from the priestly tradition in which the priest stood a few rungs up the cosmic hierarchy closer to God from which that preacher could presume to speak for God and tell the people a few rungs below, right vs. wrong.

Nevertheless, problems accompany being right. Claiming to be right in a sermon creates a moral hierarchy in which the preacher stands in a superior, dominant position. The survival-of-the-fittest implication that accompanies any hierarchy poses for listeners a threat, which increases their anxiety. Furthermore, one is not close to people up or down the rungs of a hierarchy. Indeed, one can be right or be close. Finally, being right sets one up for a fall. With right vs. wrong pronouncements being flung about, the minister could someday wind up on the wrong side of some line. Indeed, over time the dominant, right position can feel tenuous, accompanied by wariness of the underlings and the need to keep them down. Kept down, they might gather steam for a revolution.

To avoid right vs. wrong language, I might make emphatic statements but as my subjective preference: "I prefer peace to war."

Furthermore, to avoid being right, one embraces mystery. One might begin writing a sermon knowing what one will say and hit a point of confusion and realize: "I thought I knew what I knew, but I don't anymore." One enters the mystery, gropes around, and eventually encounters something unexpected but surprisingly true and finishes the sermon. The choreographer, Agnes DeMille, describes this vulnerable process in kinesthetic language: "One leaps in the dark."[5] Similarly, a village shaman would enter the wilderness for days, fasting, praying, and encountering ultimate mystery, and then return to the village with an important message. The shaman leaps into the dark, lands somewhere, and reports to the village what one has discovered. One may not be a shaman, but going into the mystery while writing a sermon weaves vulnerability into its message. Conversely the rote, known sermon, is not so vulnerable.

Guiding this leap, DeMille adds, "There is one clue: what moves one is theirs. What amuses or frightens or pleases one becomes by virtue of one's emotional participation a part of one's personality and history."[6] An idea, a story, or an experience that carries an emotional jolt, disrupts, shakes the ground under one's feet, and catches one's breath hints at ultimate mystery and therefore is grist for a sermon. That grist milled into a sermon expresses something powerfully and vulnerably true for the preacher, while the exploration of a mystery in the process of creating the sermon keeps the sermon humble and avoid pretentious righteousness.

Just as I do not want to speak in dominant role, I also want to avoid the subordinate. The subordinate voice complains and flings up its hands in despair in the face of the powers that be, which reinforces hopelessness. Instead, I would explore possibilities and express hope.

THE SYSTEM IS A WHOLE

Right vs. wrong language divides a system, which increases the its anxiety. Furthermore, if right vs. wrong, divisive language becomes normal in your congregation, then people would join you in widening differences, escalating tensions, and polarizing. The congregation could then approach any differences in terms of right vs. wrong and take adamant, uncompromising positions on matters such as how to repair the roof.

A healthy, secure system is a whole. Instead of dividing the system with right vs. wrong language, one can articulate the wholeness of that system, while still respecting its distinct elements. To avoid polarizing the system, I suggest accepting that system's polarities, not as moral opposites but as complementary. The yin-yang symbol is an image of a complementary polarity. One half is flowing into the next, and the second is flowing into the first. Each side has a little of the other. The whole contains and needs both polarities. On this note, Ken Burns speaking on the origins of jazz saw it as a confluence of sacred gospel music and secular blues.[7] The two opposites interacting, he observed, created jazz, something beautiful.

To support further congregational wholeness, I try to define the bond that caused everyone present to vote with their feet and enter this church building on this Sunday, that bond being the congregation's identity. Therefore, every Sunday I define our identity by saying, "As I see it, we are a support community for people on various journeys toward ultimate goals, such as love, or peace, or union."

I hope this identity statement, heard many times, sinks in and orients people to the larger purpose of our religious enterprise. When that purpose is clear, the church enterprise has meaning. I Indeed, the minister's job is to articulate the larger matters of identity, mission, and vision, thereby giving meaning to church life.

Another way to preach on behalf of the whole congregation involves describing an aspect of its identity, such as its history. Revealing its history has the effect of showing the congregation its collective journey, which can give the people confidence as they journey further. It is also a way of appreciating and applauding the members—a loving recounting of the founders and of those who have kept the faith.

If they are stuck and confused, revealing to the congregation their previous times of struggle can convey the message: "We have handled challenges before." Recounting previous challenges can place the current challenge in the context of the long view, which can lift them out of the weeds of their current predicament.

Telling the history also counters the impulse to hide. Anxiety feeds secrets and cabals, as people protect themselves and hide. Secrets form triangles in which insiders know, and outsiders do not. As long as the secret is a secret, those insiders remain inside and the outsiders out. Such rigid insider/outsider positioning is unhealthy. The preacher can collude with that impulse to hide by hiding historical information. But telling the history exposes secrets. Transparency unlocks the triangle and lets everyone be in the know. Telling the history also welcomes visitors in. It suggests that everyone is welcome to be an insider.

THERE MAY BE WHOLENESS, BUT DON'T FORGET FREEDOM

A preacher may at times speak for everyone by stating that we all experience the same thing. Lines like: "We hear about the famine in _____, and we feel sad and helpless about the suffering of others. We see the photos of emaciated children, and we weep."

Very touching, but this supposed unity of emotion carries problems. Lumped together with everyone, I have less freedom. The preacher might suppose that we all would appreciate the unity that accompanies thinking and feeling the same thing, but I still like to have my own thoughts and feelings. Secondly, lumped together into a mush, I have less of a self and cannot relate as a whole autonomous person to other distinct selves. I want to have my distinct self and to contact other distinct selves. It also appears that the preacher cannot manage the anxiety that comes with differences, so he or she is proposing no differences. Finally, the preacher is announcing my thoughts and feelings, which are in my head. That preacher has not asked me and does not know what I think or feel. I protect my head from the preacher's invasions by resisting the message of the sermon.

On the other hand, I know that the content, concern for others' suffering, is morally blameless. I experience a conflict between wanting to resist the sermon and wanting to agree with its morally blameless content. I sit in worship resisting, but feeling guilty about my resistance, all in a tangle rather than opening to the spirit.

Systems theory helps by reminding preachers that the system is a whole but, like a salad, contains distinct elements. Just as one would not run a salad in a blender, making it mush, one would not mush together the distinct personalities that together form the congregational system. Expressed differently, the healthy system balances wholeness and love, with freedom and individuality. Your sermons can contribute to this balancing by speaking for the system's wholeness, while still respecting the autonomy of the system's members and leaving individuals free to think for themselves.

To avoid running the congregation through a sermonic blender, I am careful with "we." I use "we" when I know it is true: "We are human beings." Or I temper the generalization: "*As I see it*, we are a support community ...." Or I offer evidence for my inclusive language: "Having spoken to many of you, I have gathered the consensus that we are a support community ...." Or I would temper it with "I imagine many people might feel _____." Or I can state how I feel: "I see hungry children, and I feel helpless." If this expresses how others feel, fine. They can also have a different experience. Or I'd simply report on the situation and let people feel what they will.

SPEAKING THOUGHTFULLY BY BEING SERIOUS

Ideally, one says it straight. One speaks truth with the seriousness that truth deserves. That vulnerable expression of truth can trigger the preacher's anxiety. What if others reject my truth? What if they reject me? Anxious about possible rejection, one could then speak one's truth but make a little dismissive joke or gesture about it that implies, "Oh, ha ha, never mind." One would then be preemptively dismissing one's message so that if others dismissed it, no surprise: it has already been dismissed. That preemptive dismissal protects the preacher, and if protection is called for, there must be a threat somewhere. Furthermore, if you say something important and follow it with a joke, people will hear the important message, then the message being undermined, and not know whether to take the message seriously or not.

The full-throated utterance of one's truth reminds me of this passage from Marianne Williamson:

> Our deepest fear is not that we are inadequate. Our deepest fear is that we are powerful beyond measure. It is our light, not our darkness that most frightens us. We ask ourselves, Who am I to be brilliant, gorgeous, talented, fabulous? Actually, who are you not to be? You are a child of God. Your playing small does not serve the world. There is nothing enlightened about shrinking so that other people won't feel insecure around you. We are all meant to shine, as children do. We were born to make manifest the glory of God that is within us. It's not just in some of us; it's in everyone. And as we let our own light shine, we unconsciously give other people permission to do the same. As we are liberated from our own fear, our presence automatically liberates others.[8]

Furthermore, speaking one's vulnerable truth with the seriousness of that truth shows safety. When the speaker demonstrates his or her safety, that invites others into safety where they can speak their truth.

SPEAKING THOUGHTFULLY BY BEING PLAYFUL

On the other hand, uniform seriousness can be evoked by, and then reinforce, systemic anxiety. Instead, being playful in a sermon can jog things out of serious, earnest ruts. As you speak from a playful vantage, that suggests that you are on the thought side of the reflex vs. thought continuum where your mammal brain is working, and people can join you there.

To become playful, it helps to give people have responsibility for themselves. If I am responsible for their salvation, weighed down by the profundity of my role, I'll get serious. On the other hand, if the people's spiritual sources provide them salvation, and if I am just a witness and guide, I can be lighter.

It also helps to take myself lightly. I am not the be-all-to-end-all. I may have important things to say as I witness and guide them, but in the end, it is not about me. It is about their spiritual journeys.

I am also not their servant, which would require me to be earnestly pleasing. Instead, I am an equal and a co-journeyer.

Journeying itself invites humor. That humor comes from the liminality of a journey. The word "liminality" originates in the Latin word *līmen*, meaning "a threshold."[9] Crossing a threshold, leaving the familiar walls and roof, journeying into the unknown, one experiences this liminal state and its unknowns, ambiguity, and openness. The unknowns of role and landscape bring anxiety, but people sometimes transcend that anxiety and find freedom and playfulness. For instance, pilgrims in Chaucer's *Canterbury Tales* told each other humorous stories.[10] On the spiritual journey, you might find your own transcendent lightness and tell your congregation: "I don't know where we are going or how we will get there, but here we go!"

DIRECT AND INDIRECT EFFECTS

A sermon has direct and indirect effects on people. Preaching a sermon is like tossing a manuscript into a hurricane, not knowing where its pages will go. Directly I might convey an insight or comfort people. Indirectly, and without intending to, I might influence someone's career change.

Preachers can assume that others are taking in the information one offers and are responding directly and objectively to what is being conveyed. No. People are not computers taking in data. Your sermonic words are more like a Rorschach, which people will filter and interpret subjectively. But you think maybe you can say it so clearly that everyone comes away with the thoughts you want them to have. This effort requires a lot of control, and applying control gives evidence of anxiety. And it won't work anyway.

Sometimes people hear something in the ballpark of what you had intended, but try as you might, sometimes you say X and people hear Y. Weeks after preaching a sermon, someone will tell you how important that sermon had been to them, and they will state what they heard you say, and sometimes they understood your message, but other times they heard something else, or they picked up one small point and ran with it, because that point moved them. When that happens to me, I just nod and appreciate that they found something in that sermon, despite that discovery being miles from what I intended.

Expecting subjectivity and direct and indirect effects when I preach, I lay out symbols and images that are powerful to me. If they move me, I surmise they will resonate with others, although I do not try to manage or manipulate what that resonance will be. For example, here is a powerful symbolic image: "Jesus wept" (John 11:35, KJV). When people hear that, they have many responses: think about their own pain; wonder how God can weep; feel comforted; feel sad. Conveying an image that moves me, I hope the listener is also moved and accept that how they are moved is particular to them and outside my control.

INDIRECT EFFECTS: MAKE UP STORIES

Stories express imagination, which emerges from the thought side of the thought-reflex continuum. Imagination offers a playful antidote to earnest absorption with facts. Such oh-so serious attention to facts might be expressing the lizard brain at work in a state of anxiety. On the other hand, the storytelling preacher implies it is safe enough to imagine, which invites everyone into safety. (Knowing people expect sermons to be factual, it would be ethical to preface fiction with: "All of the stories I tell are true, although they may not adhere scrupulously to actual facts.")

According to the novelist, Francine Prose, good storytelling incorporates three elements: something has to happen, often a life turnaround; a little magic occurs; and the characters evoke compassion.[11] The story of a sympathetic character experiencing a magical change along the lines of "I once was lost, but now am found"[12] would fit her model.

Stories can range in content. In Chapter 3, I outlined the four stories: union, tragedy, the journey, and the empirical.[13] You might gravitate toward one or two of these themes. Despite that gravitation, covering all four themes over time might give your stories a sense of completeness.

Not overtly being about them, the story is indirect, and yet people gain insight with indirect interventions rather than direct pressure. The story says: "Oh, this is not about you ..." but in a subtle way it is, and its images and events can work their way into people's imaginations through a backdoor they did not realize they left open. For example, hearing the story of the prodigal son, people might wonder how they are like the young son, the older brother, or the father.

LET'S DO SOMETHING

Many sermons are about something, but a sermon can also do something. Indeed, systems theory looks at process — what people are doing as they say what they are saying. A sermon can do something when it transcends being about something. So instead of a sermon about love, a sermon that narrates someone's struggles and humanity would evoke love. A sermon can talk about the spiritual journey or take a spiritual journey by exploring a mystery. A sermon can be about God or be from God. Inspired by the Walt Whitman line: "I find letters from God dropt in the street ...."[14] what would a letter from God say?

MODEL THE PROBLEM-SOLVING PROCESS

A sermon can show people how to solve problems by following the problem-solving process. The problem-solving process begins by naming the problem in a way all can agree. Addressing the problem of war, I guess that people would agree: "Wars hurt people." Wars and their painful effects can be further explored. The sermon can brainstorm a bunch of ideas, some plausible, some implausible, regarding what to do about war. "Solve transnational problems through the problem-solving process," sounds plausible. The less plausible, "Decorate the Pentagon with doves and hearts," could also be included. After some brainstorming, select your favorites. State why. "I like the idea of addressing transnational problems through the problem-solving process, because it has a good chance of actually solving problems." The next stage of the problem-solving process, implementation, is difficult to get up and do in the middle of a sermon. But you can discuss where and how the implementation of your ideas could happen. You can add the final step of the problem-solving process, evaluation, as you comment on how your idea is already succeeding in the world.

As you walk through the problem-solving process in a sermon, you show how it is done, which supports its internalization by the congregation. Pretty soon everyone will be using the problem-solving process.

FOR EXAMPLE ...

To demonstrate what I try to do when I lead worship, here are my standard opening words *(with annotations).*

(Every Sunday the first words I offer give a verbal cue that worship is beginning:)

Good morning. May peace be in your hearts. Through the energy of freedom and the warmth of love, may you live the fullness of being alive, and in that fullness, find peace. Through justice and understanding may humanity be at peace. And may all of life on earth live together in balance and peace.

(I also hope invoking peace calms people.)

It is good to be with you all this morning. I am honored to be visiting a congregation served by my colleague, the Rev. Smith. And I want to thank John Doe for sharing the service with me this Sunday.

(I am usually a guest, and I like to appreciate my hosts.)

I would like to welcome anyone who might be visiting this morning. I think it takes some courage to enter the doors of an unfamiliar *(I don't say "strange")* congregation, so I extend my welcome and applaud your courage.

(With this welcome, I hope to affirm the visitors and cue the congregation that their guests have done a difficult thing just to appear in their church. I hope this appreciation of the visitors encourages the members to speak to these risk-takers at coffee hour.)

To introduce this congregation to our visitors, I presume that like other congregations in our denomination, this is a support community for people on various journeys toward ultimate goals, such as truth, or peace, or love.

(Here I articulate our identity for both visitors and members. I want the visitors to understand what they have found—maybe it is attractive. And I want the members to be clear what they are here for: to support each other, to journey, and to seek something ultimate.

As I define the religious tradition, I am speaking vulnerably and am exposing us all. That we can all be exposed implies that we are okay and safe.

I also believe it is healthy for a community, as it is for an individual, to know its identity, and that as people hear their identity defined, they can hold it with greater clarity.

I have named "support" and the thing we do, which increases the odds that support becomes the normative standard for people's behavior.

"Various journeys" suggests we each are free to take our own journey. My spiritual journey might be contemplative, and others' activist. No one is pressed into someone else's journey.

The "ultimate goals" phrase enlarges the scope of our mutual endeavor. We are journeying toward something grand and meaningful. Petty agendas pale in comparison. Furthermore, our ultimate goals distinguish us from a secular community.

Each Sunday I offer three ultimate goals, drawing from truth, peace, love, transcendence, meaning, oneness, union, holiness, wholeness, the sacred, or liberation. You might have your own ultimate goals based on your tradition and theology.

Now that I have named our ultimate goals, I continue ...)

One of the ways we support each other is by ... (and I pick from a list of how we support each other)

understanding the journey quality of life
seeing our relatedness

appreciating connections
inviting the Holy Spirit
add your own

(Then I tie this method of support to our history, traditions, and/or theology.)

One of the ways we support each other is by inviting spiritual support. In our history, we have long invited the spirit through prayer in the belief that prayers will be heard and answered. Today we still pray, offering our deepest yearning to God.

(Then I tie this tradition of support to the sermon of the day.)

And that's what today's service is about: how prayer invites spiritual support. I offer this service out of my caring for you and my desire to support you on your journeys. I hope that as you journey you find freedom and love and live the full richness of being alive.

(I offer my caring, because I do care about them; this caring motivates my calling to the ministry and my interest in worshiping with them. Saying that I care also defines me and thus makes me a little vulnerable.

Knowing that they are cared about, I hope, supports people in feeling safe and being vulnerable themselves. As its members feel vulnerable but secure, the system leans on the thought side of the thought-reflex continuum, which is healthy for the system and everyone in it. Furthermore, when safe, they can open to their spiritual sources and welcome the spirit.

I also express my hope that their journey not be an endless slog through the wilderness, but arrive somewhere: freedom, love, and the richness of being alive.

I deliver these opening words from memory and out in front of the pulpit as another form of vulnerability. By being so exposed, I want to convey to people that I am safely held in spiritual hands, which means they too can find safety in the spirit.

These are also my words. I don't hide behind someone else's words, no matter how eloquent. As such I am, again, defining myself and speaking vulnerably.

Generally, I like to introduce the service with what we are here to do and why in the context of what it means to be a religious community. Seeing its point and purpose I hope makes the worship service more meaningful.)

CONCLUSION

There is more to preaching than meets the ear. Indeed, preaching to a congregational system from a secure pulpit shows people that they too can join the preacher in security.

QUESTIONS FOR REFLECTION

Considering the last sermon you heard, how was it protective of the preacher? How was it disclosive, making the preacher vulnerable?

Considering your sermons, how do they express caring or support for your congregation?

NOTES

1. Carl Jung, "Psychological Types" in *The Portable Jung* ed. Joseph Campbell (New York: Penguin, 1951/1971), 178–270.

2. Edward Whitmont, *The Symbolic Quest* (New York: Harper & Row 1969).

3. Ralph Waldo Emerson, "The Divinity School Address" in *Ralph Waldo Emerson: Selected Prose and Poetry,* 2nd Edition, ed. Reginald Cook (New York: Holt, Rinehart, and Winston, Inc. 1838/1969), 56–71.

4. William Miller and Steven Rollnick, *Motivational Interviewing* (New York: Guilford, 2002).

5. Agnes de Mille, *Leaps in the Dark,* ed. Mindy Aloff (Gainesville, FL: University Press of Florida, 2011).

6. Ibid.

7. Geoffrey Ward and Ken Burns, *Jazz: A History of America's Music* (New York: Knopf, 2000).

8. Marianne Williamson, *A Return to Love: Reflections on the Principles of "A Course in Miracles"* (New York: Harper Collins, 1992).

9. *Oxford English Dictionary,* 3rd Edition, s.v. "liminal."

10. Geoffrey Chaucer and Nevill Coghill, *Canterbury Tales* (London: Penguin Books, 1951).

11. Francine Prose, "How to Tell a Story" (lecture, Bread Loaf Writers' Conference, Ripton, VT, August 1987).

12. John Newton, "Amazing Grace" Music: Virginia Harmony, 1831, harmony by Austin Cole Lovelace (1772).

13. Jackson Carroll and Carl Dudley, *Handbook for Congregational Studies* (Nashville: Abingdon Press 1986).

14. Walt Whitman, "Song of Myself" in *Walt Whitman: Complete Poetry and Collected Prose* (New York: The Library of America 1855/1982).

12

The Spirit

In the spirit's, in God's, embrace, people are loved, supported, and safe. As Rebecca Parker puts it: "There is a love holding me. There is a love holding you. There is a love holding all. I rest in this love."[1] I believe we all rest in this love. When serving others depletes us, the spirit refills us. When straining to fulfill the incessant tasks of ministry, in the spirit's hands we rest. When buffeted by the emotional dramas of ministry, the spirit offers unconditional love and thus security. Security trends us to the thought side of the thought-reflex continuum. Guided by thought, rather than reflex, we effectively lead and heal our congregations.

We receive spirit without our effort, and it fills and sustains us. Effortless and sustaining, spirit is like our breath. The word "spirit" comes from the Latin, *spiritus*, meaning breath.[2] We receive breath, usually without our conscious effort, and it fills and sustains us. When filled with breath, our need for oxygen met, our bodies relax. When filled with spirit, our spiritual needs met, our souls relax.

Spirit meets our need for vitality by being a life force, an energy that keeps us alive and dynamic. It is a fire that glows deep within, a voice that says yes to being alive.

Spirit supports our need for belonging by being about oneness. In spirit, all is one. Spirit sees wholeness and oneness, not separations or divisions. Spirit lives in connections with the divine, with nature, with our inner life, with each other, and with all that is. Included in this oneness, we belong.

Spirit supports our need for love by, again, being about oneness. Spirit reminds me I am connected to the person facing me and to everyone.

Spirit supports our need for clarity by being a source of wisdom. Insight arrives, courtesy of the spirit.

Spirit supports our need for meaning by calling us to devote our lives to valued concerns that transcend our selves, such as other people, our congregations, or the holy.

In a spiritual experience, we receive from an infinite source. It is a well that does not run dry.

WILL AND SPIRIT

The spirit is complemented by one's personal will. Spirit is the source of life's raw materials; will chooses what to make of them.[3] Spirit is like a muddy spot on a hillside where water has welled up before it is channeled into a stream. So life's raw materials well up from a spiritual source. Our will directs them or channels them into actions. Spirit involves receiving; will involves volition, action, and control.

Unfortunately, people have trouble trusting the spirit, it being mysterious and out of our control. It defies common sense to depend on something one cannot control, to relax and float on the infinite ocean. Instead, people emphasize what they know, control, and easily trust: the will. And it sounds so mighty to have a powerful will. "I am the master of my fate. I am the captain of my soul."[4] Therefore, if I can just learn enough, do enough, work hard enough, be perfect enough, I can earn peace.

That application of will can work for a while, but without opening to the spirit, people strain. It would be like running a marathon while breathing through a straw. One can do it; the spirit gives something, but one struggles. Even when one emphasizes will, the spirit quietly nourishes. Indeed, the "master of my fate," "captain of my soul" poet first thanks the gods for his unconquerable soul.

Nevertheless, the will likes to be in charge. It says, "Let me handle your spiritual life. I know how to manage grace." But spiritual experience is received, not managed. To trust the spirit and relax the will it helps to take a spiritual quest during which one experiences the spirit's grace.

THE SPIRITUAL JOURNEY

A spiritual journey can take a lifetime; it can take a minute.[5] As a newly minted minister, I took a spiritual journey one day at a ministers' meeting. During a discussion of our meeting format, I sat quiet, afraid, really, of my older, seemingly wiser colleagues. I wondered: "What am I afraid of?" Looking at the mostly men of the group at that time, I thought of my father. I had admired my dad. He was funny; everyone liked him. He was the most important person in my life, so I wanted him to like me.

But once in a while as a kid, when I expressed a feeling he didn't like, he would crush it. If I was angry and tried to explain it, he'd say, "You're just rationalizing." Though I didn't know what rationalizing was, he didn't like it, so I didn't want to do it. If I was sad, he'd say, "You're just feeling sorry for yourself." Afraid of being a bad son, and of him not liking me, I developed a persona of emotional control around my father.

My experience is common. A child learns what one's parents can handle and to be the person one's parents want one to be. When parents can't handle a daughter's power and anger, she accommodates. When parents deny a son's sensitivity, he becomes stoic. As a child presents that palatable image, the parents love and support that child, ensuring the child's survival. That's the child's contract with parents: I present what you can handle; you ensure my survival.

The child's coping strategies coalesce into a self-image or persona—one's conclusions regarding who to be, how to behave, and how to relate to others.[6] I then cling to my persona. I can presume that this self-image is my self, making it my only option for how to be in the world. Furthermore, my self-image helped me survive childhood, making it valuable.

But as I present a palatable persona to the world, that does not let others know the real me and leaves me lonely. Furthermore, I can be so invested in my self-image that I do not know my own inner reality. And maintaining a divide between my facade and my real self causes anxiety. Finally, having to relate to someone else's persona grows boring.

When people want to relax on the spiritual ocean and trust enough to be real with others, they embark on a spiritual journey, as I did at that ministers' meeting. I realized, I'm sitting in a room full of fathers and am still being the cautious, "good" son, afraid of losing my father's love. But a still, small voice inside me asked: What would I do if this fear did not stop me? Father figures all around me, what do I want to do? I felt then trust, and with it, courage, and did something I'd never done at a ministers' meeting. I spoke up and proposed a format for our meetings. I offered a motion. That was a spiritual journey.

The journey begins when the hero realizes something needs to be faced. I had to face my lingering and unnecessary fear of my father's judgment. In another example, Prince Siddhartha, who had been sheltered from all pain by his father, happens upon an old man, then a diseased man, then a corpse, and then a monk. These encounters unsettle him, and he realizes something needs to be faced: suffering, death, and the "something more" to life. One night he slips away from the palace to begin his journey in the course of which he becomes the Buddha.[7]

There is a fascination with this something-to-be-faced.[8] Though fearsome, deep inside the hero it seems attractive, like a mountain that calls you to climb, at some risk to yourself, but that stands like the home of secrets or a portal to power. Maybe on this mountain Yahweh will speak to you from a burning bush and tell you to remove your shoes because you stand on sacred ground and then give you a glimpse of ultimate truth (Exodus 3:5, RSV).

On the journey, the self-image will have to die. Indeed, spiritual change involves death and rebirth, in contrast to will-directed change that involves choosing new ways to think and behave. Facing its end, the self-image can stop the journey by insisting it is needed and is the only way one can be.[9]

When the hero ignores his or her self-image and embarks on the journey anyway, he or she is given aid from a protective figure. The helpful crone, a teacher, a minister—such figures give the hero amulets, sayings, potions, hints that reassure and promise success. Theseus is given a thread to spool out as he explores the labyrinth and then to follow back to its entrance. Perseus is given a mirror through which to look at Medusa.[10]

Amulets in hand, the hero faces the threshold into the unknown. Guarding the threshold stand pairs of opposites: life and death, good and evil, beauty and ugliness. As a boy, I faced the opposites of good son vs. bad son.

As the hero faces these paradoxes, the self-image again resists.[11] It might suggest: "Choose one side, and make it something others will like." But as long as I was choosing to be the cautious son, I was not crossing a threshold into the unknown of who I am.

Not holding to one opposite or the other, the hero journeys through them into the unknown. In my case, I pushed through my good-son–bad-son opposites, in search of myself.

Having passed the threshold, the hero finds a strange landscape populated with ogres and dragons, violence and seduction. Odysseus encounters the violent Cyclops and seductive Sirens.[12] In effect, one is struggling with the less laudable aspects of oneself, one's inner ogres, in the arduous development of self-awareness.[13]

Despite even successful struggling, the hero does not conquer this unknown world but is swallowed by it. Jonah is swallowed by the whale (Jonah 1:17, RSV). Persephone is captive in the underworld.[14] Jesus is entombed (Matthew 27:57–61, RSV). Although Odysseus escapes the Cyclops and evades the Sirens, he remains swallowed, wandering through mysterious seas for twenty years.[15]

So swallowed, the hero appears to have died. Jonah's shipmates give him up as lost. With Persephone in the underworld, winter grips the earth. Jesus is mourned. Suitors line up to marry Penelope. My cautious-son self-image dies. People feel lost, yet as Robert Frost says, you become "lost enough to find yourself."[16]

When the good son in me has died, ministers, father figures surround me. In mythology, these are gods who offer both life and danger.[17] One father, Yahweh, permits calamity and death to befall Job, and when Job confronts Yahweh about this, Yahweh answers, but not with an explanation. From a whirlwind, this father declares, "Gird up thy loins now like a man; Hast thou an arm like God? Canst thou thunder with a voice like him?... Where wast thou when I laid the foundations of the earth?" (Job 40:6–7, 38:4, KJV).

Though Job's God makes no attempt to vindicate himself, still Job is satisfied. He says, "Now my eye sees thee; and therefore I ... repent in dust and ashes" (Job 42:6, KJV). Job's repentance is not logical: he has done nothing wrong, but the self-image and its logic have died. Now self-image-less, Job glimpses the entire span of the universe from God's eye view, which satisfies his soul. He can now trust the spirit, symbolized by Yahweh, who then rewards Job with a new house and family and 140 more years of life (Job 42: 10–17, KJV).

On some journeys the hero confronts not a father but a mother, portrayed in myth as the Queen Goddess of the World.[18] Like the father, she too is ambivalent. She represents the promise of perfection and the threat of destruction. One Hindu portrait of this cosmic mother gives her four arms, one with the "fear not" gesture, another bestowing gifts, another brandishing a bloody saber, and the fourth holding a severed head.

Facing these mother-goddesses and father-gods the successful hero reviews one's experience of one's parents, this time from God's-eye view. Viewing one's childhood from this cosmic perspective, the hero transcends nursery disappointments and childhood dramas. Furthermore, alongside this perspective comes the receiving of the spirit's support.

This spiritual support allows the hero to let die self-protective ideas of who one is, developed and relied upon in childhood, and supports the birth of, or initiation into, adulthood. In my case, hearing the still, small voice of spiritual support encouraged me to move from being the cautiously "good" son to assume my adult identity.

At the journey's end, the hero or heroine returns home with the life-giving message that the spirit offers infinite support. In my case, I offered a suggestion for our meetings. I realize, with my motion I may not have bestowed a life-giving elixir upon my colleagues, but I did give them more evidence of being spiritually supported than I would have by sitting quiet and afraid.

In mythology, the hero's return from the journey restores the world. As one fairy tale concludes: a prince, looking for a princess, enters a castle that has been under a spell and sleeping for one hundred years. Everyone is asleep, seemingly dead. Searching the castle, he finds the princess also asleep. At last, there she is: the end of the journey. He marvels at her beauty, leans over, and kisses her.

She opens her eyes, awakes, and looks at him fondly. Together they come down the stairs, and the king wakes and the queen, and the entire courtly estate; and all look at each other with big eyes. And the horses in the court stand up and shake themselves; the hunting dogs jump and wag their tails; the pigeons on the roof draw their heads out from under their wings, look around, and fly across the field; the flies on the wall walk again; the fire in the kitchen brightens, flickers, and cooks the dinner; the roast begins to sizzle; the cook gives the scullery boy a box in the ear that makes him yell; and the maid finishes plucking the chicken.[19]

Jesus lives. Persephone emerges from the underworld, and spring blooms. Odysseus returns to Ithaca. The Buddha teaches a way to enlightenment. I offer a motion. The hero, having journeyed through his or her personal terror, having died and been reborn, surpasses fear. Good and bad, life and death, divine and human, it is all one. The hero floats on a sea of Being, alive and aware. Therefore, on the journey the hero finds spiritual support which engenders trust in the spirit's infinite buoyancy.

As a corollary result of the journey, the hero moves past fearing what is and needing the application of will to control it. Indeed, at the ministers' meeting at first I feared rejection and managed my presentation of myself to prevent that rejection. But on my little journey, I faced that fear, found something spiritual I could trust, and emerged with less need to be afraid and to control. I freed my voice, spoke, and let what would happen happen. My colleagues heard my proposal and turned it right down, but that didn't matter. Having been buoyed up by the infinite ocean of spirit, I could relax control, speak my truth, and accept whatever followed.

ACCEPTANCE AND ACTION

Acceptance has little effect on pain but does ease suffering. I define pain as the inevitable blows life delivers, and suffering as one's attempts to avoid pain, or to hold the pain at bay, and the pain grabbing you anyway. Suffering involves the fear of pain, anxious attempts to run away from it, the pain itself, and the chagrin that follows one's failed attempts to escape pain. The Buddhist contemplative Shantideva summed it up: "Those seeking to escape from suffering hasten right toward their own misery."[20]

Adding to one's suffering is one's dependence on others to make it better. When a child wants something to be different, he or she, having little personal agency, cries and so insists someone else do something, like provide nourishment or change one's diaper. Adults can still express a child's demand that someone else ease one's suffering. Yet having little control over others, one can demand and demand with little effect, the futility of one's efforts compounding one's suffering.

The spiritual journey supports one in being with what is, rather than insisting on what is not. When one encounters god or goddess on the journey, one learns that there is something infinite, which transcends the unsatisfactory present, and which offers infinite support, which heals the heart and satisfies the soul. So okay, my parents were imperfect and, okay, the present is not perfect, but I can say "yes" to what is because, like Job, I glimpse it all from a god-like vantage.

Paradoxically, the hero who accepts what is becomes a change agent. That change agent acts not with the child's flailing pressure on others, but with the adult's agency over oneself. At the ministers' meeting, I did not sit and look glum and wait for them to ask me what I wanted. I gained agency over myself and voiced a proposal.

As I act, and as I belong to the system, my action changes the system. I made a personal change to go from quiet and afraid to speaking up and making a motion. I changed, and that changed my ministers' group ... slightly. The group went from one that could overlook me as if I were not even there, to one that had to reckon with my presence and preference and then decline my proposal. A victory! The spiritual journey replaced a self-image that feared being rejected and could only wait for others to change things, with a self that no longer feared rejection and could take its own action on behalf of change.

When behavior goes from being benignly difficult, as at my ministers' meeting, to overtly difficult, as when people are being hostile, that hostility can threaten an insecure self-image. If difficult behavior attacks one's self-image, and if one believes that self-image is all one is, attacks upon it will feel quite threatening. But the journey also shows me that I am more than my self-image. I am linked to the infinite and to God, from whom I draw sustenance and support. In the midst of difficult behavior, I can relax, knowing I am larger than my self-image; I am united with all that is and am supported by God.

The acceptance of what is, is also known as mindfulness.[21] Mindfulness recommends being aware of a sensation, such as pain, with less liking and disliking, less judging, less labeling, and instead opening to what is, and treating it as information. That awareness prevents one from escalating from a sensation, to a judgment of the sensation, to aversion, to tension. Simple awareness of what is moderates reactivity.

Awareness does not mean doing nothing about pain, but it does mean slowing the rush to relieve it, which allows one to learn from it. Pain gives diagnostic information about what is, which can guide ministers into their own healing action. For example, a minister found her congregation to be unfriendly and cold, resisting change and distrusting her leadership. After two years of service, she felt angry, discouraged, and ready to resign. But she stepped back from her judgments and noticed a sensation: a knot in her stomach whenever she was going to church. She observed this sensation, not to judge it as good or bad, nor to change it, but as information. Remembering the reflex-thought continuum, she interpreted the sensation as her digestive system responding to threat by shutting down. She inferred that if she felt threatened at church, maybe everyone at church felt a little threatened.

She decided to address fear in the system by offering safety. She became friendly to her perceived enemies. She guessed that they too felt threatened, perhaps by her. Viewing her enemies and then everyone as less of a threat, she was more relaxed with them. They saw her as less of a threat and relaxed around her. The system grew less threatening, and the knot in her stomach eased.

In one of the churches I served, I felt lonely. I sensed myself hardening against that loneliness and thinking blaming thoughts about my parishioners, as if they were doing this loneliness thing to me. I schemed ways to reform them. But instead of mounting a reform campaign, I opened to the loneliness. As I did, I guessed that if I felt lonely, others did too. I realized that if they were living with loneliness and were still sticking with the church, they must be loyal to each other and hoping to find belonging in their community, which caused me to admire them and gave me hope.

To address the loneliness in the system, I changed myself. I thought that being understood assuages loneliness, so I sought to listen more deeply to my parishioners and offer them understanding. This listening encouraged their openness with me, which increased their openness with each other. The congregation grew more intimate, less lonely.

I think this acceptance as an alternative to reforming people addresses one of Friedman's complaints: that much of what passes for "helping" is motivated by anxiety and as such is not helpful.[22] The not-helpful helping involves the escalation of a problem from a sensation to a discomfort to an aversion from that discomfort to the helper pressuring the helpee to relieve the helper of that discomfort. The "helpful" person is saying: I am uncomfortable; you fix my problem by benefitting from my "help."

The alternative to unhelpful "helping," or pressuring someone else to change for one's benefit, involves being aware of a discomforting sensation and gaining information from the sensation about one's system. One applies that information about the system to change oneself, that change influencing the system in a way that eases the original discomforting sensation.

Furthermore, when I surrender and accept what is, my well-being occurs not because of good things happening to me, but because of my relaxed relationship with what is. Being responsible for my relaxed relationship with what is, I am less dependent on the functioning of others for my well-being. This freedom from dependency on others eases my pressure on them to let me "help" them on my behalf, thereby giving others the space to be who they are.

LEADERSHIP

The spiritual journey prepares one to offer spiritual leadership guided by acceptance rather than control, willingness rather than willfulness, and surrender rather than mastery. Surrender in leadership involves sensing where people's energy is going and joining that. I may not always want exactly what the congregation wants, but if the congregation has energy for it, I am a fool to block it. They may know better than me what is best for their community. The flip side involves seeing where my own energy is going and going with that. I may not always want to champion my vision; it may not be politically correct or expedient. But if the energy of my truth is behind it, I would be hobbling myself to block it. To the people, yes. To my self and my vision, yes. Their visions and my visions can interact in a creative tension.

Another surrender involves allowing events to take their course with less management of their outcome. This surrender finds guidance in the Tao Te Ching's questions: "Can you love people and lead them without imposing your will? Can you deal with the most vital matters by letting events take their course?"[23] Having taken the spiritual journey, and having appraised vital matters from the perspective of the eternal, one moderates one's anxiety about outcomes. Less anxious, one demonstrates trust.

Technically, leading without managing outcomes involves articulating the identity, mission, and vision of the congregation, advocating for a healthy decision-making process, and then letting what will be be. This leadership supplies the big picture, which provides meaning. It guides the process, which provides safety. It trusts the people to work out the details, which provides them ownership of their community, empowerment, and the opportunity to journey with each other.

Conversely, to manage outcomes would raise the system's anxiety. If the minister speaks of trust but manages outcomes as if they do not trust, the not-trusting actions would be speaking the loudest. Furthermore, the minister who manages outcomes for one's own benefit sits enthroned at the apex of the system's hierarchy, making the system work for that minister. Such self-aggrandizing leadership emphasizes the survival-of-the-fittest structure at the expense of we're-in-this-together, which raises the system's anxiety. To bring less anxiety, one demonstrates security by being neutral about outcomes, setting aside what is good for oneself and working on behalf of everyone.

GOD'S SUPPORT FOR WHOLENESS

To think theologically about wholeness and related peace, God has contributed by expanding through history God's scope of support. At first, in ancient times, people waged war on other people, and their gods joined the battle not only against enemy people but also against their enemy's gods. But when trade in the ancient world supported prosperity, working together became more attractive. God made peace with trading partners and their gods. For example, while once Yahweh invited Israel to plunder the enemy Moabites (Zephaniah 2:9, RSV), in the later-written Book of Ruth, God welcomes Ruth, a Moabite, into a loving Hebrew community.[24]

In Hebrew scriptures, God further moves from caring for one nation, Israel, to caring for all nations. As a benediction for this evolution, God offers Noah, after the flood, a rainbow, as a sign of a "covenant between me and you and every living creature" (Genesis 9:15, RVS). God's expanding scope of support parallels the expanding scope of human affiliation from kinship-based clans to villages, to cities, to states, to nations, to federations of nations. With that expanding affiliation has come greater wholeness among humanity and increased peace.

Jesus, appearing later in history, furthers the theme of union and peace by offering that most difficult teaching: "Love your enemy" (Matthew 5:44, RVS). And when I love my enemy, they are no longer my enemy, and lo, I am at peace with them.

How to do this difficult thing? Paul, in his letter to the Romans, introduces redemption, writing that we are all loved and redeemed by God (Romans 5:18, RVS). He expresses not a survival-of-the-spiritually fittest order, with spiritual winners and losers, but a we-are-all-redeemed-together order. Indeed, the spirit is about wholeness and union, and so does not divide humanity. We are all equally and infinitely accepted.

PILGRIMAGE

On your journey you explore a wilderness in the midst of which you find spiritual support for being yourself. Having blazed a trail in this wilderness, you can support other individuals on their journeys to be themselves: the shy person gaining a voice in worship, the bossy leader learning to listen. You can foster small support groups in which people leave behind protective ideas of how to relate, open to each other more deeply, and share their stories, their despairs, and their healing.

Analogous to the individual journey, the entire community can take a pilgrimage from the known to the unknown to find something spiritual and become more fully themselves. The congregation's pilgrimage can begin with a problem that defies simple, technical solutions. As it journeys with its problem, the community crosses a threshold into the unknown, where they leave behind limiting assumptions and behaviors to find new perspectives, unknowns, ambiguity, and openness. The members of a partisan church, in a fight to the death, begin to listen to each other. Listening, they wander into an unfamiliar way of being. They let die their normal partisan self-images and view themselves as more of a union.

As guides, we can acknowledge that entering the unfamiliar can leave people feeling lost and uncomfortable, as the psalmist describes:

Some wandered in desert wastes,
finding no way to a city to dwell in;
hungry and thirsty,
their soul fainted within them. (Psalm 107:4–5, RVS)

Although difficult, we know such lostness is expected, not a threat, and leads to discovery. Indeed Psalm 107 continues with: "Then they cried to the Lord in their trouble, / and he delivered them from their distress" (Psalm 107:6, RVS). Having once been lost but now found gives ministers security, and our security calms the journeying community when it is lost.

Ideally, people who are lost can replace the requirement that they always feel good, with surrendering and opening to spirit. They learn that spirit enters where people are broken and needing and cannot solve their problems through will alone. Your prayers that thank the spirit for its grace, or that yearn and open to receiving from the spirit, can reassure people that the spirit is supporting their pilgrimage.

As guides, we do not fix their lostness or provide some service to relieve them of discomfort, which would be acts of will. Instead, we trust the process of death and rebirth. In that dying, people jettison ideas and assumptions that may have worked in the past but that fail to address the present. The partisan congregation sees conflict as useful in the past, but no longer. Following this loss can be the birth of who the people are now.

The leader can support one's pilgrims by offering them a vision of the Holy Land just over the horizon. A vision of something great gives meaning to the discomfort that accompanies forty years in the desert. Furthermore, the leader expressing a vision is standing out of the weeds and seeing the entire landscape, which is calming.

On Sundays, preaching, worship, and ritual can speak of the journey and its mysteries, as if to say: "we are not always going over safe and easy ground." In the spirit of risky pilgrimage Annie Dillard writes: "It is madness to wear ladies' straw hats and velvet hats to church; we should all be wearing crash helmets. Ushers should issue life preservers and signal flares; they should lash us to our pews."[25]

Paradoxically, play accompanies a difficult journey. On that arduous journey, when people open to the spirit, that spirit offers security, and with security comes playfulness. A fairy tale portrays this play. In it the hero is stuck underground at the bottom of a well and given up for dead. This hero sees a flute hanging on the wall and remarks, "This is no time for play." Indeed, it is not, and he paces and despairs. But after pacing the floor smooth, he does try the flute, and with each note, in this tale, a gnome appears, and the gnomes fly him out of the well. After despair, he plays, and play liberates.[26]

To encourage play at a church that was somewhat depressed, I invited the men of the board—sober, middle-aged executives and scientists at the major company in town—to become "The Flying Zambini Brothers" and to perform fake acrobatics at the church's variety show, complete with a lot of running around in circles, flexing of muscles, and bowing. They let go of sober, depressed ideas of who they were and adopted the new idea that they could be as dopey as their minister.

THE JOURNEY OF ORGANIZED RELIGION

Looking at a larger context, I think organized religion has a spiritual journey to undertake. Congregations and denominations are declining in membership numbers. My systemic diagnosis proposes that this decline is occurring because the old identities and purposes of organized religion are less needed and the new identities and purposes of religion have yet to be found. For instance, when ancient people feared warfare, they created an alpha God who smote their enemies. When people were miserable, they lifted their eyes to heaven and longed for release. When people lived in feral chaos, they created laws that gave societies order so needed and salvific that those laws were seen as written by the gods. When people lived with immoderation and ill manners, religion upheld moral codes in support of self-control.

But today we live in a safer, more comfortable world. Warfare and violence have declined.[27] Living standards are generally higher everywhere than they had been in, say, 1800.[28] Most of the world is governed by the rule of law. People are pretty well-mannered. Therefore, we have less need for warrior gods, heavenly succor, divine laws, and moral controls.

I wonder about the purpose of church today. I value communities and see them as meaningful, but if congregations are not rooting for their alpha God, longing for heaven, creating laws, or imposing morality, what is our faith community ultimately for? What value, identity, or guiding purpose could churches fulfill?

I believe individuals still benefit from a community within which they receive support for the risky opening of their souls, listening to God, and entering into the mysteries of the spirit. Congregations can continue to support those spiritual journeys.

People also benefit from harmonious communion with other people. We are social animals who need each other. Therefore, giving people a place where together they belong, play, sing, work, and move through the rites of passage remains a meaningful function for the church.

People also need support from each other. Spiritual communities can continue to extend divine love to comfort the afflicted.

Congregations can also address what I see as the two central challenges facing humanity. First, the survival-of-the-fittest hierarchy persists, to our detriment. In economic circles, it contributes to a widening disparity of wealth, which is correlated with, if not causal to, public illness and social problems. Research finds that the world's more economically equal societies foster greater public health, less substance abuse, greater mutual trust, deeper communal bonds, and more happiness than less equal societies.[29] Therefore, the we're-in-this-together experience, which congregations offer, provides a healthy relief from the economic hierarchy. Congregations also connect us to our brothers and sisters, who, if they suffer, may motivate a cure: economic equality.

Secondly, although humanity is less often at war with itself, it remains at war with nature, resulting in climate change and species extinction. Nature is our source of life, and if it collapses, the bell tolls also for humanity. Therefore, for human survival, it is of ultimate concern that religion keeps expanding the "we" of we're-in-this-together beyond humanity to include the animals, the oceans, the trees, and all of life.

Supporting spiritual journeys, offering a home for human relationships, creating egalitarian communities, and joining humanity with the whole of life would be my visions for the purpose of the church. What would be yours? What saving grace could people find in religious communities? What could churches give the world now that saves the world?

CONCLUSION

The spirit is about ultimate oneness, which aligns spirit with systems theory's emphasis on the wholeness of systems. The leader who experiences spiritual oneness finds support and security from spiritual sources. That secure leader is able to guide one's whole congregational system on its pilgrimage toward its spiritual sources.

QUESTIONS FOR REFLECTION

How do you experience comfort or support from your spiritual source?
How is spirituality difficult for you?
When have you experienced "helping" that seemed to be motivated by the helper's anxiety? How did that "helping" feel? When have you been a "helper" as a defense against your own anxiety?
How would you love people and lead them without imposing your will?

NOTES

1. Rebecca Parker, "There is a Love" in *A Child's Book of Blessings and Prayers*, ed. Eliza Blanchard (Boston: Skinner House, 2008), 1.

2. *Oxford English Dictionary*, 3rd edition., s.v. "spirit."

3. Gerald May, *Will and Spirit* (San Francisco: Harper & Row, 1982).

4. William Ernest Henley, "Invictus" in *Poems* (Warwickshire, UK: Read Books, Ltd., 1888/2013).

5. Joseph Campbell, *The Hero with a Thousand Faces* (Princeton, NJ: Princeton University Press, 1949).

6. Edward Whitmont, *The Symbolic Quest* (New York: Harper & Row, 1969).

7. Huston Smith, *The World's Religions* (New York: Harper Collins, 2009).

8. Campbell, *The Hero with a Thousand Faces*.

9. Ibid.

10. Ibid

11. Ibid.

12. Homer, *The Odyssey*, trans. Robert Fagles (New York: Penguin Classics, 1997).

13. Campbell, *The Hero with a Thousand Faces*.

14. Edith Hamilton, *Mythology: Timeless Tales of Gods and Heroes* (New York: Little, Brown and Company, 2011).

15. Homer, *The Odyssey*.

16. Robert Frost, "Directive" in *The Poetry of Robert Frost*, ed. Edward Connery Lathem (New York: Holt, Rinehart and Winston, 1969).

17. Campbell, *The Hero with a Thousand Faces*.

18. Ibid.

19. Jacob Grimm and Wilhelm Jacob, "Brier Rose" in *The Compete Fairy Tales of the Brothers Grimm*, 3rd edition, trans. Jack Zipes (New York: Bantam Books, 1812/2003).

20. Shantideva, *A Guide to the Bodhisattva Way of Life*, trans. A. Wallace & B. A. Wallace (Ithaca, NY: Snow Lion, 1997).

21. Jon Kabat-Zinn, *Mindfulness for Beginners* (Boulder, CO: Sounds True, Inc., 2012).

22. Edwin Friedman, *Generation to Generation: Family Process in Church and Synagogue* (New York: Guilford, 1985).

23. *Tao Te Ching*, trans. Stephen Mitchell (New York: Harper & Row, 1988).

24. Robert Wright, *The Evolution of God* (New York: Little, Brown & Company, 2005).

25. Annie Dillard, *Teaching a Stone to Talk* (New York: Harper and Row, 1982).

26. Jacob Grimm and Wilhelm Jacob, "The Gnome" in *The Compete Fairy Tales of the Brothers Grimm*, 3rd edition, trans. Jack Zipes (New York: Bantam Books, 1812/2003).

27. Steven Pinker, *The Better Angels of Our Nature* (New York: Viking, 2011).

28. Richard A. Easterlin, "The Worldwide Standard of Living since 1800." *The Journal of Economic Perspectives* 14, issue 1, (2000), 7–26.

29. Richard Wilkinson and Kate Pickett, *Spirit Level* (New York: Bloomsbury Press, 2011).

13

Conclusion

Faced with any leadership opportunity, be it a problem to solve, a program to develop, or a sermon to preach, you can be guided by mechanistic theory or systems theory. (Figure 13.1 depicts these leadership options.) Guided by mechanistic theory, you might see the congregation as collection of separate elements. You might diagnose a problem as some flawed aspect of the congregation. You might change the congregation by fixing or eliminating the broken cog in its machinery. Unfortunately, that intervention might divide the system between the healthy and the broken, and the use of pressure could exacerbate the system's anxiety.

On the other hand, guided by systems theory, you would remember that the congregation is a whole. You make your diagnosis, discerning how you are being affected by the system's illness. You understand that a symptom may be localized in one aspect of the congregation, but it is an understandable representation of illness within the whole system.

You prepare to intervene by working on your own security. To change the system, you know that any move you make anywhere in the system influences the whole system, so you move yourself and your participation in the system in the direction of health. Knowing that both what you do and how you do it are influential, you practice constructive processes. Understanding direct and indirect effects, you plant seeds and wait to see what sprouts.

The hoped-for effects of your interventions are wholeness—the congregation's diverse members collaborating and cooperating as one community—and, second, safety—the congregation's members experiencing security, trending them to live on the thought side of the thought-reflex continuum where they behave with moderation and can think with flexibility and creativity. Whole and safe, the congregation lives out its missions to support people's spiritual lives and to offer God's love to the world.

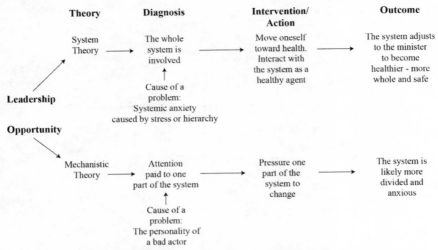

Figure 13.1 Leadership guided by systems theory or mechanistic theory.

Appendix A

Situations

This appendix applies systems theory to congregational situations.

THE BIG SLEEP

In your second year of parish ministry you are bored. Committee meetings are boring. Nothing much is happening in the congregation. You are bored by your own sermons.

First Thought

Oh well, not so bad; I'll just sleepwalk my way through this ministry.

Second Thoughts

Boredom is a sign that people are reactively avoiding and hiding from something important but threatening. What is so scary?

Maybe the congregation is afraid of conflict and avoiding it by dwelling at stage one, promoting peace at any price, that price being boredom. Such pseudo-community is not authentic or meaningful for people. Plus, if a conflict is being avoided, it will fester and later explode.

I want my vocation to be inspiring to me, as well as others, not a snooze-fest.

Actions

Show security, rather than fear, by being vulnerable. Disclose principles, visions, and goals.

Preach a sermon that takes an unpopular stand. Welcome people's opposing views. Show that differences are not as threatening as people might guess.

Sleuth out about what issues are being avoided. Look into the history of the congregation for taboo events and experiences and gradually begin to talk about them. Flooding them with deep, dark secrets might be overwhelming, but a gradual exposure to the phobia of openness can show them that openness is not the end of the world.

In general, deepen the conversation. Take up ultimate, spiritual concerns.

THE SLACKER SOCIETY

A few years into your ministry almost no one is volunteering to do anything. The stalwarts pitch in but complain of burnout. Invitations for involvement fall flat. The scarcity of volunteers worries you.

First Thought

My congregation is full of lazy bums!

Second Thoughts

They are not inspired by the identity and purpose of the congregation, and so they see no meaning in its activities.

Committee activity is meaningless because the board is doing all the meaningful work.

There is little reward for involvement.

We have an anxious system in which people are hiding, perhaps from judgment, by not acting.

Actions

Articulate the identity, mission, and vision of the congregation. This offers people the larger rationale for their activity, making that activity meaningful and motivating.

Give committees more meaningful assignments. Distinguish the board and its governance role from committees and their ministry.

Appreciate publicly those who do participate.

Address systemic anxiety by being vulnerable. Address the fear of judgment by acknowledging one's own mistakes. Quote Fiorello LaGuardia: "When I make a mistake, it's a beaut!"[1]

MISSIONS IMPOSSIBLE

On a retreat, the congregation explores its mission. Half the congregation wants the church to set up a homeless shelter, develop a lobbying effort, give money to peace and hunger groups, and draft position statements on social issues. The other half wants the church to offer spiritual support, to hold meditation and tai chi classes, and to refrain from political activity. Each affirms their mission to be true to the origins of the religion and declares they cannot live in a church that pursues the other's agenda.

First Thought

This rift is going to rip the church asunder. We're doomed.

Second Thoughts

We have a principled conflict over an activist vs. a sanctuary mission. The good news is that people are thinking hard about the purpose of the church. The bad news is that they have dug in their heels and are resisting compromise. The conflict has pulled them into high systemic anxiety where they react with a rigid, fight-or-flight response, rather than with flexibility and creativity.

They are at the pre-contemplation stage of change, saying "no" to acceptance of their differences.

Actions

From a neutral and validating perspective, explore the activist and sanctuary missions, their history and values.

Describe the congregation as on a journey. Link its current journey to other episodes in its history and to other communities that have weathered controversies.

Don't push too fast for change. Express empathy for the difficult emotions people are going through in the midst of this tension.

Appreciate how deeply people in the congregation have thought about this matter. Applauding their concern about substantive principles might make it safe for them to think even more deeply, where they might find a way to reconcile.

Offer an "I have a dream" speech, envisioning how this standoff could be reconciled in support of both the sanctuary and activist missions.

Invite representatives from both sides to dialogue. Moderate the dialogue and coach the participants in speaking in a way that is easy to hear and in listening accurately. Invite individuals to reflect back the other side's perspective. Invite members from each side to speak as if they were from the opposing side.

Hold Listening Circles to explore the congregation's mission.

OH, AND, BY THE WAY, YOU'RE FIRED!

You have been minister of a congregation for a few years, and things seem to be okay, but at a congregational meeting Buster asks the assemblage what would be the minimum number of votes required to dismiss you.

First Thought

I am being pushed into a corner, and I have to fight back. I will gather allies against this incipient movement against me.

Second Thoughts

People might be afraid of me and reluctant to approach me with their complaints and suggestions.

They may be setting up a fight, which could polarize the church.

This might be a move to intimidate and silence me.

Maybe I have been pushing for change, and the system is seeking homeostasis by jettisoning me.

Actions

Play with paradox by being neutral about one's tenure. Offer friendly support for the movement to dismiss. Show them the dismissal article in the bylaws and give them space to meet, such as your office.

Ask Buster directly whether he has any issues with you that he has had trouble expressing. Respond with empathy and problem-solving.

Invite feedback from all sources. Survey the congregation, asking what they want you to do more of, less of, and the same. Report back what you have learned and what you are doing with that information.

Check with lay leaders about the pace of change. Is it too much, too fast?

A BRIDGE TOO FAR

The congregation decides to become more diverse and calls you, an advocate of diversity, to its ministry. You bring multicultural sensibility, and people join representing demographic groups heretofore rarely seen in the congregation. All is well, except that conflicts flare up in pockets around the congregation: the choir director vs. the religious education (RE) program, the worship committee vs. the treasurer, and people complain about the administrator, who seems to be doing as fine a job as she always has.

First Thought

All this squabbling is silly and unjustified.

Second Thought

Although they took action, the congregation actually occupies the contemplation stage of change regarding diversity, and yet is ambivalent about the action they took. Now they are in a bind, stuck with the diversity they professed to want but for which they were not ready. It would be politically incorrect to speak against diversity, so the anger in the system is directed at other issues.

Action

To support their contemplation, acknowledge from a neutral perspective the pros and cons of diversity. Letting them explore their contemplation stage of change would release pressure related to their bind, hopefully resulting in less squabbling.

Furthermore, after they explore the contemplation stage of change, they can progress to the preparation and action stages. At that action stage, having caught up to their idealistic but premature decision, they will be less conflicted, more integrated.

CONSIDER THE LILIES

You have worked hard, serving a congregation for fifteen years. One day your board president gives you the feedback that you have been too involved in the organization of the church and become too powerful. She adds that she and other lay leaders find you making too many decisions and advocating too hard for your agendas.

First Thought

Those ungrateful so-and-sos. After all I do for them, they reward me with complaints.

Second Thoughts

Maybe I am overfunctioning to protect myself from criticism and to make myself indispensable. Furthermore, maybe my overfunctioning is a symptomatic reaction to anxiety in the congregation of which I am not aware. Maybe my board president is a less anxious member of the system and is asking me to join her in moderated anxiety.

Maybe I see the membership as the dominant party whom I, the subordinate, have to serve. Maybe I control too much out of a fear of mistakes, reflecting the system's anxiety about mistakes.

Maybe the church used to need a boss to bring order out of chaos, and I was that boss. But now a more stable church has less need for a boss and wants to develop a more egalitarian structure.

Actions

Accept the board president's calming leadership, and moderate your own reactivity. Work on yourself, meditate, exercise, pray, get a dog, go to a movie.

Rather than seek to please them, invite them to journey. Preach on the spiritual journey. Invite them in small groups to consider the spiritual side of their lives. Ask powerful questions about what life means.

To adjust the organizational structure of the congregation, propose the governance and ministry model.

To support shared leadership, delegate. See that the board and committees have meaningful tasks.

In a meeting with lay leaders, list with them your tasks, their tasks, and your shared tasks. Stick to your tasks. If they struggle with their tasks, support, but refrain from doing their tasks for them. Let them learn.

ORDAIN ME, OR ELSE

You are beginning your second year at your congregation. Your beloved RE director, who has served the church for twelve years, and has overseen a thriving children's program, expresses her wish to be ordained as a minister of religious education. Your denomination's polity allows a congregation to ordain anyone they wish, but the RE director has not received a graduate degree in ministry or in education, and you are skeptical about this proposed elevation of her into an ordained person. You express this skepticism, and she threatens to resign if you block her ordination.

First Thought

This is a power-grab by the long-tenured RE director against the neophyte minister. I can't let her win.

Second Thoughts

She has a position—ordination—but behind that position is a valid need. I want to understand that need and try to meet it. I have a need, too, which is to respect and value ordination as a rite of passage. This is an opportunity to negotiate.

My mission is to guide a process toward an outcome that is less about me and more about what is best for the congregation and its mission.

Actions

Explore what the RE director needs behind her ordination position. Seek ways to meet those needs that I and the rest of the congregation could feel good about. Follow the principles of negotiation by speaking for and respecting principles rather than pressure.

Continue to be friendly and supportive of the RE director. Applaud her skills and gifts.

Explore the mission of the congregation. Use that mission to guide this and other decisions.

DÉJÀ VU ALL OVER AGAIN

You have served this congregation for five years, and every spring, as you are excited about the next year's programs and projects, a financial crisis derails that planning. Worry about money takes over.

First Thought

These people are snatching defeat from the jaws of programmatic victory.

Second Thoughts

Maybe the financial crisis is a symptom of systemic anxiety. In their anxiety, they might fear making mistakes. A program action would expose them more than inaction, so they hide by refraining from action.

They say they want to develop new programs and contribute to the community, but maybe their words belie their real wish, which is to keep the church quiet and small, their personal involvement modest.

Maybe they are passively balking at the program ideas because I have not vetted them thoroughly and gained their assent.

Actions

If they fear making mistakes, make the system safer. Empathize with the fear of making mistakes. Offer the assumption that we are okay, even when imperfect. Offer the thought that mistakes offer an opportunity for learning. Give positive reinforcement for any actions they do take.

Assess their identity. See if they are not as activist as they might want to appear. Validate whatever identity defines them, making it okay to be who they are. Accepting their identity could move them to consider a vision of who they might want to be.

Vet the program ideas with individuals and small groups. Modify these ideas with people's input. Weigh with people the pros and cons of the proposed actions.

JACK VS. JILL

Despite your leading workshops and sermons on conflict resolution, two members, Jack and Jill, have a rift. Jack meets with you about this, and you suggest he contact Jill with an offer to mend the rift. Jack does and shows you Jill's reply: "You and I have differing agendas at this church. No further discussion is needed."

First Thought

It is my responsibility to persuade Jill to make peace with Jack.

Second Thoughts

Jack and Jill have a conflict in which Jill views cutting off as a reasonable option.

The training I have offered in conflict has successfully motivated half of this feud, Jack, to reconcile. That's progress.

Actions

Talk to Jill about her rift with Jack, not to persuade her to soften her stance, but to hear her side and offer her empathy. If she pulls you to take her side against Jack, stay explicitly neutral. Validate her experience of difficulty with Jack, acknowledging her anger and other attending emotions, without agreeing that he is an evil person. Hope that validating her story might calm her down.

Attend to all the relationships in the system, making sure the air is clear and that harmony is the norm. Make the cutting-off option an outlier.

Acknowledge that although harmony is normal, conflicts still occur. Offer behavioral standards that keep conflicts from escalating. Include the standard that people seek to resolve their conflicts with each other.

Give Jack pastoral support.

A LITTLE DISCORD

You have served a congregation for a few years and have often disagreed with the music director over which hymns to sing. You learn that the music director complains to the choir about you. This music director precedes your tenure as minister, is beloved by the choir, and is both a staff member and a member of the church.

First Thought

This means war, and I am in a weak position. And how dare she bad-mouth me to the choir!

Second Thoughts

The music director is in a power struggle with me. Maybe the system sets up power struggles.

The music director does not feel safe enough to take his complaints directly to me. Maybe the rest of the congregation does not feel safe to complain directly.

Maybe the congregation views itself as composed of separate fiefdoms, the choir being one such fiefdom, rather than as a unity.

Actions

Develop a closer, trusting relationship with the music director. Consider with him the process that attends our disagreements. Develop more humane and productive processes. Offer your hope that he and you can cooperate and collaborate on worship more successfully. Let the music director win battles, while you win the war by becoming a trusted supervisor of the staff.

Invite the entire congregation to bring their issues with you to you. Set up an evaluation processes, gauging progress toward goals, and asking the congregation what from you they would like more of, less of, and the same.

Create a staff covenant that includes the expectation that the staff support each other. Include as well the standards that intra-staff conflicts remain within the staff and that staff members do not undermine each other before the congregation. If the music director is not on board with those standards, view him as at the pre-contemplation stage of change. Empathize with his position. If he moves to the contemplation stage, weigh the pros and cons of these standards with him and the rest of the staff.

Strengthen contracts, board policies, and job descriptions. You could include in the standard staff contract a clause that states that undermining one staff member before the congregation would violate the principle of staff unity and be cause for dismissal. Maybe such a clause is coming too late to be included in the music director's contract, but including this clause in future contracts would prevent this problem from recurring.

Clarify the minister's role as chief of staff and your power to supervise, hire, and fire. You may not want to fire the music director, but it would help you, and any future minister, to clarify the minister's role.

I DON'T WANT TO GO TO THE OFFICE

You begin your settlement to find that the church administrator is antagonistic toward you. She liked your predecessor, and, despite your charming personality and imminent skills, she remains chilly toward you. She does her job: handling newsletters and orders of service, and answering the phones, and does not refuse the minor tasks you request, but she spins your words to make you look bad. When you suggested the church rent its space to a daycare, she tells others that you "ordered" the church to rent its space. She is divorced, lonely, and not in good health. She has loyal friends within the congregation, whom you believe would fear that without this job, she would be at a total loss.

First Thought

Make a case for her lack of cooperation, and ease her out.

Second Thoughts

The church has reached the action stage of change by calling you as their new minister, but the administrator remains at the pre-contemplation stage of this change.

It would require a huge campaign to oust the administrator. She has not violated her contract, so the ouster would look like a personal vendetta. Those loyal to her would fight it and, in the process, see you as a ruthless autocrat, not as their minister.

This administrator might well be a thorn in your side, but the damage to church unity resulting from scapegoating her would make matters worse.

Indeed, the administrator could even hope you try to oust her, shifting you from being the shiny new minister to someone corrupt and evil. Being seen that way would make your ministry a slog.

The administrator, in her resistance and skepticism, could be a symptom of distrust or fear of autocracy in the congregational system. Removing her would inflame the system's distrust and fear.

Actions

Work with her as best you can. Treat her with respect. Refrain from charging at the red cape of insubordinance she waves in front of your nose.

Take up the other interests you have in your ministry.

Express appreciation of her to her and to others. As she is undermining you, your compliments would be paradoxical.

Empathize with her regarding how much she misses your predecessor and how difficult this transition has been for her.

Investigate your predecessor's style of leadership as it contributed to distrust in the system of which the administrator is symptomatic, not to make that predecessor look bad but to give you insight into the system.

Instead of waging an offense against her, protect yourself from the administrator with a good defense. Put your "suggestions" in writing so that if she makes them into "orders," you have a paper trail showing otherwise.

If you guess that the administrator is a symptom of the system's distrust of autocracy, strive for openness, transparency, and the democratic processes. Play the long game, hoping that as the congregation grows in trust and health, she will feel more at peace and become more cooperative.

As with the situation with the music director, or with any staff difficulty, develop and apply covenants, contracts, board policies, and job descriptions to make it clear to all what any staff person is expected to do.

A FAILURE OF VERVE

You have an activist agenda and wish to promote social justice in the community and in the world. You preach often on the problems and ills of society. You lift up the great things the church could do. You proclaim that God's love is manifested in action. But your words fall flat. The people listen to your sermons and nod, but their level of action remains low.

First Thoughts

They are failing at their responsibility. I need to push them harder, maybe complain that they are failing and invoke some guilt.

This is not a good pastoral fit. I should serve a leader church with an activist mission.

Second Thoughts

Maybe I am exhorting, and the exhortation induces resistance. Furthermore, guilt inducement, although traditionally popular in religious circles, would express my own helpless anxiety and not inspire people.

Actions

Present models of religious activists.

Reinforce actions the people are already taking.

On behalf of modeling, take on your own action projects. Make the projects fun. Invite some well-respected individuals to join you in your projects. Make the social action project with the minister a special thing.

Hold an identity workshop and explore the congregation's mission, key story, and other aspects if its identity. Be open to any vision ideas that emerge.

NOTE

1. "Mayor Admits O'Brien Appointment a Mistake," *The New York Times*, February 12, 1941.

Appendix B

Self-Definition Exercises

Throughout this book, I have promoted leadership that is secure enough to be self-defining. To define yourself, it helps to know who you are. You are a compendium of your beliefs, likes, wants, values, story, principles, etc. I offer these exercises to support your clarity regarding your identity.

1. Write a one-sentence definition of the congregation.
2. Write a one-sentence personal credo, starting with: "I believe ..."
3. Write fifty sentences that begin with "I like ..."
4. List your wants, completing the sentence that begins "I want ..." as many times as you want.
5. Write a statement describing your values. What do you care about most deeply?
6. Describe a time in which you felt at peace or in awe.
7. Write a one-sentence definition of your ministry.
8. List the key principles that guide your ministry.
9. Distill the message of all your sermons into one sentence.
10. Carl Jung began his autobiography with the sentence: "My life has been the story of the self-realization of the unconscious."[1] Write your one-sentence autobiography.
11. Write your visions for your congregation.
12. List what you want people in your congregation to experience.
13. What would be a symbol of yourself as a leader?
14. What biblical or historical figure do you hold as a model for leadership? What about that figure's leadership do you emulate?

15. Name your personal gifts for leadership. List what gifts are needed from other people to balance, complete, or complement your own.
16. Fill in the blanks: "As a minister I want to _____ (verb) _____ (subject of the verb) because that would _____ (the ultimate effect of that action on the subject), and it would _____ (the ultimate effect on that action on yourself)." (For example, "As a minister I want to support the development of communities because that would enrich others' lives, and it would bring fulfillment to myself.")
17. When are you "in your element"? Where are you? What is happening? What are you doing?
18. Choose a simile for your ministry. When I am at my pastoral best I am like a ...
19. What constitutes a good life?
20. What does it mean to be a good person?
21. What three qualities would characterize your personality?
22. When you retire, how would you want to be remembered?

NOTE

1. Carl Jung, *Memories, Dreams, Reflections*. Aniela Jaffé. ed., Clara Winston, Richard Winston translators. (New York: Random House: 1961)

Appendix C

History of Systems Theory

Through human history, systems theory has slowly developed. This appendix looks at when and how people understood that elements interact to compose a whole system, as well as the related systems theory themes of multiple causality, direct and indirect relationships, and process dynamics.

For much of human history, people's thinking was concrete and not consistent with the more-than-meets-the-eye quality of systems theory. They saw the sun cross from one horizon to the other and concluded it was traveling across the sky. They looked to the horizon and concluded that the world was flat. They viewed people outside their clans as threats. Mysterious phenomena that defied concrete understandings were seen as caused by the gods.[1]

Perhaps the earliest systemic thinking occurred when protohumans began to make tools, about 2.5 million years ago.[2] They grasped the indirect relationship between a rock and the tool they could craft from that rock.

These early humans lived in small kinship-based bands. When disputes arose within these bands, the disagreeing sides parted ways.[3] This practice of dividing suggests that these primal bands did not appreciate or seek to preserve the wholeness of their communities.

About 50,000 years ago, human societies began to grow.[4] For these larger societies to function, and not just split when times grew rancorous, people began to value maintaining their community's wholeness. They also developed more sophisticated interpersonal processes than splitting when times grew difficult. For instance, they learned reciprocity,[5] a process in which a good turn for my non-kin neighbor prepares that neighbor to do a good turn for me. About 100,000 years ago they also developed language, which uses an auditory expression to represent a thing. The process of reciprocity, and the indirect relationship between a sound and a thing, required elementary systems thinking.

239

About 15,000 years ago, some people shifted from nomadic to settled life. They then paid attention to the grasses and grains growing in their vicinity, learning how to cultivate the nutritious and weed out the others.[6] As they planted a seed, trusting that it would transform into a plant they could later eat, they learned the systems theme of delayed effects.

When early farmers developed surpluses, they could trade. Trading expanded the wholeness of a community to include one's trading partner. That larger whole supported further systems thinking.

To handle the interpersonal complexities of reciprocity, language, and trade, people grew smarter and evolved bigger brains.[7] The abstract complexity of systems thinking benefited from this increased intelligence.

As societies grew into cities, they needed more complex structures to maintain order, and so they developed laws.[8] These laws, in theory applying to and benefiting everyone, supported the wholeness of these societies. Supporting wholeness, their creation involved systems thinking.

The wider enlargement of human societies supported further systems thinking. In the fifteenth century, Europe contained some five thousand political units, each governed by a warlord.[9] When one of these five thousand warlords defeated another, that victor's territory grew, resulting in fewer but larger political units. A warlord ruling a larger territory became a king. Indeed, by the nineteenth century, political units had coalesced from five thousand to two hundred larger kingdoms. These kings disliked raids and vendetta by knights within their kingdom because dead peasants and ruined crops were costly to the kingdom, so kings applied their military might to stopping knights from battling each other.[10] As such these kings were considering the benefit of their whole kingdoms and were practicing systems thinking.

The right of someone to be king, though, remained mysterious and, therefore, understood to be ordained by God. King Arthur grasped the sword, Excalibur, signifying by divine right that he was king. With God ordaining leaders, people assumed little influence on how they were led.

The year 1651 marked a small increment in people's assumption of political power with the publication of *Leviathan* in which Thomas Hobbes theorized how leaders best govern.[11] If people such as Hobbes could think about how they are best governed, maybe they, and not just the gods, could influence governance.[12]

People's influence in government was further supported by Jean-Jacques Rousseau's *Social Contract*, published in 1762. He described citizenship as grounded in the consent of the governed.[13] If people are consenting to how they are governed, maybe their consent could take the form of a vote, planting the seed of democracy, government "of the people, by the people, for the people."[14] In a democracy, everyone's voices influence each other, an example of multiple causality. In a democracy, if I change my opinion, that influences the whole ... slightly.

The history of science supported systems thinking, as scientists developed understandings of the world that defied concrete common sense. In the early 1500s, Copernicus proposed that the earth rotated around the sun.[15] Galileo, during the late 1500s and early 1600s, further theorized that two bodies of differing weights would fall at the same speed.[16]

Isaac Newton in 1666 furthered systems thinking by describing gravity as an invisible force that influenced the interaction of objects.[17] Despite this interactive theory, Newtonian physics was generally mechanistic as it viewed matter as composed of "small, solid, and indestructible objects."[18] Further-more, Newton and other scientists tended to separate objects from their context before studying them. As such they did not respect the interactions of elements in a system.[19] In 1863, Tennyson expressed this mechanistic scien-tific method in his poem, "Flower in the Crannied Wall" in which he uproots a flower from its environment and muses about this now-separate object.[20]

Flower in the crannied wall,
I pluck you out of the crannies,
I hold you here, root and all, in my hand,
Little flower—but if I could understand
What you are, root and all, and all in all,
I should know what God and man is.

In economics, the understanding of the interdependent system of economic exchanges supported the development of systems thinking. The first econo-mist, Adam Smith, offered in 1776 an explanation of this economic system. He wrote that when individuals pursue their self-interest, the "invisible hand" of supply and demand supports the stable production and consumption of goods and services.[21] He stated that the baker supplies us with bread out of self-interest in gaining an income from its purchase. When bakers compete with other bakers, they keep their prices low. But if there are too many bakers, the glut of bread in the market lowers the prices further, which causes some bakers to become tailors. Understanding this invisible network of mutuality reinforced systems thinking.

In natural history, scientists began to appreciate that the whole of nature is composed of its many elements, all interacting with each other—the central systems theory theme. During his career over the early to mid-1800s, Alex-ander von Humboldt viewed nature as an interconnected system, a "living whole" in which a "great chain of causes and effects" means "no single fact can be considered in isolation."[22]

Darwin, in the mid-1800s, supported systems thinking with his theory of evolution.[23] His unification of all species as having evolved from a common origin advanced people's understanding of the wholeness of nature.

Concurrently, new developments in physics questioned the Newtonian or mechanistic orthodoxy. For instance, scientists Michael Faraday and James Clerk Maxwell observed electric and magnetic forces causing more complicated interactions between objects than gravity.[24]

During the early twentieth century, physicists went further in viewing matter not as building blocks, but as interactive. For example, in 1905, Albert Einstein proposed a new theory of relativity in which space is not three dimensional, and time is not a separate entity. Both interact to form a four-dimensional continuum: "space-time."[25] According to this theory, different observers will sequence events in time differently according to the speeds at which those observers are moving. Einstein also proposed that mass is not an inert building block but becomes energy when travelling at the speed of light squared ($E = MC^2$).[26]

Ernest Rutherford in 1911 further showed that atoms were not little building blocks, but regions of space within which moved even smaller objects: electrons, protons, and neutrons.[27] He also showed that, depending on how they were observed, subatomic units could appear as particles or as waves.

Neils Bohr observed that subatomic particles assumed their properties in their relationships with other particles, writing: "Isolated material particles are abstractions, their properties being definable and observable only through their interaction with other systems."[28] Werner Heisenberg spoke further of matter not as composed of objects, but of interactions: "The world appears as a complicated tissue of events, in which connections of different kinds overlap or combine and thereby determine the texture of the whole."[29] Understanding matter as defined by the interaction of its elements supported systems thinking.

In biology, systems theory was developed further by Ludwig von Bertalanffy through his career beginning in the 1920s. For one thing, he coined the term "Systems Theory."[30] In 1968, Bertalanffy wrote a history of systems theory in which he defined a system as "a set of elements standing in interrelation among themselves and with the environment."[31]

Bertalanffy disagreed with the "Crannied Wall" assumption that components of a system could be analyzed as independent entities. Instead, he believed that a system is characterized by the interactions of its components and by "the non-linearity of those interactions."[32] Championing the systems idea of multiple causality, he noted, "we must think in terms of systems of elements in mutual interaction."[33] He then studied elements within the wholeness of their natural environment.

Furthermore, Bertalanffy stated that the same systems dynamics occur in any and all systems: "There appear to exist general system laws which apply to any system of a certain type, irrespective of the particular properties of the system and of the elements involved."[34]

In medicine, through much of history, people viewed illness as mysterious and thereby caused by metaphysical agents, such as demons, the cure being the rituals of a witch doctor. Later, noxious air, known as miasma, was seen as a cause of illness.[35] In 1670, Anton van Leeuwenhoek, peering at objects with greater magnification than ever used before, discovered microorganisms.[36] Who knew? Louis Pasteur, during the 1860s, showed that microorganisms were responsible for spoiling beer, wine, and milk.[37] He heated liquids to kill such bacteria, a process that came to be known as pasteurization. Pasteur thought, if microorganisms could contaminate beverages, they might also infect people. Joseph Lister followed in 1865 to develop antiseptic procedures for surgery.[38] Medicine proceeded to develop antibiotics to fight off toxic microorganisms.[39] This link between illness and objects that cannot be seen was consistent with the more-than-meets-the-eye quality of systems theory. On the other hand, the idea that a toxin is a tiny object that can be fought off and eliminated is consistent with mechanistic theory.

Medicine moved further toward systems theory with the discovery of immunity, which supported the multiple causality theme.[40] Because of immunity, toxin A does not automatically infect body B. Finding that additional factors such as sleep, stress, love, and physical exercise, all affect the immune system, added to the multiplicity of causality.[41]

Leadership theories have also become more systemic. We have gone from the "great man" theory of leadership to seeing the interactions of systems and leaders as causing historical events.[42]

Further supporting systems theory is humanity's trend to ever-larger societies.[43] Instead of dividing when things get tense, people have affiliated in groups that have grown from clan, to city, to state, to nation, to federation of nations. To support working together, people have formed transnational organizations, such as the United Nations, charged to support practices and policies that benefit the whole of humanity.

Supporting the understanding of systems theory's abstract relationships is humanity's increasing intelligence, measured by rising IQ test performances.[44] As noted above, this rising IQ reflects humanity's continued shift from concrete to abstract thinking.

Systems theory was supported by developments in psychology. Originally, mental illness was seen as mysterious and as originating from metaphysical causes, such as in Salem, Massachusetts, witchcraft. In contrast, Freud, in the early twentieth century, viewed the causes of psychological problems as unconscious conflicts originating in childhood.[45] His theory that childhood history could influence an adult's life was consistent with systems theory's theme of indirect causes. Although Freud made a step toward systems thinking, he still focused on the individual, rather than the relationship system.

During the mid-twentieth century, Murray Bowen shifted from treating the individual in isolation to understanding the person within their relationship system.[46] He developed concepts such as "differentiation" and "chronic anxiety" to explain the interaction of individuals within systems. Rabbi Edwin Friedman trained with Bowen and applied Bowen's concepts to congregational life.[47] He taught that congregations were systems replicating the dynamics of a family or of any other system.

Finally, as you understand and apply the idea that the interaction of elements creates a whole, you continue this development of systems theory.

NOTES

1. Robert Wright, *The Evolution of God* (New York: Little Brown, 2009).

2. Jared Diamond, *The Third Chimpanzee* (New York: Harper Perennial, 1992).

3. Tim Flannery, *The Eternal Frontier* (New York: Grove Press, 2001).

4. Ian Morris, *Foragers, Farmers, and Fossil Fuel* (Princeton: Princeton University Press, 2015).

5. Ibid.

6. Ibid.

7. Michael Tomasello, "Social Cognition and the Evolution of Culture" in *Piaget, Evolution, and Development,* ed. Jonas Langer and Melanie Killen (Mahwah, NJ: Erlbaum, 2008), 221–45.

8. Steven Pinker, *The Better Angels of Our Nature* (New York: Penguin, 2011).

9. Ibid.

10. Ibid.

11. Thomas Hobbes, *The Leviathan,* ed. C. B. MacPherson (London: Penguin Books, 1651/1982).

12. Pinkner, *Better Angels.*

13. Jean-Jacques Rosseau, *The Social Contract and Discourses*, trans, G. D. H. Cole (New York: Dutton, 1762/1950).

14. Abraham Lincoln, "Gettysburg Address" in *Abraham Lincoln: Speeches and Writings Vol. 2 1859–1865,* ed. Don Fehrenbacher (New York: Literary Classics of the United States, 1989).

15. Thomas Kuhn, *The Copernican Revolution, Planetary Astronomy in the Development of Western Thought* (Cambridge, MA: Harvard University Press, 1985).

16. Drake Stillman, *Essays on Galileo and the History and Philosophy of Science, Vol 1* (Toronto: University of Toronto Press, 1999).

17. Isaac Newton, *The Principia* (Oakland, CA: University of California Press, 1687/2016).

18. Ibid.

19. Andrea Wulf, *The Invention of Nature* (New York: Knopf, 2015).

20. Alfred Tennyson, "Flower in the Crannied Wall" in *The Complete Works of Alfred Lord Tennyson* (Ware, England: Wordsworth Editions Limited, 1994).

21. Robert Heilbroner, *The Worldly Philosophers* (New York: Simon and Schuster, 1999).

22. Wulf, *The Invention of Nature*.

23. Charles Darwin, *The Origin of the Species: 150th Anniversary Edition* (New York: Penguin, 1859/2003).

24. Nancy Forbes and Basil Mahon, *Faraday, Maxwell, and the Electromagnetic Field* (Amherst, NY: Prometheus Books, 2014).

25. Albert Einstein, "On a Heuristic Point of View Concerning the Production and Transformation of Light," *Annalen der Physik* 17, no. 6 (1905): 132–48.

26. Albert Einstein, "On the Electrodynamics of Moving Bodies," *Annalen der Physik* 17, no. 10 (1905): 891–921.

27. Ernest Rutherford, *Radioactive Substances and Their Radiations* (Cambridge, UK: Cambridge University Press, 1904).

28. Niels Bohr, *Atomic Physics and the Description of Nature* (Cambridge, UK: Cambridge University Press, 1934).

29. Werner Heisenberg, *Physics and Philosophy* (New York: Harper Torchbooks, 1958).

30. Ludwig von Bertalanffy, *General Systems Theory, Foundations, Development, Applications* (New York: George Braziller, Inc., 1968).

31. Ibid.

32. Ibid.

33. Ibid.

34. Ibid.

35. *A Dictionary of Public Health* "miasma theory" ed. John M. Last (Westminster College, Pennsylvania: Oxford University Press, 2007).

36. Brian Ford, *The Leeuwenhoek Legacy* (Bristol and London: Biopress and Farrand Press, 1991).

37. Mary Ellen Bowden, Amy Beth Crow, and Tracy Sullivan, *Pharmaceutical Achiever: The Human Face of Pharmaceutical Research* (Philadelphia, PA: Chemical Heritage Press, 2003).

38. *Cambridge Illustrated History of Medicine*, ed. Roy Porter (Cambridge, UK: Cambridge University Press, 2001).

39. Ibid.

40. Ellie Metchnikoff, *Immunity in Infective Diseases,* trans. F. G. Binnie (Cambridge, UK: Cambridge University Press, 1905).

41. Sheldon Cohen, "Social Relations and Susceptibility to the Common Cold" in *Emotion, Social Relationships, and Health,* ed. Carol Ryff and Burton Singer (Oxford, UK: Oxford University Press, 2001), 221–232.

42. Warren Bennis, "The Challenges of Leadership in the Modern World," *American Psychologist* 62, no. 1 (January 2007): 2–5.

43. Morris, *Foragers, Farmers, and Fossil Fuel.*

44. Pinker, *The Better Angels of Our Nature.*

45. Sigmund Freud, *The Freud Reader*, ed. Peter Gay (New York: Norton & Co., 1995).

46. Michael Kerr and Murray Bowen, *Family Evaluation* (New York: Norton, 1988).

47. Edwin Friedman, *Generation to Generation: Family Process in Church and Synagogue* (New York: Guilford, 1985).

Bibliography

Basch, Michael Franz. *Doing Psychotherapy*. New York: Basic Books, 1980.

Barna, George. "Why Pastors Leave the Ministry." *Fuller Institute, and Pastoral Care, Inc.*, 2014. https://feic.org/wp-content/uploads/2014/10/Why-pastors-leave-the-ministry.pdf.

Bateson, Gregory. *Steps toward an Ecology of Mind*. New York: Dutton, 1972.

Baumeister, Roy and John Tierney. *Willpower*. New York: Penguin Books, 2012.

Becker, Penny. *Congregations in Conflict*. Cambridge, UK: Cambridge University Press, 1999.

Behfar, Kristen and Christina Black. "In Defense of Indirect Confrontation: Managing Cross-Cultural Conflict." *Leadership and Organizational Behavior*, April 3, 2017, University of Virginia, Darden School of Business. https://ideas.darden.virginia.edu/2017/04/in-defense-of-indirect-confrontation-managing-cross-culture-conflict.

Benjamin, Lorna Smith. *Interpersonal Diagnosis and Treatment of Personality Disorders*. 2nd ed. New York: Guilford Press, 1996.

Bennis, Warren. "The Challenges of Leadership in the Modern World." *American Psychologist*, vol. 62, no. 1 (2007): 2–5.

Bertalanffy, Ludwig von. *General Systems Theory: Foundations, Development, Applications*. New York: George Braziller, Inc. 1968.

Blackwell, Lisa S., Kali H. Trzesneiwski, Carol S. Dweck. "Implicit Theories of Intelligence Predict Achievement across an Adolescent Transition: A Longitudinal Study and an Intervention." *Child Development*, vol. 78, no. 1 (January–February 2007): 246–63.

Boers, Arthur Paul. *Never Call Them Jerks: Healthy Responses to Difficult Behavior*. Herndon, VA: The Alban Institute, 1999.

Bohr, Niels. *Atomic Physics and the Description of Nature*. Cambridge, UK: Cambridge University Press, 1934.

Bourne, Edmund. *Anxiety and Phobia Workbook*. New York: MJF Books, 1995.

Bowden, Mary Ellen, Amy Beth Crow, and Tracy Sullivan. *Pharmaceutical Achievers: The Human Face of Pharmaceutical Research*. Philadelphia, PA: Chemical Heritage Press, 2003.

Bowen, Murray. *Family Therapy in Clinical Practice*. Lanham, MD: Jason Aronson, Inc., 1990.

Bradley, Bill. "Bill Bradley Quotes." *ThinkExist.com*. Accessed January 21, 2015. http://en.thinkexist.com/quotation/leaders_should_be_collaborative-modest-and/151084.html.

Bridges, William. *Transitions*. New York: Da Capo Press, 2004.

Brody, Gene, Zolinda Stoneman, Douglas Flor, and Chris McCracy. "Religion's Role in Organizing Family Relationships: Family Process in Rural, Two-Parent African American Families." *Journal of Marriage and the Family*, vol. 56, no. 4 (1994): 878–888.

Bruns, Roger. *Martin Luther King, Jr: A Biography*. Greenwood Publishing Group, 2006.

Buechner, Frederick. *Wishful Thinking: A Seeker's ABC*. San Francisco: Harper 1993.

Campbell, Joseph. *The Hero with a Thousand Faces*. Princeton, NJ: Princeton University Press, 1949.

Carroll, Jackson and Carl Dudley. *Handbook for Congregational Studies*. Nashville: Abingdon Press, 1986.

Carter, C. Sue "Neuroendocrine Perspectives on Social Attachment and Love." *Psychoneuroendocrinology*, vol. 23, no. 8 (1998): 779–818.

Churchill, Winston. *The Gathering Storm*. New York: Houghton Mifflin, 1948.

Clergy Self-Care Renewed: How Clergy and Congregations Can Prevent Burnout and Support Healthy Living. Mental Health Ministries. www.MentalHealthMinistries.net. http://www.mentalhealthministries.net/resources/brochures/clergy_burnout/clergy_burnout_self-care.pdf.

Cohen, Sheldon. "Social Relations and Susceptibility to the Common Cold" in *Emotion, Social Relationships, and Health*, edited by Carol Ryff and Burton Singer, 221–232. Oxford, UK: Oxford University Press, 2001.

Cozolino, Louis. *The Neuroscience of Psychotherapy*. New York: Norton, 2010.

Davidson, Richard, and Sharon Begley. *The Emotional Life of Your Brain*. New York: Penguin, 2012.

Dalberg-Acton, John Emerich Edward. "Letter to Bishop Mandell Creighton." April 5, 1887, in *Historical Essays and Studies*, edited by J. N. Figgis and R. V. Laurence. London: Macmillan, 1907.

Darwin, Charles. *The Origin of the Species*.150th Anniversary Edition. New York: Penguin, 1859/2003.

Diamond, Jared. *Guns, Germs, and Steel*. New York: Norton, 1997.

Diamond, Jared. *The Third Chimpanzee*. New York: Harper Perennial, 1992.

Dillard, Annie. *Teaching a Stone to Talk*. New York: Harper and Row, 1982.

Earley, Jay. *Self-Therapy*. Larkspur, CA: Pattern System Books, 2009.

Easterlin, Richard A. "The Worldwide Standard of Living since 1800." *The Journal of Economic Perspectives*, vol. 14, no. 1 (2000) 7–26.

Einstein, Albert. "On a Heuristic Point of View Concerning the Production and Transformation of Light." *Annalen der Physik*, vol. 17, no. 6 (1905): 132–48.

Einstein, Albert. "On the Electrodynamics of Moving Bodies." *Annalen der Physik*, vol. 17, no. 10 (1905): 891–921.

Ellison, Christoper G., David A. Gay, and Thomas A. Glass. "Does Religious Commitment Contribute to Individual Life Satisfaction?" *Social Forces*, vol. 68, no. l. (1989): 100–23.

Ellison, Christoper G. "Are Religious People Nice People? Evidence from the National Survey on Black Americans." *Social Forces*, vol. 71, no. 2 (1992): 411–30.

Emerson, Ralph Waldo. "The Divinity School Address" in *Ralph Waldo Emerson: Selected Prose and Poetry*, 2nd ed., edited by Reginald Cook, 56–71. New York: Holt, Rinehart, and Winston, Inc. 1838/1969.

Enright, Robert. *Forgiveness Is a Choice*. Washington: American Psychological Association, 2001.

Epictetus, *The Enchiridion*. Radford, VA: Wilder Publications, 2012.

Estes, Clarissa Pinkola. "Letter to a Young Activist during Troubled Times." https://www.mavenproductions.com/letter-to-a-young-activist.

Fallon, Jim. *The Psychopath Inside: A Neuroscientist's Personal Journey into the Dark Side of the Brain*. New York: Penguin, 2013.

Ffytche, Matt. *The Foundation of the Unconscious: Schelling, Freud, and the Birth of the Modern Psyche*. Cambridge, UK: Cambridge University Press, 2011.

Fisher, Robert, William Ury, and Bruce Patton. *Getting to Yes*. 3rd ed. New York: Penguin, 2011.

Flannery, Tim. *The Eternal Frontier*. New York: Grove Press, 2001.

Forbes, Nancy and Basil Mahon. *Faraday, Maxwell, and the Electromagnetic Field*. Amherst, NY: Prometheus Books, 2014.

Ford, Brian. *The Leeuwenhoek Legacy*. Bristol and London: Biopress and Farrand Press, 1991.

Forsyth, Donelson. *Group Dynamics*, 6th ed. Belmont, CA: Wadsworth Cenage Learning, 2014.

Frankl, Victor. *Man's Search for Meaning*. New York: Pocket Books, 1946/1963.

Freud, Sigmund, *The Freud Reader*, edited by Peter Gay. New York: Norton & Co., 1995.

Friedman, Edwin. "Bowen, Theory and Therapy" in *Handbook of Family Therapy, vol. II.* edited by Alan S. Gurman and David P. Kniskern, 134–170. New York: Brunner/Mazel, 1991.

Friedman, Edwin. *Generation to Generation: Family Process in Church and Synagogue*. New York: Guilford Press, 1985.

Gabbard, Glenn. *Psychodynamic Psychotherapy in Clinical Practice*. Arlington, VA: American Psychiatric Publishing, 1990.

Gamet, Sandra. "Listening Circles Integrative Project Paper." Master's thesis, Christ Seminary, 2005.

Goleman, Daniel. *Social Intelligence*. New York: Random House, 2006.

Goleman, Daniel, McKee, Annie, and Boyatzis, Richard. *Primal Leadership: Realizing the Power of Emotional Intelligence*. Boston: Harvard Business School Press, 2002.

Greenberg, Leslie. *Emotion-Focused Therapy*. Washington, DC: American Psychological Association, 2002.

Greenburg, Leslie and Safran, Jeremy. *Emotion in Psychotherapy*. New York: Guilford Press, 1987.

Guerin Jr., Philip J., Leo F. Fay, Thomas F. Fogarty, and Judith G. Kautto. *Working with Relationship Triangles: The One-Two-Three of Psychotherapy*. New York: Guilford Press, 1996.

Gutkowaska, Jolanta, M. Jankowski, S. Mukaddam-Daher, and S. M. McCann. "Oxytocin Is a Cardiovascular Hormone." *Brazilian Journal of Medical and Biological Research*, vol. 33, no. 6 (2000): 625–33.

Hamilton, Edith. *Mythology: Timeless Tales of Gods and Heroes*. New York: Little, Brown and Company, 2011.

Handal, Paul J., Wandamarie Black-Lopez, and Stephanie Moergen. "Preliminary Investigation of the Relationship between Religion and Psychological Distress in Black Women." *Psychological Reports*, vol. 65, no 3. (1989): 971–5.

Heifetz, Ronald. *Leadership without Easy Answers*. Cambridge, MA: Belknap Press of Harvard University Press, 1994.

Heifitz, Ronald, Marty Linsky, and Alexander Grashow. *The Practice of Adaptive Leadership: Tools and Tactics for Changing Your Organization and the World*. Cambridge, MA: Harvard Business Press, 2009.

Heilbroner, Robert. *The Worldly Philosophers*. New York: Simon and Schuster, 1999.

Heinrichs, Jay. *Thank You for Arguing*. New York: Three Rivers Press, 2013.

Heisenberg, Werner. *Physics and Philosophy*. New York: Harper Torchbooks, 1958.

Henley, William Ernest. "Invictus" in *Poems*. Warwickshire, UK: Read Books, Ltd., 1888/2013.

Hersey, Paul and Ken Blanchard. *Management of Organizational Behavior 3rd Edition – Utilizing Human Resources*. Upper Saddle River, New Jersey: Prentice Hall, 1977.

Hobbes, Thomas. *The Leviathan*. London: Penguin Books, 1651/1982.

Hodgkinson, Virginia A, M. Weitzman, and A. Kirsch. "From Commitment to Action: How Religious Involvement Affects Giving and Volunteering" in *Faith and Philanthropy in America: Exploring the Role of Religion in America's Voluntary Sector* edited by Robert Wuthnow and Virginia Hodgkinson. San Francisco: Jossey-Bass, 1990.

Hoffmann, Robert. *No One Is to Blame*. Palo Alto, CA: Science and Behavior Books, Inc., 1971.

Homer. *The Odyssey*, translated by Robert Fagles. New York: Penguin Classics, 1997.

Hotchkiss, Dan. *Governance and Ministry: Rethinking Board Leadership*, Second Edition (Lanham, MD: Rowman & Littlefield, 2016).

Hughes, Dan. "The Communication of Emotions and the Growth of Autonomy and Intimacy within Family Therapy" in *The Healing Power of Emotion*, edited by Diana Fosha, Daniel Siegel, and Marion Solomon, 280–303. New York: Norton 2009.

Jung, Carl. "Aion: Phenomenology of the Self" in *The Portable Jung*, edited by Joseph Campbell, 139–162. New York: Penguin, 1951/1971.

Jung, Carl. "Psychological Types" in *The Portable Jung*. edited by Joseph Campbell, 178–270. New York: Penguin, 1951/1971.

Kabat-Zinn, Jon. *Mindfulness for Beginners*. Boulder, CO: Sounds True, Inc., 2012.

Kahn, Michael. *The Tao of Conversations*. Oakland, CA: New Harbinger Publications, 1995.

Kahneman, Daniel. "The Riddle of Experience vs. Memory." *TED: Ideas worth spreading*. Video file. February 2010. https://www.ted.com/talks/daniel_kahneman_the_riddle_of_experience_vs_memory?language=en.

Kegan, Robert and Susan Laskow Lahey. *Immunity to Change*. Boston: Harvard Business Press, 2009.

Kerr, Michael and Murray Bowen. *Family Evaluation*. New York: Norton, 1988.

King, Martin Luther. *Letter from the Birmingham Jail*. San Francisco: Harper, 1994.

Kohut, Heinz. *The Analysis of the Self*. New York: International Universities, 1971.

Kohut, Heinz. *The Restoration of the Self*. New York: International Universities Press, 1977.

Kome, Penny and Patrick Crean, eds. *Peace: A Dream Unfolding*. San Francisco: Sierra Club Books, 1986.

Kouzes, James, and Barry Posner. *The Leadership Challenge: How to Make Extraordinary Things Happen in Organizations*. San Francisco: Jossey-Bass, 2012.

Krause, Neal. "Religion, Aging, and Health: Current Status and Future Prospects." *Journals of Gerontology: Series B*, vol. 52B, no. 6 (1997): 291–3.

Kuhn, Thomas. *The Copernican Revolution: Planetary Astronomy in the Development of Western Thought*. Cambridge, MA: Harvard University Press, 1985.

Last, John. "miasma Theory" in *A Dictionary of Public Health*, edited by John M. Last. Westminster College, Pennsylvania: Oxford University Press, 2007.

Lehr, Fred. *Clergy Burnout*. Minneapolis: Fortress Press, 1991.

Lincoln, Abraham. "Cooper Union Address" in *Abraham Lincoln: Speeches and Writings Vol. 2 1859–1865*, edited by Don Fehrenbacher. New York, NY: Literary Classics of the United States, 1989.

Lincoln, Abraham. "Gettysburg Address" in *Abraham Lincoln: Speeches and Writings Vol. 2 1859–1865*, edited by Don Fehrenbacher. New York, NY: Literary Classics of the United States, 1989.

Linehan, Marsha. *Cognitive Behavioral Treatment of Borderline Personality Disorder*. New York: Guilford Press, 1993.

Lu, Stacy. "Mindfulness Holds Promise for Treating Depression." *Monitor on Psychology*, vol. 46, no. 3 (2015): 50–3.

Maas, James. *Power Sleep*. New York: Harper Collins, 1998.

Machiavelli, Niccolo. *The Prince*. New York: Harper Collins, 1532/2012.

MacDonald, G. Jeffrey. "Congregations Gone Wild." *The New York Times* (New York), August 7, 2010.

MacLean, Paul. *The Triune Brain in Evolution*. New York: Springer, 1990.

Mann, R. D. "A Review of the Relationship between Personality and Performance in Small Groups." *Psychological Bulletin*, vol. 56, no. 4 (1959): 241–70.

Maslow, Abraham. "A Theory of Human Motivation." *Psychological Review*. vol. 40, no. 4. (1943).

Matthews, Lawrence. "Theology and Family Systems Theory in Dialogue" in *Leadership in Ministry*, edited by Israel Galindo, 164–186. Middletown, DE: Didache Press, 2017.

May, Gerald. *Addiction and Grace*. New York: Harper Collins, 1988.

May, Gerald. *Will and Spirit*. San Francisco: Harper & Row, 1982.

Maykus, Janet and Penny Long Marler. "Is the Treatment the Cure: A Study of the Effects of Participation in Pastoral Leader Peer Groups." April 2010. Austin, TX: Austin Presbyterian Seminary, 2010. http://www.austinseminary.edu/uploaded/continuing_education/pdf/SPE_Survey_Report_and_Analysis_April_2010.pdf.

McKay, Matthew and Patrick Fanning. *Self-Esteem*. 2nd ed. Oakland: New Harbinger, 1992.

Metchnikoff, Ellie. *Immunity in Infective Diseases*. Translated by F. G. Binnie. Cambridge, UK: Cambridge University Press, 1905.

Millon, Theodore. *Disorders of Personality*. New York: John Wiley & Sons, 1981.

Morris, Ian. *Foragers, Farmers, and Fossil Fuel*. Princeton: Princeton University Press 2015.

Newton, Isaac, *The Principia*. Oakland, CA: University of California Press, 1687/2016.

Norcross, John. "The Therapeutic Relationship" in *The Heart and Soul of Change*, 2nd ed., edited by Barry Duncan, Scott Miller, Bruce Wampold, and Mark Hubble, 113–141. Washington, DC: American Psychological Association 2010.

Ogden, Pat. "Emotion, Mindfulness, and Movement" in *The Healing Power of Emotion*, edited by Diana Fosha, Daniel Siegel, and Marion Solomon. New York: Norton, 2009.

Oswald, Roy and Speed Leas. *The Inviting Church*. Herndon, VA: The Alban Institute, 1987.

Pierce Carol, and Bill Page. *A Male/Female Continuum: Paths to Colleagueship*. Laconia, NH: New Dynamics Publications, 1986.

Papp, Peggy. *The Process of Change*. New York: Guilford Press, 1983.

Parker, Rebecca. "There Is a Love" in *A Child's Book of Blessings and Prayers*, edited by Eliza Blanchard, 1. Boston: Skinner House, 2008.

Peck, Scott. *The Different Drum*. New York: Touchstone, 1998.

Pinker, Steven. *The Better Angels of Our Nature*. New York: Viking, 2011.

Porter, Roy. "Hospitals and Surgery" in *Cambridge Illustrated History of Medicine*, 202–245, edited by Roy Porter. Cambridge, UK: Cambridge University Press, 2001.

Prochaska, J. O., and W. F. Velicer. "The Transtheoretical Model of Health Behavior Change." *American Journal of Health Promotion*, vol. 12, no. 1 (1997): 38–48.

Proeschold-Bell, Rae Jean and Sara LeGrand. "High Rates of Obesity and Chronic Disease among United Methodist Clergy." *Obesity*, vol. 18, no. 9. (2010): 1867–70.

Rendle, Gilbert. *Leading Change in Congregations: Spiritual and Organizational Tools for Leaders*. Herndon, VA: Alban Institute, 1998.

Richardson, Ronald. *Creating a Healthier Church: Family Systems Theory, Leadership, and Congregational Life*. Minneapolis: Fortress Press, 1996.

Rogers, Carl. "A Theory of Therapy, Personality, and Interpersonal Relationships, as Developed in the Client-Centered Framework" in *Psychology: A Study of Science*, edited by Sigmund Koch. New York: McGraw-Hill, 1959, 184–256.

Rogers, Carl. *On Becoming a Person, A Therapist's View of Psychotherapy*. New York: Houghton Mifflin, 1961/1989.

Rosenberg, Marshall. *Nonviolent Communication, A Language of Life*. Encinitas, CA: Puddle Dancer Press, 2003.

Rothauge, Arlin. *Sizing Up a Congregation for New Member Ministry*. New York: The Episcopal Church Center, 1983.

Rosseau, Jean-Jacques Rosseau, *The Social Contract and Discourses*, translated by G. D. H. Cole. New York: Dutton, 1761/1950.

Rutherford, Ernest. *Radioactive Substances and Their Radiations*. Cambridge, UK: Cambridge University Press, 1904.

Rye, Mark. S., Kenneth I. Pargament, M. Amir Ali, Guy L. Beck, Elliot N. Dorff, Charles Hallisey, Vsudha Narayanan, and James G. Williams, "Religious Perspectives on Forgiveness" in *Forgiveness: Theory, Research, and Practice*, edited by Michael E. McCullough, Kenneth I. Pargament, and Carl E. Thoresen. New York: Guilford Press, 2000, 17–40.

Sapolsky, Robert. *Why Zebras Don't Get Ulcers*. 3rd ed. New York: Henry Holt, 2004.

Scarf, Maggie. *Intimate Worlds*. New York: Ballantine Press, 1997.

Schaller, Lyla. *The Change Agent*. Nashville: Abingdon, 1972.

Schoenfeld, Timothy J., Pedro Rada, Pedro R. Pieruzzini, Brian Hsueh, and Elizabeth Gould. "Physical Exercise Prevents Stress-Induced Activation of Granule Neurons and Enhances Local Inhibitory Mechanisms in the Dentate Gyrus." *Journal of Neuroscience*, vol. 33, no. 18 (2013): 7770–7777.

Seligman, Martin. *Learned Optimism*. New York: Vintage Books, 2006.

Shantideva, *A Guide to the Bodhisattva Way of Life*, translated by A. Wallace & B. A. Wallace Ithaca, NY: Snow Lion, 1997.

Siegel, Daniel. *The Developing Mind*. New York: Guilford Press, 1999.

Skinner, B. F. *The Behavior of Organisms*. New York: Appleton-Century, 1938.

Smith, Huston. *The World's Religions*. Anniversary edition. New York: Harper Collins, 2009.

Smith, Tom. " Job Satisfaction in the United States." Chicago: University of Chicago (2007). http://www-news.uchicago.edu/releases/07/pdf/070417.jobs.pdf.

Steinke, Peter. *Healthy Congregations, A Systems Approach*. 2nd ed. Herndon, VA: The Alban Institute, 2006.

Stillman, Drake. *Essays on Galileo and the History and Philosophy of Science, Vol. 1*. Toronto: University of Toronto Press, 1999.

Stogdill, R. M. *Handbook of Leadership: A Survey of Theory and Research*. New York: Free Press, 1974.

Tao Te Ching, translated by Stephen Mitchell. New York: Harper & Row, 1988.

Tattersall, Ian. *Masters of the Planet*. New York: Palgrave Macmillan, 2012.

Tennyson, Alfred. "Flower in the Crannied Wall" in *The Complete Works of Alfred Lord Tennyson*. Ware, England: Wordsworth Editions Limited, 1994.

Thomas, Kenneth W. and Ralph H. Kilmann, *Thomas-Kilmann Conflict Mode Instrument*. Palo Alto, CA: Consulting Psychologists Press, 1971.

Tomasello, Michael. "Social Cognition and the Evolution of Culture" in *Piaget, Evolution, and Development*, edited by Jonas Langer and Melanie Killen, 221–245. Mahwah, NJ: Erlbaum, 2008.

Turner, Frederick. *Beyond Geography*. Rutgers, NJ: Rutgers University Press 1992.

Vitello, Paul. "Taking a Break from the Lord's Work." *The New York Times* (New York), August 1, 2010.

Walsh, Roger. "Lifestyle and Mental Health." *American Psychologist*, vol. 66, no. 7 (2011): 579–92.

Ward, Geoffrey and Burns, Ken. *Jazz: A History of America's Music*. New York: Knopf, 2000.

Watson, Jeanne, Rhonda Goldman, and Greet Vanaerschot. "Empathic: A Postmodern Way of Being?" in *Handbook of Experiential Psychotherapy*, edited by Leslie Greenberg, Jeanne Watson and Germain Lietaer, 61–81. New York: Guilford Press, 1998.

Whitmont, Edward. *The Symbolic Quest*. New York: Harper & Row, 1969.

Wilkinson, R. G. *Unhealthy Societies: The Afflictions of Inequality*. London: Routledge, 1996.

Williams, Mark, John Teasdale, Zindel Segel, and Jon Kabat-Zinn. *The Mindful Way through Depression*. New York: Guilford Press, 2007.

Williamson, Marianne. *A Return to Love: Reflections on the Principles of "A Course in Miracles."* New York: Harper Collins, 1992.

Winthrop, John. "A Modell of Christian Charity," a sermon written in 1630 on board *The Arbella on the Atlantic Ocean*. Boston: Collections of the Massachusetts Historical Society, 1838.

World Health Organization. *World Report on Violence and Health*. Edited by Etienne G. Krug, Linda L. Dahlberg, James A. Mercy, Anthony B. Zwi, and Rafael Lozano. Geneva, Switzerland: World Health Organization, 2002.

Wright, Robert. The Evolution of God. New York: Little, Brown & Company, 2005.

Wulf, Andrea. *The Invention of Nature*. New York: Knopf, 2015.

Wuthnow, Robert. *Acts of Compassion: Caring for Others and Helping Ourselves*. Princeton, NJ: Princeton University Press, 1991.

Yalom, Irwin and Molyn Lesczc. *The Theory and Practice of Group Psychotherapy*. 5th ed. New York: Basic Books, 2005.

Zweig, Connie and Steve Wolf. *Romancing the Shadow*. Emeryville, CA: Alibris, 1998.

Index

Page references for figures are italicized.

About the Author

The Rev. Ken Reeves, PhD, is a member of the clergy and a licensed clinical psychologist. He has an MDiv and has served congregations as a pastor and in interim roles. He has an MS and a Certificate of Advanced Study in pastoral counseling and a PhD in clinical psychology. Ken has a therapy practice and conducts psychological evaluations of ministers and candidates for the ministry. He has taught at Andover Newton Theological School and conducted continuing education workshops for clergy. He resides in Massachusetts with his family. He can be reached through his website: thewholechurch.com.